More praise for *A Gathering of Fugitives*

". . . Diana Anhalt finally gives voice to the passions that led a generation of remarkable artists and activists into exile in Mexico and to the fears that kept them strangers to their children — and to American history for too long."
— Tony Kahn, Host and Special Correspondent of PRI's "The World" and executive producer of "Blacklisted," on NPR

"With courage, humor and a compassionate heart Diana Anhalt brings to life her parents story and that of a group of unsung American leftists, whose passionate pursuit of social justice led them to flee McCarthyism for a fascinating and somewhat troubled exile south of the border."
—Margaret Hooks, author of "Tina Modotti: Radical Photographer" and "Guatemalan Women Speak"

". . . a rich, historical contribution that painfully reminds us that non-conformity is not without costs and pain."
—Stanley I. Kutler, Fox Professor of American Institutions & Law University of Wisconsin

"With courage and authority, Diana Anhalt has written a powerful and extraordinary historical account of American citizens in Mexico during the McCarthy era, and their lives afterward. *A Gathering of Fugitives* makes sure we do not forget these dreamers, visionaries and fugitives in search of hope and truth."
—Marjorie Agosín, Wellesley College

". . . a thoughtful, penetrating, ground-breaking look at a very unusual childhood. In 1950, when Ms. Anhalt was eight years old, her parents, American Communists, uprooted the family from the Bronx and emigrated to Mexico. There, they found a community of about 60 American families, all seeking refuge from the persecutions of the Cold War. This book beautifully documents their lives—what they running from, what they were running toward."
— Tony Hiss, author of "The View from Alger's Window: A Son's Memoir"

Also by the author

Anthologies
(Contributor)

Every Woman Has a Story
Red Diapers: Growing Up in the Communist Left
Leap Years: Women Reflect on Change, Loss and Love
With a Little Bit of Salt

A Gathering of Fugitives

*Dearest Jean –
without you this
book would not
have been possible—
and I really mean
that
with love,
Diane
Feb. /02*

American
Political
Expatriates
in Mexico
1948-1965

Diana Anhalt

Archer Books

Published in the United States by:
Archer Books
P. O. Box 1254
Santa Maria, CA 93456

Printed in Canada

First edition

Cover photo of map © 2001, Photodisc, Inc.
Cover photo of author courtesy of Mauricio Anhalt

Library of Congress Cataloging-in-Publication Data

Anhalt, Diana, 1942-
    A gathering of fugitives : American political expatriates in
Mexico, 1948-1965 / Diana Anhalt.
        p. cm.
    Includes bibliographical references.
    ISBN 1-931122-03-2 (pbk.)
        1. Americans--Mexico--History--20th century. 2. Political
refugees--Mexico--History--20th century. 3. Political refugees--
United States--History--20th century. 4. United States--Politics
and government--1945-1989. 5. Communism--United States--
History--20th century. 6. Anti-communist movements--United
States--History--20th century. 7. Internal security--United
States--History--20th century. I. Title.

F1392.A5 A64 2001
325'.21'08913072--dc21
                                                    2001046394

E-mail: gathering@archer-books.com
Web site: http://www.archer-books.com

For the two 'M's in my life: Mauricio and Mexico.
They have made all the difference.

Contents

Acknowledgments

In the course of writing this book I knocked on many doors, reintroduced myself to people who hadn't heard from me for forty years or more, and asked favors of total strangers. I was rarely turned down.

Those I spoke to had strong feelings about the expatriate experience and this period in history. However, my interpretations and the conclusions I reached here are entirely my own. I take full responsibility for the contents of this book, a book that never would have been written without the combined efforts of scores of people.

Anita Boyer, Jean Butler, Max Shlafrock, Berthe Small, Morton Sobell and "Keith," (who has asked to remain anonymous), adopted my project—and me—even when they didn't always agree.

My husband Mauricio and my friends Richard Delgado, Margaret Hooks, Nancy Rocha, Carla Hagen-Sorenson, and Jean Stefancic read and re-read my work, made corrections, offered advice, goaded me on and shamed me into persevering. Their input and encouragement proved invaluable.

I am also grateful to Victor Rabinowitz for clarifying some legal issues and to Don Kirschner, Alan Wald, Harvey Klehr and Ellen Schrecker whose constructive feedback and vast knowledge in the area of American Communism proved invaluable.

For answering my questions, opening doors, and steering me in the right direction, I would particularly like to thank Marjorie Agosín, Bobbi Graff, Ambassador Jorge Alvarez Fuentes, Patricia Galeana, Lee Gruenfeld, Juan Manuel Gomez Gutierrez, Pedro Guillermo Hoth, Tony Kahn, Ann

Kimmage, Stanley Kutler, Marcela Lombardo, Arnaldo Martínez Verdugo, Roberto Morín, Victor Navasky, Alisa Shapiro Ratusnik, Harriet Reisen, Merrily Weisbord and Ira Wood.

I am grateful, as well, to Abbott Small for his translation of Luisa Moreno, Michael Pincus of Bolerium Books, Library of Congress researcher Morey Rothberg, and Lawyer Katherine Meyer, who sued the FBI on my behalf. To John Taylor-Convery, Rosemary Tribulato and the people at Archer Books, my thanks for their hard work, patience and trust.

Special recognition goes to all those who appear here and to those I interviewed, but was unable to include. Each of them addressed my questions, answered my letters and phone calls, loaned me books and documents, and gave generously of their time and knowledge. They became my surrogate ancestors, contributed scraps of information and helped me piece together the stories of our communal pasts. I will always be grateful for their confidence, their enthusiasm and, above all, for returning my parents and my story to me.

D. A.

Prologue

A Personal History: Why We Fled the Bronx

I sat at my grandmother's kitchen table. She fed me *challah* and honey on Fridays, a slice of toasted Wonder bread with honey any other day of the week, and a cup of weak tea. "I was born in Poland," she told me, "but when people ask me where I'm from, I say America. Better you shouldn't know about Poland, Cossacks, pogroms."

My grandmother pulled me closer, her maroon sweater rough against my cheek, and I smelled her talcum powder and, more faintly, moth balls. "I fled in the night with my father's youngest sister. To leave without saying good-bye, that is a terrible thing."

After dinner and before we drank our tea she curled my hair with a curling iron heated on the range, dampening the ends with spit, coiling the tendrils onto the hot rod. Today, whenever I hear the word 'pogrom,' I smell burning hair. A miniature moon, a reflection cast by the overhead lamp, floated on the surface of my tea. ' That is why,' I thought, 'her tea—three teaspoons of sugar and a dribble of milk— was the best I'd ever tasted. It tasted like the moon.'

The day we vanished from the Bronx I was to be the apple blossom in the third grade festival. I'd purchased pink crepe paper for my costume and cut, gathered and stapled it together in four layers so my tutu would stand straight out. When I learned we were leaving—"Just for a while," my mother told me—I cried. "My teacher will never forgive me. I promised, I promised." And I couldn't help wondering whether our disappearance wasn't in some way related to my grandmother's fleeing Poland. Maybe an unwritten commandment? "Jews must leave their birthplaces!" But there were no Cossacks, not even a whiff of burning hair.

Instead, my uncle Aaron drove us to the airport in my father's dark blue Studebaker on a rainy day late in 1950. A pink and green crocheted blanket spread over our knees, my four year old sister Judy, my cousin Donna—who was allowed to miss school for the occasion—and I, sat in the back seat. We ate bananas and marshmallows, sang camp songs, and planned my birthday party. I would turn nine in January. Upon arriving at the airport I gave Donna the chocolate turkey I'd been saving for Thanksgiving, and she promised to keep it until my return so we could eat it together.

I recall a precipitous departure, but I'm mistaken: My father's friend, Edward (Eddy) Lending, told me, "I ran into [your father] on 42nd Street and 5th Avenue in 1950. I don't think we had met in the intervening twelve years, since I'd gone to Spain. And I was fond of him. We sidled into Bickford's for coffee and a long chat. I told him about Mexico, that if I could manage to establish a reasonable economic basis for living there we were going to migrate. Two days before our departure, [your dad] was on the phone. 'Guess what?,' he enthused, 'We're leaving for Mexico in a month.'"[1]

Under pretense of employment with my Uncle Ben's company, Warren Manufacturing, my father procured passports and, in a gesture I imagine must have appealed to his sense of humor, had my mother type out an official-looking letter on my uncle's company stationary. It was addressed to the American Commercial Attaché at the U.S. Embassy in Mexico City: "Our Sales Engineer, Mr. Meyer Zykofsky, will arrive shortly for the purpose of surveying the manufacturing possibilities there and will call on you at your convenience."

So there must have been time to plan and pack the four suitcases, three pieces of hand luggage and two boxes we took along. My father included his jazz recordings, books and two oils painted by my uncle Herman. My mother, whose culinary abilities rarely extended beyond opening a can of tuna fish, insisted on packing her *Settlement Cookbook*. (So infrequent were her incursions into the kitchen, she stored back copies of *The Daily Worker* in the oven.) She also took her typewriter and approximately three inches of blue yarn attached to the knitting needles, the result of her attempt to knit a baby's

1. Edward Lending, letter to author, May 19, 1992.

sweater when she was pregnant with my sister four years earlier. (Shortly before my brother's birth in 1954 she pulled it out again. We discovered the same piece of knitting, still attached to the needles, stuck away in a lower drawer when she died.) I was allowed to bring my Brownie camera, my ice skates and a gray corduroy jumper with red hearts and flowers on it, of which I was particularly fond. I don't remember saying good-bye at the airport but I do remember the plane. I followed the airline stewardess down the aisle. A passenger glanced up from her book to ask, "Where are you going, dear?"

"To California," I replied.

"Well, if you're going to California, you're on the wrong plane because this one is going to Mexico."

I trotted back up the aisle to tell my parents, just in case they didn't know. "What! We didn't tell you we were going to Mexico? Well, it doesn't matter. California and Mexico are neighbors, you know."

I must have asked my parents why we left the States. They never told me or, if they did, I don't remember their answers but, at some level I knew, just as I knew it was better not to probe. Much of what was said in our family—in most families, I suppose—was communicated through silences and evasions: the turned back, a flushed face, the hand tightening into a fist. I learned early on what questions not to ask at the same time I understood what the silences meant. I think I knew that they—my small mother, moving through life like a brisk wind in her tweeds and sensible pumps, clutching a large brown handbag; my father, handsome, irreverent and dogmatic, a man people listened to and everyone, except possibly my mother, deferred to—were on the run. And I grudgingly accepted that, along with the conviction that our leave-taking was primarily intended to make my life miserable. Years later I would resume my questioning. My parents were dead by then, but this time I got some answers: from relatives, friends, fellows in exile and the FBI.

My parents, Belle Friedman and Meyer—usually called Mike— Zykofsky were born into immigrant families newly arrived from Eastern Europe and, as they never ceased to remind me, their lives were tough, far tougher than mine. By the time they were eleven or twelve they were working odd jobs. ("Your mom, she tutored kids after school," my mother's youngest brother, Ben, told me. "I just shined shoes. And look at me today. Today I'm a millionaire. There's no place like America!")

My mother's mother rented out the living room sofa to boarders, immigrants harder up than they were. When they could afford the occasional chicken, she killed and plucked her own because it cost a penny less, and spoke bitterly of her husband, a carpenter, because he was chronically unemployed and spent most of his time in the synagogue: "In the old country he was an atheist. Here he finds God!" (He refused to eat her chickens because they weren't kosher.) At fifteen my mother got her first real job as a cashier in a cafeteria after changing her name from Sarah Bella Friedman to Belle Frees because most places wouldn't hire Jews.

I know even less about my father. The eldest of four children, he had lost his mother when he was fourteen. He seldom spoke of his childhood. But there was one story he told over and over again until it grew into family myth, *Adele and the Breaded Veal Cutlet*. Before his father—a tailor and natty dresser with a twinkle in his eye (referred to irreverently by my cousin Donna as 'Hot Pants' Zykofsky)—remarried, my father's younger sister, my aunt Adele, did the cooking. One night she hurriedly heated oil in a pan, breaded the meat in a powdery substance poured from a packet, and flung it onto a hot skillet. When my father entered the kitchen, large bubbles were rising out of the oil toward the ceiling. Adele, who couldn't have been older than thirteen, burst into tears. "There's something wrong with this meat," she sobbed, "and there's no money for more."

My father seized the remaining cutlets—still uncooked— and spreading each to its full size, rinsed them under the faucet. "Now you can cook them. See? You used detergent instead of flour."

I think the story appealed to him because it showed him to be exactly as he fancied himself—a resourceful individual, a hero perhaps, smarter than most of us, and fully in command of a situation, whether comic or tragic; although the comic brought out the best in him. (He had an irrepressible sense of humor about everything except his politics and a vast collection of puns: His favorite was the one about the cannibal who suffered from a belly ache because he boiled a "friar.")

A year after meeting at a Young Communist League function in 1935, Belle and Mike, with their parents' blessings, ran off to Albany, New York where they married in secret rather than risk losing their job benefits were their marriage to become known. Both were employed by the Works Project Administration (WPA) and organized educational activities for street gang members, out of school and out of work.[2]

I don't suppose anyone taught them to hate the Depression or resent poverty. Experiencing it was enough: The stench of rotting food or a backed-up toilet in unheated hallways, the eviction of tenants unable to pay rent, bread lines, the challenge of finding a decent job if you were Jewish, Catholic, Asian or Black, and the possible loss of it if you demanded a living wage; the corruption of ward politics, deplorable working conditions and, of course, a fear of fascism, convinced them of the system's injustices and drew them and their like to the Communist Party.

I imagine communism attracted youngsters of my parents' generation and background because they despaired at the state of their society and had faith in mankind's ability to change. Unlike earlier generations of Communists, they had no desire to recreate Little Russias on American soil.[3]

This young, energetic, well educated generation considered themselves Americans. But they came of age in a society where the Communist Party alone addressed their concerns for reform. Although the Party had a private agenda, the vast majority of its members was fiercely committed to reform. They were drawn by a passionate sense of purpose: The Party held out hope, and hope fueled their souls.

Belle and Mike's first few years together must have been been rough. My grandmother threw out her boarders and they shared her living room sofa until they could afford their own place. According to his FBI dossier, my father, a machinist, worked for ten different firms between April, 1938 and April, 1944 in fields as diverse as aircraft, metallurgy, printing, optics and transformers. My mother worked as a cashier, a

2. Edward Lending, interview with author, August 28, 1991.
3. Nora Sayre, *Previous Convictions: A Journey through the Fifties*, New Jersey: Rutgers University Press, 1995, p. 353. Sayre emphasizes that differing attitudes toward Russia separated my parents' generation from earlier Communists, many of them East European immigrants. These were more likely to live out a lifestyle reminiscent of the old world, recreating Russian traditions—the food, dress, customs—out of familiarity or admiration.

bookkeeper, a clerk—whatever she could get. Although they had been top students, they couldn't afford college full-time. Mike attended evening classes in business administration at the City College of New York for two years and in production design at the Laboratory School of Industrial Design. Though little time remained for recreation they did spend an occasional weekend at Camp Unity. The first interracial adult summer camp in the United States, it was subsequently investigated on grounds of having been a Communist indoctrination center.

The year I was born, 1942, the United States joined the war effort. In 1944 my father did. As a married man with a child he was not subject to the draft, but he volunteered and was sent overseas. Two years as a machinist in a transportation corps in France and Belgium strengthened his political inclinations.

FBI sources[4] also claim that he and my mother became registered members of the American Labor Party (ALP) following the War and remained so until 1949. A short-lived but influential political pressure group, the ALP played an active role in New York State politics. It supported a variety of progressive candidates associated with established parties or ran their own people—my father among them—for local, state and federal office. By the time my parents became active, the Communist Party controlled a faction of the ALP.

Bureau information further discloses that my father became the ALP chairman for Parkchester, the Bronx community we lived in. He also donated $75, a considerable sum in the 1940's, to the Civil Rights Congress,[5] "the most successful Communist Front of all time."[6] Those same sources also reveal my parents' association with the National Committee to Win the Peace, Progressive Citizens of America, American Youth for Democracy, the Young Communist League and the International Workers Order, all influenced, to some extent, by the Party.

Following his discharge from the Army in February, 1946, my father was employed as a salesman for the La Salle offset

4. Federal Bureau of Investigation, Meyer Zykofsky, May 26, 1954, NY100-118463.
5. After six Blacks were convicted of murder in Trenton, New Jersey in 1948, the Civil Rights Congress took up their cause and conducted a widespread campaign for publicity and funds throughout the country.
6.Mary Jo Buhle, Paul Buhle & Dan Georgakas, Eds., *Encyclopedia of the American Left, IL*: University of Illinois Press, 1992, p. 134.

printing firm. At the suggestion of his employer, a personal friend, he used the name Mike Zyke, an easier name to remember than Meyer Zykofsky.

My mother worked for the Lighthouse, an organization for the blind, but when my father was sent overseas she found full time work as a bookkeeper in the garment district. According to the FBI, she was employed at Temple Emanuel in the Bronx in 1946, but I believe she only volunteered there occasionally because she approved of the Rabbi's politics. As the mother of a young child, the only way to keep her job was to find low-cost day care for me. Together with a group of working mothers, she established the still-extant Parkchester Nursery on Tremont Avenue, within walking distance of Unionport Road, where we lived.

I remember the nursery school: I broke out in hives after eating a peanut butter and jelly sandwich for lunch, and a boy in my group named Joey ate crayons and taught me the words 'stinker' and 'shit.' Nor will I ever forget my humiliation at discovering, as I slid down the sliding pond on a cold autumn morning, that I'd forgotten to put on my underpants.

My first political memory, however—I must have been five or six—was of my mother ringing doorbell after doorbell in our apartment building in Parkchester soliciting signatures to integrate our housing development. I trailed after in my bathrobe and bedroom slippers. No doubt I recall the event, not because I was impressed by the 'cause,' but because my mother was rarely home during the day unless I was sick. (That would explain the bathrobe and bedroom slippers.)

The second such memory concerned riding the elevator with a neighbor who lived on the eighth floor. I was carrying my roller skates, one in each hand, so she pressed the elevator buttons and, as the doors closed she said, "You know what I just did, Diana? I voted for your father. You be sure to tell him, O.K.?" Then the doors opened. I don't recall whether I ever conveyed the message but I do remember asking my father if he had run for president.

Looking back on the event from a distance of some fifty years I can only assume that I remember it so well because, at some level, I sensed it was precisely this, my father 'running for president,' which triggered our leaving. The Primary elections for New York City's tenth assembly seat, which he did run for, were held on August 22, 1950. When the final count was tallied on November 7 of that same year, my father received 3,486 votes out of a total 47,184 cast, fewer than any of his opponents. By then, we had been in Mexico for close to a month.

"When the McCarthy period became a daily part of our lives," writes a family friend, "I can understand the apprehension your parents felt, since your father had been so public in his political activities."[7]

The left wing was keenly aware that it was walking on thin ice. Between 1949 and 1950 incident upon incident heightened their sense of vulnerability: Found guilty of contempt, the Hollywood Ten went to prison, the Communists triumphed in China, twelve American Communist leaders were found guilty of 'conspiring to advocate the violent overthrow of the government,' the United States pledged to support South Korea, Alger Hiss was convicted of perjury, and left-wing unions were expelled from the CIO.

Even the non-political were alarmed: Sally Bloch, my mother's closest friend, recalls attending a meeting with my parents sometime in the '40s, making out a check for Spanish Civil War Veterans, and worrying about it for years; my cousin Donna tells of her parents removing book jackets and replacing them inside out so titles were hidden from view; my uncle Dave struck my father's name from his directory, listing only a phone number.

My parents were also frightened, frightened enough to take off. Perhaps they were driven by the conviction, held by many Party members, that fascism would inevitably take root in the United States as it had in Germany. Could they have perjured themselves by signing Loyalty Oaths?[8] Was it possible they now feared detection as did others who went to Mexico? Or were they merely escaping what they believed was an oppressive situation? "If anyone asks, tell them we're in Mexico on business," my mother told me repeatedly. But if that were true, where was the business? Why were we barely getting by? Why had they

7. Lillian Kittner, letter to author, December 7, 1993.
8. In order to obtain or keep a job, the government and many private industries required their employees to sign loyalty oaths, i.e. sworn statements to the effect that they were not, and never had been, members of the Communist Party. If a present or former Party member signed one they could be charged with lying under oath.

told everyone, including me, we were going to California? Why did they change our last name to 'Zyke?'

Shortly before I was to start school in Mexico my parents told me they had shortened our last name: "To Zyke, it rhymes with Mike. Zykofsky, after all, is awfully hard to pronounce in Spanish."

"It's also hard in English," I reminded them, and proceeded to write 'Zyke' on all my school notebooks. Then within weeks, they changed their minds—much to my disgust. This meant blacking out all the e's in order to change them to o's and, though I took care not to smudge, 'Zykofsky' did not look as good as 'Zyke' had.

We arrived in Mexico at the same time the C.P.U.S.A. was sending hundreds of trusted members into hiding. When twelve Party leaders, arrested in January of 1949, were convicted under the Smith Act, steps were taken to assure the Party's continuity and provide a semblance of leadership and structure. A chosen few were sent to Mexico City. Could my parents have been among them? I asked A.B. Magil, who lived there from early 1950 through July, 1952 as a correspondent for the Party paper, *The Daily Worker*. He didn't remember having met them and doesn't believe they belonged to the underground.[9]

I still don't know, despite FBI allegations, if my parents were Party members. A friend once told me my ignorance was a way of protecting myself from the truth: I was afraid to discover they had been. She was wrong. I was afraid to discover they hadn't. If they were, I could forgive them, or at least understand their tearing me away from my home, my school, my country. But no one, except me, seemed to care why they had moved to Mexico. Not even the FBI. They wouldn't start investigating Belle and Mike until three years after they had left the States.

At about the same time, I started dreaming that my front tooth fell out while I was nibbling on the eraser end of a pencil. I kept pushing the tooth back into the gum, where it wobbled unsteadily only to fall out again. Not until years later did I realize I was the tooth, yanked out of my life by the roots, roots never to cleave to bone again, at least not in a conventional sense. I must have lost my childhood then or even earlier, when I lost my grandmother. Her death was close enough to our

9. A. B. Magil, interview with author, January 20, 1993.

departure for the two incidents to blur. After that, I was invaded by a sense of loneliness and loss, and I probed the empty spaces of my being like a tongue searching for a missing tooth.

Chapter One

The Impulse:
When the Left Left and Went to Mexico

I was only eight years old when my family fled the Bronx in the fall of 1950, and they didn't confide in me. If they had, things would have been a whole lot easier. I wouldn't be writing this book, trying to piece together the details of their lives and—as it turned out—other peoples' lives as well. Along with their homes, their former identities and, sometimes their names, they left behind the assorted odds-and-ends: personal papers and newspaper clippings, old ties, an empty filing cabinet, a beach umbrella. The inconvenient parts, the details which might have encumbered them, they supressed. They were twice exiled: from their environment and from their former identities.

I hung onto the memories. My parents couldn't take those away, but memories are unreliable and, with time, I learned to distrust mine. I still clutched at them, of course, because they were all I had and, in the end, I did reconstruct a past for myself. But first I had to identify those people who could return it to me, discover why, like my parents, they had migrated to Mexico and, once there, what experiences we had shared in common. I ended up with an unwieldy hodge-podge of facts—many of which I ended up discarding—and the realization that coherence and order, like a model economy or the perfect body, is something you might set your sights on but are unlikely to achieve.

Of course, when we arrived in Mexico in October of 1950, I didn't know all this. There were a lot of things I didn't know. For example, I had no idea how how far I was from the Bronx—until I saw the palm trees. The palm trees clinched it. I had never seen any except in Dorothy Lamour films or in my illustrated copy of *Robinson Crusoe*, but now long rows of them lined the grounds of the Shirley Courts Motel.[1] They drove home to me the distance we had travelled—that and the bread boy. I caught sight of him our first morning in Mexico City. He darted by on his bicycle, his red shirt billowing out behind him, a bread-heaped basket balanced on his head. A car honked and cut him off. I caught my breath, but he simply swerved, squeezed his black-bulbed bicycle horn, and glided off down the street.

We had breakfast at *Sanborn's* because it was recommended in *Terry's Guide to Mexico* as a safe place to eat. After paying the bill, my father gave me a large twenty centavo coin, then equivalent to approximately two and a half U.S. pennies. I clutched it in my fist, and soon my hand was black creased and sweaty and smelled like lead. As we made our way single-file down the narrow sidewalk, dodging other pedestrians headed in the opposite direction, street vendors and the occasional stray dog, my parents took turns encouraging my four year old sister, Judy, to walk and, when she refused, carrying her. I brought up the rear, my dark blue sweater knotted around my waist, the camera hung around my neck, carrying *Terry's Guide* and a bottle of soda pop, a rare treat prohibited me in the Bronx. (In Mexico it became my daily fare. Water never crossed my lips until we moved into an apartment and installed an *Electropura* bottled water stand. I even remember brushing my teeth with ginger ale, although my sister claims I'm mistaken.)

We reached a corner. My parents stepped off the curb and proceeded to cross the street. Just then a bony hand darted out and grasped my arm. I turned to see an ancient beggar, barefoot and dressed in rags imploring me out of a toothless mouth in words I couldn't understand but knew the meaning of. She wanted something. My soda? My twenty centavo coin? As I opened my fist to give it to her I remember thinking, 'This is mine. It's the only one I have. Why should she have it?' I yanked my arm out of her grasp, yelled "No" and crossed the street at a run. My parents hadn't noticed, and I said nothing. But for the rest of the day I felt as I had when my mother

---

1. I later learned that the hotel most favored by newly arrived political expatriates was the Hotel Reforma, until they discovered it was crawling with agents. After that, they referred to it as the "Hotel Informer."

caught me pouring my milk down the drain and shouted, "How could you? Children are starving in Europe." As a child of the left, I was supposed to know better. How many times had I been told how lucky I was not to have been born Jewish in Germany or Black in the South? Now I would have one more unfortunate minority to worry about.

We walked all the way to the main square, the *zocalo*, where my father purchased a newspaper from a passing vendor. He settled down on a park bench, my mother alongside him. Although his only previous encounter with Spanish had been half a dozen *Berlitz* classes, he translated the gist of it anyway, occasionally consulting his English/Spanish pocket dictionary. The one article I remember—no doubt altered somewhat in translation and with the passage of time—had to do with an increase in grave robberies. Local officials reported that family members had taken to sleeping in cemeteries immediately following burials in order to discourage thieves from making off with the coffins, for which there was a growing demand on the black market.

My sister and I sat on the dust scented grass. It was brittle and dry, but when I pulled out a stalk and nibbled at its still green root it was sweet, sweeter than the playground grass back home. Mid-morning traffic streamed by. There were the familiar sounds: honking horns, screeching brakes, wailing sirens and others less familiar such as the gong-like clamor of a garbage truck bell, church bells, the steam whistle on a sweet potato cart, the shrill twitter of a knife sharpener's pipe and, from a food stand, the rhythmic clapping of palms shaping small rounds of corn dough into tortillas.

The Cathedral loomed before us, and men in work clothes leaned against its wrought iron fence. Some carried signs: *albañil*, *electricista* or *pintor*. Others wore them around their necks or placed them on the ground at their feet. Occasionally, a passerby would engage one in conversation and the two would depart together. After consulting his dictionary, my father explained that these were workmen—bricklayers, electricians, painters—waiting for clients. "Well, Belle," my father joked, "if worse comes to worse I can always hang a sign around my neck and see what happens." Judy and I hooted with laughter, but my mother didn't crack a smile.

For close to fifty years, I've managed to repress that memory of my small, grim-faced mother sitting beside my father on a park bench in the center of Mexico City, and today, when I summon it up, I can't help but feel guilty for never having given her much thought. She must have felt completely powerless and very much alone. I can still visualize her in this very same spot in front of the Cathedral with its barefoot street vendors, stray dogs, the babble of Spanish, traffic sounds and bells asking herself, as I'm sure she must have, "What the hell am I doing here?"

I probably asked myself much the same thing, and I know what my answer would have been: "My parents made me." Still, that didn't keep me from feeling as if I'd been "evicted from my life."[2] I was miserable, and I blamed it on my parents. Only now, ten years after I started digging for the answers, do I realize they did do a few things right: They left me a little money in the bank, good teeth, and one hell of a family story. What a pity they never got around to telling it to me—not the whole thing anyway. All I got was an occasional tantalizing peek into their pasts. (Like skilled strip-teasers, they never entirely revealed themselves.) They were afraid.

After we left New York, reality wobbled beyond my control, like the tooth in my dream. I had been thrust into a new life, but didn't want to give up the old one. How dare my parents separate me from my previous existence? How could I be expected to adopt a new identity if I didn't know why? But no one explained. If I were to describe my personal history, it would be a history of living without one: I was totally excluded from my parents' political commitments, which I never really understood, in a movement I never really understood (and in some ways still don't). Thus, my story—what little there was of it—was about not knowing.

Belle died in 1986 and Mike in 1989, shortly before I turned fifty, and although they went slowly, I was still astounded, the way very small children are when things refuse to live up to their expectations. At some level I must have believed that before taking such a drastic step my parents would, at the very least, ask for my permission, let me know their intentions. But no, they just died. And worse yet, they did so before answering my

2. Phrase coined by Chilean poet Marjorie Agosin.

questions. On the other hand, I recognize that if they hadn't died they probably wouldn't have answered them anyway. (Some of the people I spoke to told me they had never explained why they had gone to Mexico to their own children, and I can't help wondering if my parents would have confided in somebody else's child.)

That's when I decided I would have to settle for whatever answers I could get. Now that so much time had elapsed, I figured most people would speak to me openly, and they did— about the witch hunts and their experiences in Mexico and about some of the 'famous communists' residing in the country. However, many claimed not to have left the States for political reasons. Unless their identities were so well known there was nothing left to hide, secrecy and its companion, discretion— the corollaries of exile—circumscribed their lives.

The small group of controversial Americans who found refuge in Mexico during the late '40s and throughout the '50s, while not political exiles in the conventional sense—neither they nor any of the others I ever spoke to made a formal request for sanctuary—had, for all intents and purposes, left the United States because their present or former association with the Communist Party or Popular Front groups closely associated with it, made them vulnerable to persecution were they to remain. Their stories are full of passion, intrigue and misguided ideals, but most of all they are elusive. This is a community, which, if you were to ask many of its members, never really existed. (The unknown exiles I call them.)

They reminded me of the people author Betty Friedan wrote about in her investigation on aging.[3] Whomever she interviewed eliminated themselves from the study because they claimed—no matter what their chronological age—that they weren't old enough to be included. People in their sixties told her to speak to those in their seventies and the seventy year olds said, 'speak to the eighty year olds,' and so forth. Others might age, but no one she interviewed empathized with the stock images of maturity—senility, poor health, impotence— because these simply did not apply to them. It is possible a few of the people I spoke to were incapable of regarding themselves as political expatriates because, here too, the negative

3. Betty Friedan, *The Fountain of Age*, New York: Simon & Schuster, 1993, p. 21.

stereotypes—fugitive, disloyal, politically unreliable—rarely applied. That wouldn't make my work any easier.

Nevertheless, some of these unknown exiles, the oldtimers for example, were better known—or less unknown—than the others because they were less afraid. Artists and intellectuals for the most part, a few had fought with the Republican forces in Spain, and all had arrived in Mexico by 1948. But, unlike the others, they couldn't be categorized according to their reasons for having left the States and, in general, were a mixed group. Because most of them had known my parents and thus were more likely to discuss their experiences, they would be a good group to start with.

"Call Conlon Nancarrow. I'll give you his number," long-time family friend, Eddy Lending, who had fought with him in Spain, told me. Nancarrow, a composer, had arrived in 1940 and, although I had never met him, I had heard he was a musical genius who later became known internationally as the "father of electronic music."[4] He had mastered all the major instruments by the time he was six, conducted the Ohio Symphony Orchestra when he was thirteen, and devised the 11-tone scale. I also learned—from Eddy—that he was interested in gourmet cooking and racy literature.[5] That was what I had to go on.

Over the phone his voice was the voice of a much younger man, so when I met him I was startled by his frailty. His eyes were sunken, his color ashen, and his sparse Van Dyke beard faded to the color of his skin. He was said to be a shy, private person and I had been warned: "You'll have to draw him out." But when he met me at the gate, he took hold of my briefcase, grasped my elbow, and led me slowly through the large garden to the front entrance. "Well," he said, "I really hope this isn't one of those traditional kinds of interviews."[6]

The house's reputation had also preceded it: It was built by Mexican artist Juan O'Gorman, whose small bas-relief in the entrance of the National University's Library resembles the one he created for Conlon Nancarrow's garden years earlier.[7]

4. Pablo Espinoza, "El autoexilio interior de Conlon Nancarrow," *La Jornada*, sección cultural, November 24, 1993, p. 31.
5. Edward Lending, letter to author, January 2, 1996 with enclosure dated December 30, 1995 addressed to Yoko and David Nancarrow.
6. Conlon Nancarrow, interview with author, August 28, 1996.
7. Pablo Espinoza, *La Jornada*, p. 31.

On entering the house I felt as if I'd been there before. The white stucco walls lined with art and books, the stone floors and simple furnishings, and the picture windows fronting on the garden, were eerily reminiscent of my parents' house in the Pedregal.

Once we were seated in the living room he started to speak slowly in a soft, clear voice, and although I was sitting directly in front of him I found myself straining to hear him: "I live a very isolated life really. For about two years, you know, my health was so bad, if it hadn't been for my wife I'd be dead now, and now I'm recovering and feeling almost normal. Well, I had a stroke and—I don't know—other things. And I still have trouble remembering names and I have trouble remembering, in general. When I first got back to a sort of normality I had to learn to write again so I could sign my name to a check. And, little by little, I got so I could recover my writing. Still a little shaky but it works."

When I asked why he had moved to Mexico he laughed. (He laughed a lot during our interview.)

"The U.S. government refused to renew my passport in 1940 because of my relation with the Communist Party and the Abraham Lincoln Brigade, which I had joined because I thought it would be good to defeat Franco. Well, I didn't like the idea of becoming a second class citizen. For the first few years in Mexico I was still an American so they [the U. S. government] couldn't keep me out of the States, but after I became a Mexican in 1956 they could. There was no specific reason. It's just the whole thing. I'm a subversive, I guess."

Unfortunately, his memory was spotty and he was unable to answer many of my questions. "Yes," he would respond when I asked him about a person or an incident. "I used to know that, but I don't remember anymore."

We strolled out into the garden and he walked me back to the gate, but this time I carried the briefcase. When I said good-bye, not realizing I would never see him again—he died within a year—I asked, "Well, what do you think, Conlon? Was this a traditional kind of interview?"

"Not at all," he laughed. "You know, usually people ask me the same things they could look up in the music books. This isn't in the music books."[8]

8. Conlon Nancarrow, interview with author, August 28, 1996.

Film maker William Colfax Miller, another Spanish Civil War vet, told me he left for Mexico in '39 because, "There was no Un-Mexican Activity Committee there." When a friend told him, erroneously, that he could become an official in the Mexican Army as a result of having fought in Spain, he believed him. Once he'd arrived in Mexico he had no intention of turning around and going home.[9]

Oldtimer John Menz, who moved to Mexico on two occasions—as a student from 1946-1948 and as a political refugee from 1951-1956—had been involved in the anti-loyalty oath battle at Berkeley in the early '50s[10] and had gotten into trouble for his bold opposition to school policy during a stint at the University of Texas in Austin.[11]

While John Menz, Bill Miller and Conlon Nancarrow were well aware of the political implications in their having left the United States, some of the other early arrivals I spoke to, although open about their left wing sympathies, told me: "We had other reasons for going to Mexico. We were not political expatriates," they insisted.

The FBI, however, thought otherwise.[12] Their records refer to an American Communist Group in Mexico, the ACGM, and described them as follows: "A loosely knit organization of a prominently social nature of persons who are present and/or past members of the Communist Party of the United States and their friends and associates who share a common sympathy for communism and the Soviet Union."[13]

9. William Colfax Miller, letter to author, March, 1993.
10. Berkeley, along with many educational institutions, large companies, government agencies and privately owned businesses required employees to sign loyalty oaths swearing they had never belonged to the Communist Party.
11. John Menz, letter to author, November 27, 1993.
12. When I first decided to investigate my past I solicited my parents' FBI dossiers and additional records under the Freedom of Information Act. It took me over four years and a lawyer's intervention to get them.
13. Federal Bureau of Investigation, David Drucker, April 29, 1955, p. 4, 105-12761-(57). A more complete description of the ACGM reads as follows: "(Unidentified source) has advised that the term 'American Communist Group in Mexico City' is used to describe the association on principally a social basis of American Marxists in Mexico City. The group is composed of expellees from the Communist Party, USA; strong pro-Communist sympathizers, and individuals who still claim to maintain their membership in the Communist Party, USA. . . . The group shares in common a pro-Soviet, pro-Communist and anti U.S. point of view. The group has never been organized under Party discipline although several unsuccessful attempts to do so have been made. From time to time funds are collected which are reportedly sent to the CPUSA to support its program."

Contemporary dancer and choreographer Waldeen Falken-
stein was on all the FBI lists although she told me over the phone
that her reasons for going to Mexico in 1947 were related to her
work, not her politics, thus there no reason for me to interview
her: "Anyway dear, it's impossible. My health, you know." So I
dropped in on her anyway, unannounced, under the pretense
of delivering some magazine articles. Although surprised to
see me—she was wearing a dressing gown and her hair was
wrapped in a towel—she was cordial and answered my questions. Mexico's Department of Education had invited her
down to direct a national dance company, she told me. That
was why she had left the States.

But, in her case (and in others) the FBI did not make such
fine distinctions so, neither could I. They referred to her and
her husband at the time of her arrival—medical translator Asa
Zatz—as "closely associated with the ACGM," no doubt because
of their progressive politics and their friendship with members
of the political expatriate community and the Mexican left.

Like Waldeen, sculptor and graphic artist Elizabeth Catlett
claims her reasons for going to Mexico in 1947 were work-
related: "I came here because I admired greatly the graphics
workshop, the *Taller de Grafica Popular,* (Workshop of People's
Graphic Art) and the mural painting and so forth, the public
art." But her name too would also find its way onto the FBI's
ACGM lists and she was subject to the same kind of scrutiny
as the others.

A powerful woman with cropped hair, which sets off her
dark, deeply expressive eyes, she led me through her Cuernavaca home, a place as unpretentious as she, filled with her art
and her husband's—powerful black and white graphics and
sleek, sensuous sculptures chiseled out of marble, cast in
bronze or carved from wood— to her studio. I had been there
with my parents, who were great admirers of her work, many
years earlier. They owned one of her wooden figures, a mother
and child. (Whenever I passed it on my way to my bedroom,
I'd run my hand down its smooth flanks.)

Once seated at a work table facing her garden, she leaned back
in her chair, clasped her hands in front of her and confronted
me with a steady gaze: "O.K. What do you want to know?" She
conveyed such a sense of dignity, power and reserve that, even

though I had known her for years, I couldn't help but find her slightly intimidating. Although she is not without warmth, she is very much her own person, trying to impress no one, and I could easily visualize her staring down an unsympathetic judge or the cops lining the city streets during a demonstration.[14]

As a student, she became known for her activism in fighting injustice, a theme which often appears in her work: She participated in a Supreme Court demonstration against lynching, a hangman's noose around her neck, and demonstrated in support of other black teachers, like herself, who were earning half the salary of whites.[15] Needless to say, her close association with civil rights and labor during the '30s and '40s did not endear her to law enforcement authorities.

Prior to leaving for Mexico in 1947, she had worked at the George Washington Carver School, one of the so-called People's Schools listed on the Attorney General's list of Red Front organizations.[16]

". . . I was married to artist Charles White. . . . And then I met my present husband, [Mexican artist Francisco *Pancho* Mora], got a divorce and stayed [in Mexico]. In the late '40s I returned to Washington D.C. to give birth to my first child. I had a cousin who was a very good surgeon there and I didn't know any doctors in Mexico. That's when they were making lists and investigating and so forth. Some reporters called me about the Carver School and I said, 'I haven't had anything to do with them for over a year and a half now, and I'm going back to Mexico.'"[17]

Many of the people I spoke to, like Elizabeth Catlett, I had known as a child. But what struck me was how little I actually knew about their backgrounds. Philip and Gertrude Stein, who arrived in the summer of '48, for example, were among the first people my parents met when they arrived in Mexico, but I had no idea why they had left the States.

They greeted me warmly: "You haven't changed a bit," they

---

14. Elizabeth Catlett, interview with author, January 17, 1991.
15. Lynn Norment, "Elizabeth Catlett: Dean of Women Artists," *Ebony*, April 1993, pp. 46-50.
16. The Committee on Un-American Activities of the U.S. House of Representatives periodically published a list of those organizations and individuals who, in their judgment, were engaged in subversive activities.
17. Elizabeth Catlett, interview with author, January 17, 1991.

told me. (I was sixteen the last time they had seen me, forty years earlier.) They, however, have changed very little. Both are pale and spare and give the impression of being slightly under-nourished. Yet despite his leanness, Philip conveys a resilient strength. Gertrude's finely chiseled bone structure, tense beneath tightly stretched skin, is striking. (I didn't used to think her beautiful. She is. I remembered, instead, a waif-like figure, fragile but fueled with nervous energy.)

We sat down together around the dining room table, and I turned on my tape recorder. I had a hard time focusing on them and keeping my eyes off their walls. They were hung, floor to ceiling, with oil paintings, some by Mexican muralist David Alfaro Siqueiros with whom Philip collaborated during his ten years in Mexico; others were his own: powerful canvases painted in drab greens, blacks and browns, and boldly slashed through with red and orange. We sipped our tea, and he told me their story:

"Of course it starts in Hollywood. We had a big strike there. Our Scenic Artists, along with other craft unions, lost the strike shattering our Conference of Studio Unions' collective,[18] and I went to jail for three months because of the strike activity, and when the long 1946 strike ended in 1947—toward the end of '47, I guess—there wasn't much to do in Hollywood.

"Anyway, there was no work in the studios. I had been a scenic artist for Columbia Pictures. Then I found some work doing theatrical scenery and window decorations. Gertrude had a job in some office maintaining us a bit, and then we put on a little show. . . . But I did not leave the United States for any political reason. We weren't persecuted in any way. We didn't really feel threatened politically. That's the way it went, because we knew we could take advantage of the G.I. Bill. . . . So after the war I had a lot of time. I was going to Chouinard Art School in Hollywood, but I still had over three years left

18. Griffin Fariello, *Red Scare: Memories of the American Inquisition: An Oral History*, New York/London: V.W. Norton & Company, 1995, p. 256. The studios traditionally opposed the Conference of Studio Unions (CSU), a progressive union, and threw their support behind the corruption ridden International Alliance of Theatrical Stage Employees (IATSE), run by Chicago mobsters. In exchange for payoffs the IATSE curbed workers' demands and cooperated with studios to destroy the CSU. During the 1945 and 1946 CSU strikes IATSE thugs assisted studio and local police in violently dispersing over 1,000 strikers.

under the G.I. Bill. So we packed up. We had a little house in Canoga Park, which we sold, and left for Mexico. We went to San Miguel Allende only because there was a school there, and we could enroll as G.I.s and get our monthly stipend and study art. Gertrude studied there too, all kinds of art things—ceramics, weaving. I met Siqueiros there, and after the school was closed by a student-teachers' strike, we went to Mexico City where, for the next nine years, I worked with Siqueiros, did my own painting and had a few exhibits. Gertrude taught English."[19]

After dozens of interviews, and in spite of the Betty Friedan (Who me?) syndrome, I did manage to identify roughly sixty families. There were more, of course, but they were hard to pinpoint, in part, because political repression in the United States, as compared to elsewhere, was comparatively mild: There were no mass roundups, concentration camp internees[20] or wholesale executions. As a result, going to Mexico was for many a question of choice. (Most of the politically suspect, however unpleasant their experiences, did remain in the States and survive the witchhunts.)

Some of the people I interviewed questioned their own motives, and I imagine that many others who sought refuge here—perhaps quite a few—went undetected. Others died before they got around to telling their stories or suppressed them out of their growing disillusion with communism. A number were never identified because they avoided contact with the political expatriate community, married Mexicans and assimilated far more successfully than the rest of us, or simply chose to escape notice because they were afraid. After all, for some, keeping a low profile was one way to evade political persecution.

Fear had a lot to do with it. Fear on both sides: While political dissidents were terrified by the strident anti-Communism, the right-wing was also afraid—of a USSR strengthened by war and no longer an ally; the newly recognized destructive potential of nuclear power and the threat posed by a militant left. Added to their fears, real and imagined, was a deep-seated sense of

19. Philip and Gertrude Stein, interview with author, May 15, 1995. Philip Stein, letters to author January 22, 1995 and January 7, 1998.
20. Under the Internal Security or McCarran Act of 1950 concentration camps were established in the event of a national emergency, but were never used.

frustration and impotence. Americans, used to winning battles and moving on, became quickly impatient with the emerging Cold War. They were looking for a solution: Political conservatives—right-wing Democrats and disgruntled Republicans—out of power since Roosevelt had assumed office in 1932, promised them one. By placing the blame on the Communist Party, the New Deal and organized labor; imposing restrictive legislation and holding a series of sensational media events, they could attract voters and discredit the opposition.[21] (At a time when television was just beginning to gain widespread acceptance, they would also reach a previously unimagined number of viewers.)

Therefore, the opposition, people like my parents, afraid they might lose their jobs or be harassed or detained for having associated with suspect organizations or individuals, fled to Mexico because the deteriorating political climate at home, like the signal lights at a railroad crossing, was a sign of danger: They believed—along with the American Communist Party—that fascism was replacing democracy in the United States.

When I interviewed Alonso Aguilar, Mexican economist, writer, journalist, university professor and a long-time friend of some of the political expatriates, he said as much:

"After World War II we had trouble understanding what was going on. Up until then Americans had expressed extreme positions openly and when, in good faith, and perhaps somewhat naively, we asked what they thought of McCarthyism, what could be done about it, we encountered reserve, insecurity, even fear. . . ."[22]

The first question I asked those who had fled the States was the one my mother and I, newly arrived in Mexico, had asked ourselves: "What the hell am I doing here?" I just rephrased it: "What made you go leave home?" I turned for answers to family friends and their acquaintances: former labor leaders, 'undesirable' U.S. resident aliens, the Abraham Lincoln Brigade vets, Party organizers, Hollywood activists, and the unfriendly

21. Jeffrey Robert Ryan, *The Conspiracy That Never Was: United States Government Surveillance of Eastern European American Leftists, 1942-1959,* Doctoral Dissertation, Boston College, Ann Arbor, MI, 1989: University Microfilms International, 1991 p. 106.
22. Alonso Aguilar, interview with author, July 9, 1991.

witnesses at Congressional and State hearings. Some were members or former members of the Communist Party; others were not. All were the victims—or potential victims—of loyalty boards, investigating committees, blacklists, Cold War legislation and informers and their answers ranged from the unexpected to the ingenuous: One woman told me: "Well, we had to go somewhere and we'd never been to Mexico." Screenwriter Hugo Butler's daughter, Mary, aged five years old at the time, remembered asking her mother the same question:

"She said, 'Well, we're blacklisted.'

"'And what does that mean?' I was very young.

"And she said it meant they'd done something [so] that they wouldn't make any of our films. And I asked, 'Well, why not?'

"And she replied, 'Well, we sent too many scripts out at once.'

"And I thought, 'How stupid can you get? And what a terrible punishment.' You know, for sending too many scripts in at one time. That seemed such terrible punishment!"[23]

While people left the States for different reasons, I began to realize that their reasons for choosing Mexico were very much the same. Ever since the early days of banditry, when personal situations threatened to become distasteful or perhaps intolerable, Americans crossed over to the other side in order to elude criminal charges, evade taxes or a vindictive spouse, escape the high cost of living and of course, religious and political repression. One additional attraction was Mexico's reputation— often over-rated—as a country where, in the worst of cases, 'things could be arranged.'

So, in effect, political expatriates were simply following a time honored tradition and crossing the border into a country with a reputation for harboring fugitives: A former president, Lázaro Cárdenas (1934-1940), had given asylum to someone as controversial as Leon Trotsky,[24] opened the doors to those fleeing fascism in Europe and encouraged political diversity

23. Mary Butler, interview with author, July 28, 1991.
24. Bolshevik leader Leon Trotsky's opposition to Stalin resulted in his exile. Most countries denied him sanctuary because they didn't want to antagonize the Soviet Union.

during his regime. (Most progressives had heard of him and his contributions, and they provided a comforting, if no longer completely realistic, image of Mexico for political activists on the run.)

In addition, it was one of only two countries waiving passport requirements for U.S. citizens. (Canada was the other. However, a series of highly publicized espionage trials in the mid '40s would discourage some politicial expatriates from seeking refuge there.) Since the U.S. Government refused to issue travel documents to the politically suspect, some dissidents were unable to go elsewhere.

Even if they could, many lacked the resources. From past visits they knew life was cheaper in Mexico than in the United States, allowing them to live well on less. Furthermore, once they obtained working papers, they could operate businesses or, occasionally, find employment.

In the end, I think most of them were optimists, and Mexico's geographic location made it possible to think of flight as a temporary expedient—as indeed it was for many—almost like taking a trip. Some drove down, and all retained the option of returning as soon as things cooled off. Leaving behind homes, businesses, elderly parents and college-aged offspring, many chose to think of going to Mexico as an inter-ruption to their 'real lives.' Those who had the luxury of looking before leaping weighed all these factors before migrating. But sometimes the situation had become, or threatened to become, so difficult they had nothing to lose. The family lawyer would say, "Look, things could get worse before they get better, so scram. I'll let you know when it's safe to return."

Chapter Two

Perforated Lives:[1]
The American Political Expatriates

I've always made important decisions at airports: to drop out of college, return to Mexico, get a degree in teaching, marry my husband. I find the activity and sense of purpose inspiring. Airports make it seem so easy to move on. (Everyone is doing it.) I enjoy knowing, that for a few hours at least, I'm at an impasse, free to observe others in transit on their way to somewhere else. It makes me restless, compels me to keep on going—not just from one place in the world to another but from one place in my life to another. (If I'd been born fifty years earlier I probably would have felt the same way at railroad stations.)

I was at the Los Angeles airport on my way to Mexico and had a few hours to kill between planes when I decided to write this book. The thought had shadowed me a long time, but as I was leafing through my telephone directory wondering who I could call with my spare change I realized I knew at least a half a dozen people in California alone who would help me.

As friends of my parents, I tended to lump them all together: I remembered a close-knit group of people much like those we had known in the Bronx: warm and effusive with strong opinions and loud voices who invited us over to eat spaghetti or tacos and listen to jazz on Saturday afternoons. They exchanged

---

1. "Notwithstanding cowardices,
     I have been able to come to understand
     that my perforated life
     has been filled with the infinite . . .
     And I fervently bless the host of pain. . . ."
from "The Host of Pain," *Vendedor de Cocuyos* (*The Vendor of Fireflies*) by Luisa Moreno; translated into English by Abbott Small. Moreno, a Guatemalan civil rights activist, labor leader, and U.S. resident for 22 years, moved to Mexico in 1950 after the American Government filed deportation procedings against her. She resided briefly in Guatemala, but returned to Mexico after the CIA deposed President Arbenz in 1954.

magazines and books and answered each other's questions:
Where do you buy pickles or *The New York Times*? Do you have
to boil the milk? Can you renew your entry visa without leaving
the country? They offered each other moral and, when necessary,
financial support, and shared a liberal outlook. Most kept low
profiles and were virtually unknown outside our small circle.

But when I started contacting some of my parents' old
acquaintances, and they, in turn, referred me to others, I soon
discovered that these so-called 'political expatriates' didn't
conform my pre-packaged, pre-adolescent images of them:
They didn't always know each other, and when they did, didn't
necessarily agree on the issues or even like each other very
much. They came from highly diversified backgrounds and had
left the States for a wide variety of reasons.

Although they were united by a strong sense of camaraderie
many of them had already drifted away from the Party by the
time they arrived in Mexico, and often disagreed on key issues:
the Hitler-Stalin Pact, a change in Party leadership,[2] Stalin's
autoritarianism, Party attempts to restrict intellectual freedom, and after 1956, both Krushchev's report to the Twentieth
Congress,[3] and the Hungarian revolt.[4] Such disagreements
could often lead to discord and fallings-out.

The only pattern I could find was that they were 'lefties,'
had departed under similar circumstances during a time when
their politics were not tolerated by the general public, and—if
I stretched it a bit—fit into roughly five different categories:
the U.S. resident aliens, who as foreigners, feared they might
be deported because of their association with the left; Party
or Party press envoys; those accused of conspiracy and espionage,
the blacklisted Hollywood writers and political activists, and a
few who arrived following hearings into Communist conspiracy
in Miami.

The more people I spoke to the more I realized how little
we had known about each other and the legal issues underlying

2. When William Z. Foster replaced Earl Browder in 1945, the Party reverted to a
more rigid and doctrinaire stance, abandoning the "Popular Front" approach which
had attempted to accommodate a broader spectrum of opinion.
3. Khruschev's revelation in 1956 of atrocities committed under Stalin caused many
to leave the Party.
4. Hungary's disenchantment with Soviet rule resulted in an uprising soon quashed
by Russian troops in November, 1956.

our departures. I think this was one of the things that surprised me the most. Those in the first group, the resident aliens, for example, were all known to me as a child, and their cases had generated considerable publicity but I, and probably many of the others, had no idea they had been forced to leave the States. There was no doubt that their motives were political. As foreigners, they enjoyed none of the protection U.S. citizens are entitled to under the law and any non-citizen who belonged to a suspect organization could be deported.[5] As early as 1940, the Smith Act, also known as the Alien Registration Act, was an obvious attempt to curtail their participation in activities which, in the government's judgment, called for the violent overthrow of the United States Government, but it didn't always work.

When the Supreme Court ruled that violent overthrow was not the inevitable result of Communism, legislators came up with an easier way to deport dissidents, the 1950 McCarran Act (Internal Security Act). It solved the problem by equating Communists with subversives. Each organization was compelled to identify itself as such, to register, and disclose membership and sources of funding. Their members, if United States citizens, could be denied the right to apply for passports or renew old ones or, if resident aliens, could be subject to deportation. Immediately after it was passed in October, 1950, over President Truman's veto, an order was issued to apprehend eighty-six individuals identified as communist aliens.[6]

At around this time, some resident aliens, pressured to leave post-haste or realizing that their eventual deportation was all but inevitable, moved to Mexico. Bart van der Schelling and his wife, Edna Moore, arrived in Mexico in June, 1950: "Those were the bad days. 'In the Troubles,' as they say in Ireland," Edna recalled. She seated me in a plush armchair in her snug living room in Los Angeles, propped her cane against the side table, and served me strong black coffee.

Edna was a compact red-head whose loud voice and direct manner conveyed a misleading impression of toughness. She had been a family friend and my music teacher at the American School in Mexico City. I remembered her—diminutive, elf-like—

---

5. Many had requested citizenship, but were turned down because of their politics.
6. David Caute, *The Great Fear: The Anti-Communist Purge Under Truman and Eisenhower,* New York: Simon & Schuster, 1978, pp. 229-230.

pounding away at the piano keys and bellowing out the words to *La Cucaracha, John Brown's Body*, or *Love's Old Sweet Song* in a voice turned hoarse from tobacco. Today, forty years later, she sipped her coffee slowly, grasping the cup between both hands to keep them from trembling.

Her husband, Bart, a naturalized American citizen, had arrived in the United States from Holland with childhood buddy, painter Willem de Kooning. A fine singer, Bart performed regularly at left-wing events, cut several recordings—his renditions of Spanish Civil War songs on the Vanguard label is a collector's item—and served as a Section Commander for the George Washington Battalion during the Spanish Civil War. According to Edna:

"The laws have since changed, but during the '50s as a naturalized American citizen you couldn't be absent from the United States for more than five years running. You had to return for a certain number of weeks. But Bart had a bad heart attack around that time and couldn't return [to the United States.] Anyway, he lost his citizenship, and didn't feel like being deported. . . .

"Well, about that time, we had a house in Laurel Canyon in the Hollywood Hills, and we used to have folksong fests and meetings about once a month. Earl Robinson came by when he was around and Pete Seeger. Bart and Pete were very good friends from way back. So anyhow, we made a lot of noise singing. Somebody, some friend, came by and said, 'Watch out. Someone's been asking about you guys.' So we got the message. We felt it was time to take off. And we did. We went for a few weeks and stayed thirteen years."[7]

Others waited until deportation proceedings were initiated against them and then agreed to what was euphemistically called 'voluntary departure.' This alternative allowed possible reentry if permission were granted at a later date and was, therefore, preferable to deportation, which unconditionally eliminated any likelihood of ever reentering the United States.

Canadian Anita Boyer, a strikingly beautiful woman with a quick wit and a direct manner, chose the first option. Although not a Communist herself—"I consider myself apolitical," she

7. Edna Moore van der Schelling, interview with author, August 1, 1991.

told me—she was inclined to marry them. And not just any communist. Both her first and second husbands, Raymond Boyer[8] and Frederick Vanderbilt Field, (referred to here as Fred Field) were millionaires, had achieved notoriety—the first in Canada, the second in the United States—and had served time in prison.

The campaign against Anita began shortly after Fred finished his jail sentence. "As a foreigner I was at the mercy of the U.S. government," Anita told me. "I felt locked up. I couldn't do anything except be a housewife and live in this great big house. And oh, I went to dance classes and did these very simple things, very safe things. I had to report to the immigration authorities every six months. And every six months they would say, 'What do you do here? What do you read? Who do you see?' and so on.

"One time I went to the Immigration Office and this big fat slob asked me, 'How come, Mrs. Field, you run with the dogs? First you married Dr. Boyer and now you marry Mr. Field.' And, heart pounding and with a feeling of revulsion, I lied: 'Did it ever occur to you Mister—whatever his-name was—that I married them because they're both millionaires?'

"Well, he sat back in his chair and he laughed and he said, 'My goodness I never thought of that.'"[9]

By 1953, when Anita was forced to leave the United States, deportation proceedings against resident aliens had become vastly simplified. The 1952 Immigration and Nationality Act, also known as the McCarran-Walter Act, reduced immigration from non-white countries and tightened previous restrictions. It denied aliens residence permits for political reasons, provided for the deportation of resident aliens deemed subversive, and allowed for the deportation and loss of citizenship for dissidents who had become naturalized citizens, even if their political activities had ceased prior to 1952, the year the law was passed. It also produced a whole new crop of potential victims. Anyone associated with the Party or radical politics or, as in

8. During a series of sensational trials held in Montreal in 1947, Raymond Boyer, a McGill University research chemist, was convicted of violating the Official Secrets Act. According to his accuser Igor Gouzenko, a cipher clerk in the Soviet Embassy, Boyer was part of a group that had handed over Canadian explosives secrets to the Soviets in 1943 and 1944.
9. Anita Boyer, interview with author, February 14, 1992.

the case of Anita, an alien closely related to a 'subversive,' could now be deported.[10]

Upon quitting the United States, most political expatriates, like the van der Schellings and Anita Boyer, went straight to Mexico. Cedric Belfrage, author, film critic, journalist, and co-founder/editor of the *National Guardian*, was the exception. He had spent approximately eight years traveling throughout the world as the *Guardian*'s "editor in exile." I remembered him from the occasional Sunday we spent at his home in Cuernavaca when I was young. He was a thin, thoughtful man who smoked a pipe, and was delighted, but not condescending, when I beat him at Scrabble.

A British citizen, he had left the States in 1955 to avoid deportation following years of litigation, hearings and detentions, resulting from his close association with the left and his identification by Elizabeth Bentley, the 'Red Spy Queen,' as a Soviet intelligence source during World War II. He and his wife, Mary, settled in Cuernavaca and opened a guest house, *Casa Belfrage*, to supplement their income. A haven for South American exiles and a meeting spot for Mexican and American intellectuals, it was known in left-wing circles for comfortable accommodations, stimulating conversation and good food.

By the time I phoned Mary in 1992, Cedric had been dead for two years and Mary had not seen me in over twenty, but she sounded happy to hear from me and eager at the prospect of an interview.

"Anything I can bring from Mexico City?" I asked.

"Sure, bring *bialis*. (onion rolls)," she said.

Mary is a small, stocky, gray-haired woman in her seventies whose apologetic smile and round face, devoid of makeup, convey—mistakenly as it turned out—a calm, mild manner. As she toasted the *bialis* over the range, I peered out the window with its view of pool and rolling lawn. After we had eaten the onion rolls she suggested a house tour. The rustic interior with its stone fireplace in one corner of the living room, hand woven wool throw rugs on the floor, and simple wooden furniture, had changed little over the years. "Why don't you come some weekend and bring your friends?" she asked me. "I need to rent more rooms, attract a younger crowd." The walls in

10. Griffin Fariello, *Red Scare*, p. 18.

Cedric's study were still lined with his books and she told me she was interested in selling them. She showed me their guest book. It contained messages from pediatrician Benjamin Spock, writer Jessica Mitford, lawyer Victor Rabinowitz, folk singer Pete Seeger and the Rosenberg's sons, Robert and Michael Meerpol, among others.

Once we had returned to the living room I turned on my recorder and asked, "What made you and Cedric decide to open a guest house?"

"Well, I just couldn't see myself teaching in Mexico City at the American School, like some people we know."

(I was working at the school at the time, although I'm not sure she knew that.)

"Hey, you can't do that!" she cried, spying my tape recorder. I turned it off and started taking notes. I handed her a list of those I believed had come to Mexico for political reasons and asked her to take a look. She started to read. Upon reaching her name she crossed it off. "I was an exile, but I wouldn't have had to go if I'd had money."

She conceded that some of the expatriates might have gone to Mexico for ideological reasons, believing the United States was fast becoming fascist, but felt very few were politically motivated. As she reviewed the list she separated the names into two groups, those she liked and those she disliked. "There are the liberals and the stinking liberals," she told me.

I must have grimaced because she countered with, "I'm terrible, I know."

The majority, she told me, came to Mexico because they could have maids and live cheaply. She insisted that most of the people weren't political expatriates at all because they had come down to make money. "And the Hollywood people don't count. They had money. And I can't go along with your premise of those poor, persecuted leftists. They were rich."

I responded. "Look, after many years my folks did well here, but they came down with $1,000. That was all they had, Mary. Their life savings."

She started to cry. "I cry easily. I'm so angry." she told me.[11]

I breathed deeply and looked away from her and down at my notes. I didn't want to give her the satisfaction. But it was

11. Mary Belfrage, interview with author, March 4, 1992.

too late. I burst into tears. Certainly, nothing prepared me for her reaction, nor for my own. What in the world was I doing there? After all, I was one of scores of children who had been uprooted, but none of them were running around with a tape recorder trying to understand why their parents had left the States over forty years earlier. I had to have a motive. Either that, or I was crazy. I think, at some level, I may have been expecting some reward for my perseverance—admiration, praise, affection—and was trying to recoup something I had lost or compensate for something I'd never had. Maybe that's why Mary's reaction upset me so much. Mary Belfrage was supposed to love me, not berate me.

She felt terrible, I know. When I returned to visit with friends a few months later we sat side by side on her sofa, our arms around each other's shoulders, and smiled.

Yet, with the exception of Mary, almost everyone I spoke to was not only delighted to see me but surprisingly forthcoming about most things. When I first started my research I was afraid the majority would try to evade my questions on grounds their migrations to Mexico were not politically motivated. Upon mentioning this to Victor Navasky, publisher and editorial director of *The Nation*, who had had a lot more experience in this area than I, he said: "Just wait," or words to that effect. "You'll be surprised at the things people will tell you. All you've really got to do is listen to what they have to say." With the exception of two groups of people—those sent by the Party and those accused of espionage and conspiracy—he was right.

Most political expatriates had chosen to go to Mexico, but not everyone got to choose: People who fell into this category were among the hardest to identify and, generally, the most careful. (The father of one of my schoolmates, reputed to have been involved in the underground, agreed to see me. Then, at the last moment, he canceled, telling me he had changed his mind because his son-in-law worked for the government.)

Once the Party decided who should go, they determined the timing of their migrations and the lengths of their stays. Those sent were either journalists representing Party publications or public figures who had been openly involved in Popular Front activities.[12]

Charles Humboldt, also known as Clarence Weinstock, appears to have fallen into both these categories: He was a journalist, art critic, the editor of the cultural quarterly, *Masses and Mainstream,* and a writer of essays, poems and short stories. The people I interviewed believed he was "highly political," and a few thought he was a Party official, although little is known of his time in Mexico. Even the length of his stay is in doubt, although he apparently arrived sometime in 1952 and may have stayed as late as 1954.[13]

Others had been named by government informers, or were likely to be, and a few were merely in transit. For these last, Mexico was a corridor to somewhere else. Believing their continued presence might place them and the Party at risk, some individuals were instructed to leave the States, settle elsewhere, and go through a "watchful waiting period."[14]

Such instructions clearly reflected a change in Party policy: As early as 1947 or 1948, anticipating severe repression, the leadership adopted the idea of a clandestine organization. They stopped issuing cards, destroyed central membership lists, and formulated a plan to send hundreds of cadre into hiding in Mexico, Canada, Europe and the United States while still preserving some semblance of leadership.

In addition to those instructed to leave their homes, a small contingent lived in the shadows, the reason for their presence in Mexico virtually unknown to most of the others. Following the arrest of eleven of twelve top Party leaders[15] in January, 1949, George Watt, head of the CP National Committee's underground apparatus, told everyone he was taking a vacation and left for Mexico with his family. His real purpose was to organize a small rudimentary network in case it became necessary to send National Committee members into exile. Assisted by a

12. Between 1935 and 1940 the U.S. Communist Party formed alliances with a wide variety of progressive causes and organizations. As a result, it became more closely identified with New Deal policy, leading, in turn, to its greater accessibility and openness. When William Z. Foster replaced Earl Browder in 1945, the Party reverted to a more rigid and doctrinaire stance, abandoning the "Popular Front" approach which had attempted to accommodate a broader spectrum of opinion.
13. Barbara M. Riley, finding aid for Charles Humboldt Papers, Yale University Sterling Memorial Library, Manuscripts and Archives, Manuscript Group #721.
14. May Brooks, interview with author, July 19, 1994.
15. Party head William Z. Foster was not seized because of a heart condition.

businessman, a resident of Mexico, he put together a group of some six sympathizers, all originally from the States. Once he had set the groundwork for a Mexican connection, those left in charge were given the responsibility of establishing an effective apparatus.

Ten months later, the Party's worst fears were confirmed: Eleven CP leaders were found guilty under the Smith Act for conspiring to advocate the violent overthrow of the U.S. government. While the decision was being appealed, George Watt returned to Mexico accompanied by three well known Party members trained to operate under duress. They were to reside in Mexico and take over control of the Party if the U.S. leadership were destroyed.[16]

I first heard of the CPUSA underground from Abe (A. B.) Magil, sent to Mexico in 1950 with his wife Harriet and daughter Maggie as *The Daily Worker* correspondent. By the time I interviewed Magil in 1993, he had left the Party after 45 years, following a long career as a member of *The Daily Worker* editorial board, editor of the *New Masses*, a member of its national leadership during the 1950s, and the author of many books and pamphlets.

When I arrived at their New York City apartment their only knowledge of me stemmed from a brief correspondence and the recommendation of a mutual acquaintance. Despite this, both were cordial and spoke openly and enthusiastically about their time in Mexico, asking eagerly after old friends.

Although Harriet has nearly lost her eyesight, she moved around the apartment with assurance, placing the flowers I had brought in water, brewing coffee, leading me past shelves crammed with books and walls lined with art. She seated me at the dining room table. Behind my chair hung a photo of Frida Kahlo. It was personally dedicated and read, *"No me olviden."* (Don't forget me.)

Abe told me, "I was a Party functionary, and they asked me to go. At first, Harriet was very disappointed. . . . She was in love with France." He explained that, strictly speaking, he was not in Mexico as a Party representative, nor as part of the apparatus, but might have been perceived that way because of his

16. Peter Steinberg, *The Great 'Red Menace': United States Prosecution of American Communists, 1947-1952,* New York University PH.d. Thesis, 1979, p. 311.

position with *The Daily Worker.* "And yes, there were people who were part of the underground," although he refused to divulge names. "But I didn't have direct contact with them. I was too public."[17]

Unlike most expatriates in Mexico during the early '50s, they mixed as easily with Mexicans as with Americans, their learning Spanish early on an enormous asset. Harriet, a psychiatric social worker and the more fluent of the two, was unable to work legally because of her immigration status. Keeping busy was important, she told me: "So I volunteered at the *Centro Avila Camacho.* . . . I gave seminars in Spanish for three groups of social workers at a wonderful maternal and child care center, a model for Latin America. I went out with the nurses on their rounds to see what they were contending with, and learned as much as I taught."

For Abe, in Mexico as a journalist writing about political developments in Latin America, in general, and Mexico, in particular, it was important to move in Party circles. He and Harriet established contact with Mexican Communists and intellectuals such as painters David Alfaro Siqueiros, Diego Rivera and Xavier Guerrero; Mexican Party head Dionisio Encina, General Heriberto Jara, and Revolutionary hero, politician and Secretary of the Navy, and the *Partido Popular* founder, Lombardo Toledano. They also befriended a number of Latin American exiles, among them Venezuelan Party heads Gilberto and Eduardo Machado, the Cuban revolutionaries Carlos Rafael Rodriguez and Juan Marinello, and Chilean poet Pablo Neruda.

As a result of his close contact with the left-wing, Abe was the only American I interviewed who was able to address my questions concerning the Mexican Party. When I asked about ties between the Americans and Mexicans he responded: "I don't think the [U.S.] Party was very active in assisting the Latin American Party. It was, in itself . . . weak . . . and being persecuted, but it regarded itself, I think, as more politically developed than the Mexican Parties." He told me there was no

17. A. B. Magil, interview with author, January 20, 1993; A. B. Magil letter to author, February 3, 1993. In a subsequent letter he wrote, "Those sent to Mexico, except for myself, had the job of setting up an underground organization in the event the Party had to function illegally or semi-legally."

U.S. representative between Mexico and the United States, but that there was a Party emissary in Mexico who worked closely with Encina.

While their stay in Mexico was not without difficulties, Abe summed up his experience in the country when he said: "I remember one time sitting at my typewriter. The sun was shining in, and I thought to myself: 'Sometime I will look back on this period as a golden time.' And it was true."[18]

If Mexico was an idyllic experience for some, for others it was a dimly-lit memory, a tunnel leading somewhere else. In the summer of 1950 when Ann Kimmage boarded a train to Mexico City with her parents, Belle and Abe Chapman, and her older sister, Laura, she had no idea she would be gone for more than thirteen years.

Her father, a committed Party member since the '30s, had been editor of the Communist Jewish daily, *Morning Freiheit*, an Executive Officer of the International Worker's Order (IWO)[19] and a member of the New York State Party Committee. As a writer and authority on the Philippines he had published a number of articles and reviews for the Institute of Pacific Relations (IPR).[20] In the summer of 1951 attempts were made to subpoena him for hearings on Communist infiltration at IPR. But, by then, he had vanished without leaving a trace.[21]

Ann and I began to correspond shortly after I started my research. I was fascinated by her story. She was in Mexico briefly, although I never met her. Her memories of Mexico City as a place where shrill colors, the smell of frying oil and an undercurrent of excitement set it apart from everything she had ever known, coincided with my own. We were both the same age when we left home, had lived in New York City, and had mothers named Belle.

She sent me an early version of her gripping memoir, *An Un-American Childhood*. In it she described how a few weeks after they had settled down into a large house in the center of

18. A. B. Magil, interview with author, January 20, 1993.
19. The IWO was listed by the Committee on Un-American Activities as a subversive organization in 1947.
20. The Institute of Pacific Relations, organized to promote understanding with the Pacific rim, was accused of a pro-Communist bias and of publishing classified information.
21. Ann Kimmage, *An Un-American Childhood*, Athens & London: University of Georgia Press, 1996 pp. xv-xix.

Mexico City: ". . . agitated voices woke me up in the middle of the night. I tried to decode the rapid flow of words that reached my bedroom. The voices of my father and mother were intermingled with voices that spoke thickly accented English. The pitch of their speech was intense and passionate. Names of people I didn't know, like Sobell and Rosenberg and others, filled the house; talk of arrests and searches was brisk and agitated.

"I got out of bed to look over the banister from the top landing of the staircase, curious to see what was happening. Ashes were falling to the floor from my parents' cigarettes as they waved their hands to emphasize their words. . . . When my mother saw me hanging over the banister, witnessing this late night encounter, she matter of factly announced that we would be leaving the house. I asked, 'When?' only to be told 'Now, right now!' There was no time for me to get out of my nightgown as my sister and I were quickly ushered into a car. From the window of the moving car I watched the last flickers of the city lights vanish as we sped into the dark night countryside."

After traveling for hours over steep, winding roads they arrived at a small village and, slightly beyond, a farm surrounded by low walls. From Ann's description it was one of hundreds of modest *ranchos* which dot the Mexican landscape, a grouping of adobe structures, roofed with rugged, brick colored shingles. I can visualize the room where they were confined for months: white-washed plaster walls, low ceilings, hard-packed dirt floors, a room barely large enough for a pair of cots and two beds. They looked out onto a courtyard, dusty and desolate, where their Mexican hosts—a couple with three adolescent sons—carried on their daily routines. A few mangy dogs lolled in the shade, some chickens scratched the soil. Fear that their presence might arouse suspicion confined them to the house until sun-down. Ann had no one to speak to—their hosts spoke no English—except her sister and parents: Her sister could not explain her predicament; her parents refused.

This dark time in hiding lasted several months and ended abruptly with the arrival of three men who rapidly fired off orders to their Mexican hosts and explained, in a mixture of English and Spanish, that remaining on the farm was no longer possible. The Chapmans returned to Mexico City and were taken directly to the airport. Her father boarded a plane—to Moscow she later learned[22]— while she, her mother and her sister were flown, initially, to a city she believes may have been Amsterdam. (She remembers eating windmill shaped chocolates on a plane equipped with comfortable beds and crisp sheets, a luxury she had not known since leaving New York.) After her father joined them a few months later they settled down to a new life with an assumed identity in Prague.

Most people who were sent to Mexico stayed briefly: Chapman was there for a few months and Magil less than two years. In that respect, Sam and May Brooks were the exception: May continues to live in Mexico; Sam died there in 1963, eleven years after their arrival.

We are sitting at May's kitchen table in her small, modestly furnished home in Cuernavaca, one of several sharing a large communal garden. I hadn't seen her for over five years but she still wears her red hair closely cropped—a trademark—and retains an urchin-like air. Although painfully thin, she has lost neither her magnetism nor her energy, and conveys the warmth found in those who are genuinely fond of people. Her jerky gestures and throaty chuckle are electric; her enthusiasm and delight in conversation contagious. She darts around the compact kitchen to light the stove, heat water, grab a teacup.

She explains: "I was born in New York City [and] had that narrow, provincial view that anybody who lives out of New York is somehow inferior. . . . You know, like the cartoon in the *New Yorker* [of the guy] look[ing] at the map of the United States and [all he sees is a blowup] of New York and a piece of San Francisco. Who would have thought of living outside of New York? It was my city, I liked my life . . . and those were good years."

Sam and May's first trip to Mexico was in 1939. During the early '40s they worked with the Spanish Refugee Relief Committee (SRRC) and established a cooperative in Cuernavaca for Spanish refugees fleeing Franco. When I asked May how this enterprise was related to the Communist Party, she replied: "No, it had nothing to do with the Party. This was pure initiative on our part. It functioned for a while but then it couldn't function for too long because of politics. The Communists would not

22. Ann Kimmage, *An Un-American Childhood*, early version of manuscript, pp. 12-16, p. 51.

talk to the Anarchists, and they would talk to the Socialists, but not to the Trotskyites and so forth. [There was a] crisis all the time, and so we came to try to pull it around again and [the commune] lasted for—I don't remember how long a time, too short a time really. It began with maybe twenty-five people . . . maybe more, maybe thirty-five people. . . ."

The second time they left the United States to live in Mexico, May told me, was under far different circumstances: In 1949 when the Party first made the decision to go underground, she was singled out to organize the 'Manhattan Underground.' Her contact was J. Peters, a Hungarian citizen, who had headed the CPUSA secret apparatus until 1938, approximately.[23] When he was deported by the American government in 1948, contact was broken and she was put in touch with John Lautner, highly placed in the Party hierarchy. Shortly after their first telephone conversations, conducted in code, he asked her to meet him in the dining room of New York City's Wanamaker's Department Store. "It was like meeting the Representative of God," she told me. Soon after, he advised her that she would be unable to reach him for a while because he was being hospitalized. Then the news hit the front pages: John Lautner was a double agent. Since he testified, for the most part, in private sessions, much of his declaration remained secret but it was assumed that her name and Sam's were in the records. They left the United States in 1951, lived briefly in Paris, and then proceeded to Mexico. May told me the Party believed they might be singled out for a major case and felt there was "no need for martyrs." Although reluctant to leave, they would never have questioned Party orders, she told me. "It was a matter of discipline."

While people like Brooks, Magil and Humboldt may have been in danger had they remained in the States, there was another group at even greater risk: those accused of having spied or otherwise collaborated with the Soviet Union. The majority of these never returned to the United States, and the few who did remained in Mexico a minimum of twenty years.[24]

23. John Earl Haynes & Harvey Klehr, *Venona: Decoding Soviet Espionage in America,* Yale University Press, 1999. J. Peters also wrote the *Peters' Manual* used to instruct Youth Communist League members in organizing techniques.
24. After twenty years, in accordance with the Statute of Limitations, individuals can no longer be tried for the same crime unless they are accused of murder.

For a handful of them, not even Mexico was safe, and became the stepping stone to a Soviet bloc country—Russia, Poland or Czechoslovakia and, after the 1959 Revolution, Cuba.

Because of the magnitude of the charges and the publicity such accusations generated, rumors took on lives of their own. They were like recurring nightmares and never completely disappeared. Instead, they dropped quietly into oblivion—for a while—only to be resurrected by some new investigation. To my knowledge, about a dozen of those named in relation to espionage, conspiracy or collaboration ended up in Mexico, but, obviously, no one I interviewed actually gave that as their reason for having left the United States and rarely mentioned it in relation to others. As a matter of fact, if I had started interviewing people in 1971 instead of waiting until 1991 I might have chosen to completely eliminate 'accusations of conspiracy and espionage' as a motive for going to Mexico.

As luck would have it, shortly after I started my research, and amid considerable controversy, a large body of previously unavailable information was made public: Soviet archives were opened to foreign scholars and deciphered portions of the Venona Decrypts, intercepted wartime cable traffic between Moscow and its diplomatic offices in the United States, were published.[25] They corroborate charges by government witnesses like Elizabeth Bentley and Whittaker Chambers: Prior to and during World War II the American Communist Party actively and successfully recruited Americans to assist the Russians.[26]

One of those identified as a Soviet collaborator was New York literary agent Maxim Lieber, who lived in Mexico for approximately three years. When Whittaker Chambers testified against Alger Hiss in 1948 and 1949, he implicated Lieber and accused him of allowing his business to be used to provide legal cover for an underground apparatus. In fact, Soviet agents

25. Although the Venona Decrypts have proven a useful tool for historians some reservations do remain. In his article, "Tales from De Crypts", *The Nation*, October 14, 1996 Victor Navasky raises the following issues: How do investigators determine the identity of the individual behind the code name? How can we distinguish between knowing collaborators and unknowing ones? Can guilt be assumed in cases of omissions resulting from unretrievable material? How does one evaluate content in cases where purpose and author remain unknown?

26. Historian Maurice Isserman believes that "several score, at the very most 300 American Communists, [were] accomplices to Soviet espionage during World War II" out of the approximately 50,000 CP members during that period. "Venona," *New York Times*, May 9, 1999.

operating in Japan had used his business, American Features Writer Syndicate, as their front in the early 1930s.[27]

Lieber told interviewer Allen Weinstein he left the United States after the Party instructed him to. "They said, 'Get the hell out of here; get the hell out of here. Do you want to go to jail?' They were afraid that I was involved too much because of the Chambers thing. So I went to Mexico. . . ."[28] While Lieber claimed Chamber's accounts of Party involvement in espionage had been "overly romanticized," he conceded that, in general, they were based on fact.[29]

I had never heard him mentioned in this context before, nor, now that I think of it, any of the others—the Sterns for example. They were our 'big fish.' Martha Dodd Stern, writer and daughter of a former U.S. Ambassador to Germany, and her husband, public housing advocate Alfred Stern, were known, rather, for their considerable wealth, ostentatious life-style and unorthodox marriage. (When it came to sex, most of the self-exiled, their political tolerance not withstanding, were downright prudish. One woman told me Martha had scandalized the community when she sunbathed bare-breasted in mixed company.) Martha and Alfred were different from most of the others: They were rich, sophisticated, 'fast,' and glamorous and probably wouldn't have chosen Mexico as their home if double agent Borris Morros, a flashy wheeler-dealer turned music publisher, hadn't denounced them. (Alfred had helped finance a record company administered by Morros, which the Soviets had used as a front.) The Sterns fled the United States at the end of 1953 because, rumor had it, Martha was about to be subpoenaed and, like many of the others, she had no passport.[30]

According to recently revealed Soviet documents, which in turn, have been partially corroborated by Venona intelligence cables, it appears that Martha was originally unaware that she was being used by the NKVD through her lover, Soviet diplomat Boris Vinogradov. During the mid-thrities, she apparently gave him information extracted from her father's U.S. Embassy files in

27. Whittaker Chambers, *Witness*. New York: Random House, 1952, p.44. 28.
28. Allen Weinstein, *Perjury: The Hiss-Chambers Case*, New York: 1978, p. 404.
29. Ibid., p. 129.
30. Katrina Vanden Heuvel, "Grand Illusions," *Vanity Fair*, September 1991, Vol. 54, No. 7, pp. 223-248.

Berlin. When Stalin ordered Vinogradov's assassination in 1938, his death was not revealed to Martha. (As late as 1955 she was still inquiring as to his whereabouts.) After marrying Alfred Stern in 1938 she was helpful in identifying potential recruits for undercover work during the '40s.[31] But records indicate that, over the long term, Moscow found the Sterns of little value in the area of espionage and judged their performance "disappointing."[32]

In each of the other cases, however, the testimony of one government witness, Elizabeth Bentley, implicated at least a half a dozen American Communists or fellow travelers residing in Mexico during the '50s. Among those she named were Fred Field, heir to the Vanderbilt fortune; editor and writer Cedric Belfrage, public health worker Lini deVries, (known to Bentley as Lee Fuhr), Mildred Price Coy, Former head of the China Aid Council,[33] and Maurice Halperin.

Halperin arrived in 1953. He was described by a Mexico City friend as a "sweet, rather naive guy . . . a lovely professorial type who enjoyed playing the fiddle—badly."[34] He was a Harvard graduate with a doctorate from the Sorbonne, a well regarded scholar and political scientist, the author of several books, and the man who chaired Boston University's Latin American Studies Department. In 1945 and again in 1948[35] Bentley accused Halperin of collaborating with the Soviets during the War when he had been chief of the Latin American Division of the Research and Analysis Branch of the Office of Strategic Services.[36] She would repeat her allegations in *Out of Bondage,*

31. Allen Weinstein & Alexander Vassiliev, *The Haunted Wood,* New York: Random House, 1999 , pp. 57, 66, 69-70, 105-106. Information found in Soviet intelligence documents includes communications between Martha and Boris Vinogradov, between Martha and other Soviet contacts, information about her brother, and an exchange with Stalin regarding Dodd.

32. Weinstein, *Perjury: The Hiss-Chambers Case,* p.66.

33. Janice R. MacKinnon & Stephen R. MacKinnon, *Agnes Smedley: The Life and Times of an American Radical,* Berkeley: University of California Press, 1988, p. 314. During the War, China Relief supervised the allocation of money and supplies to the Nationalist Government in China. Mildred Price was in charge of directing medical aid reaching that country; Herbert L. Packer, *Ex-Communist Witness: Four Studies in Fact Finding.* Palo Alto: Stanford University Press, 1962, p. 58, p. 117. Bentley claimed that "[Mildred ran] the Communist unit which functioned in the Institute of Pacific Relations." Her sister, Mary Price, syndicated columnist Walter Lippmann's personal secretary, was accused of having procured confidential files for the Russians.

34. David Prensky, letter to author, June 20, 1997.

35. *Time* magazine, September 9, 1957 p. 46.

36. The Office of Strategic Services, OSS, was the precursor of the Central Intelligence Agency, the CIA.

her personal account of her life as a spy.[37]

Also incriminated by her evidence was David Drucker, an associate of the Tempus Import Company. Tempus traded with the Soviets and had belonged to the Organizational Secretary of the Bronx County Communists, Samuel Brown, and, before that, to Joseph Katz, whom Bentley identified as one of her "Soviet handlers."

I met David at his sister's home in Manhattan, a Gramercy Park brownstone with an old world flavor, straight out of a Henry James novel. In the course of the afternoon there was a continual ringing of doorbells and phones as people arrived for tea and conversation, turning our meeting into something closer to a family reunion than an interview. David's older sister, Rebeca Bernstien, piled apple cake onto plates and poured tea, her 101 years betrayed only by her slight deafness.

Although I hadn't seen David in at least twenty years, he hadn't changed much. His full head of hair was whiter than I remembered, but he had retained his dark, bushy eyebrows—which persisted in growing down rather than up—strong features and hearty manner. The slight stoop to his shoulders was more pronounced—he was above average height for his generation—but I could have sworn that his heavy, dark rimmed glasses were the same ones he had worn in Mexico. He told me he had slowed down some but was still playing tennis on a regular basis, "Only doubles, unfortunately."

Once he had seated me in the library—we thought it would be quieter there, but it wasn't—he extracted pages of notes, assorted addresses, articles, and one or two books from a briefcase. He had evidently given some thought to our meeting and proceeded to organize me, issuing instructions with just the edge of a New York accent grown more pronounced since he'd left Mexico. It was some time before I was able to focus on my main objective, his reasons for going into exile.

"Well, for ten years, from '33 to '43[38] I had been house attorney for the Amtorg Trading Corporation, a Russian owned company that represented the Soviets in trade with the United States."

37. Elizabeth Bentley, *Out of Bondage*. (With an Afterword by Hayden Peake).New York: Ivy-Ballantine Books,1988, p. 182.
38. According to the obituary obituary written by Drucker's daughter, Emily Collins, his association with Amtorg spanned from 1933 to 1945.

His relationship with Amtorg had grown out of contacts made during time he spent in Russia in the late '20s and early '30s. He continued: "I first was registered as a foreign agent for the Russians.[39] Then in 1950, we acquired this contract to represent the Chinese, and I was registered as a foreign agent for them. I think I am the only person who was registered with [both] the Russians and the Chinese. . . . The American Chinese Import and Export Corporation [was] a company that Fred Field had founded, intended to represent the Chinese in foreign trade when the new People's Liberation Army took over China. . . . Fred was the President, but actually had nothing to do with [it]. We had offices on 40 Wall Street but our stationery showed that we were on Pine Street . . . the back entrance." He laughed. "[After all] it wouldn't look nice for a company that's going to deal with China to have its offices on Wall Street."

When the Communist government assumed power, they invited Drucker to China in order to establish the first trade agreements negotiated with Americans. He arrived in February, 1950. But in September of that year the State Department confiscated his passport, and he had no choice but to return home.

"Now all of these things . . . [became] a sort of focal point for the government to investigate, and I had a number of conferences with [them] . . . and I realized that things were getting sort of warm. I had, ten years before, been subpoenaed when I worked for Amtorg [by a] Grand Jury as a result of the Nazi Pact of 1939. I had no problem as a result of that. . . . But really what forced—compelled me decidedly—to go down to Mexico was when I began to feel that things were going to happen to me here in the United States if I stayed. So I went down to Mexico in the summer of 1952 and met [some people] and they told me about the company they had, [invited me to] join them, and pointed out how easy it was to live down there, so I moved down."[40]

Despite the accusations against them, most of those identified by informers were able to live out their lives in Mexico—for a

39. Under the McCormack Act, also known as the Foreign Agents Registration Act of 1938, all agents of foreign governments disseminating propaganda in the United States were required to register as foreign agents.
40. David Drucker, interview with author, May 20, 1991.

few years at least—in relative obscurity. The Hollywood refugees, on the other hand—screenwriters, producers, directors and technicians who arrived in Mexico in the early '50s—attracted far more attention. They were probably the most glamorous and certainly the largest exiled group in Mexico. Because so many were writers they left ample written testimony. They could afford to be candid. Once the investigating committees and government witnesses had done their work, they—unlike some of the others—had nothing left to hide.

Their problems started when an anti-communist group, the Motion Picture Alliance for the Preservation of American Ideals (MPAPAI), presented the House Un-American Activities Committee (HUAC) with a long list of suspected Communists in the movie industry. Since few American cities had Hollywood's capacity to draw an audience, this opportunity to expose subversion was too good to turn down. Consequently, the congressional committee accused nineteen "unfriendly" witnesses[41] of conspiring to undermine democracy, insinuating "alien values" into their scripts, and perpetrating communism by hiring others of like persuasion.[42]

"What followed in Washington on October 18, 1947 read like a movie script," wrote Barbara Kahn, wife of screenwriter Gordon Kahn, an "unfriendly" witness summoned before the Committee.[43] "A battery of newsreel cameras and blazing photographic lights set the scene for the grandstand entrance of J. Parnell Thomas, a Republican Representative from New Jersey. Washington was tense, the city was jammed with newspapermen, magazine writers and radio commentators.[44] The public

41. Larry Ceplair & Steven Englund, *Inquisition in Hollywood,* Berkley, Los Angeles, London: University of California Press, 1983, pp. 445-446. For the most part, these were members or former members of the Communist Party. The Hollywood Ten included Alvah Bessie, Herbert Biberman, Lester Cole, Edward Dmytryk, Ring Lardner Jr.(*), John Howard Lawson, Albert Maltz(*), Samuel Ornitz, Dalton Trumbo(*), and Adrian Scott. However, an additional nine people were never called to testify . These included: Bertolt Brecht, Richard Collins, Gordon Kahn(*), Howard Koch, Robert Rossen(*), Lewis Milestone, Irving Pichel, Larry Parks and Waldo Salt. Those with asterisks (*) following their names were in Mexico for varying periods of time.
42. Griffin Fariello, *Red Scare*, pp. 257-258.
43. Barbara Kahn, Commencement Address for Alvine High School, Manchester, New Hampshire, 1972. Barbara Kahn's correspondence with author, from July 11, 1991 through the end of 1998.
44. Larry Ceplair & Steven Englund, *Inquisition in Hollywood*, pp. 275-276. Unlike Gary Cooper, a friendly witness, Lauren Bacall was in Washington D.C. to support the Committee for the First Amendment (CFA), a civil rights organization which supported freedom of speech and rallied around the accused. They chartered a plane

lined the steps and entrance of the courthouse hoping to catch a glimpse of their film idols. Hysterical fans swooned at the sight of Gary Cooper or Lauren Bacall, and the atmosphere was charged with expectation."

Rather than resort to the Fifth Amendment with its association to organized crime and implication of guilt, the nineteen decided to stand on the First, the right to free speech, in the belief that choosing to remain mute was a form of expression. But as far as the Committee was concerned, any response short of complete cooperation was unacceptable. As Chairman Parnell Thomas called up one unfriendly witness after another, each requested permission to read a brief statement summarizing his position. Permission was routinely denied, but for reasons unknown, screenwriter Albert Maltz was allowed to read his:

". . . for a full week this Committee has encouraged an assortment of well-rehearsed witnesses to testify that I and others are subversive and Un-American. It has refused us the opportunity that any pickpocket receives in a magistrate's court, the right to cross-examine these witnesses, to refute their testimony, to reveal their motives, their history, and who, exactly, they are. Furthermore it grants these witnesses congressional immunity so that we may not sue them for libel for their slanders. . . ."[45]

Responses such as his infuriated the Committee. Tempers flared, shouting matches ensued, and witnesses were forcefully dragged from the premises. After ten "unfriendlies" had been called, the HUAC abruptly adjourned the hearing, dismissed the additional nine, and cited the Ten for contempt.

But matters did not rest there. During a 1949 meeting held at the Waldorf Astoria, following what has become known as the Hollywood Trials, the studios' financial backers convinced the Hollywood bosses, originally opposed to the hearings as an infringement on their control over the studios, to abandon the Ten to their fate. In addition, the studios agreed to fire the five Hollywood Ten writers under their jurisdiction and not to

to Washington D.C., broadcasted two national radio programs, and ran ads in the papers. Other CFA supporters included John Houston, Edward G. Robinson, Humphrey Bogart, Katherine Hepburn, Danny Kaye, Myrna Loy, Fredric March, Richard Rodgers and Moss Hart.
45. Gordon Kahn, *Hollywood on Trial: The Story of the Ten Who Were Indicted*, New York: Boni & Gaer, 1948, p. 84.

reinstate any unless each atoned for past sins. Thus, the ritual of public confession, accompanied by a willingness to inform on others, was compulsory if, once dismissed as a Red, one wished to regain studio employment.

After the Hollywood Ten went to prison in 1950, following an unsuccessful appeal, investigations of the entertainment industry became an accepted practice. Between 1951 and 1958 the Committee investigated Hollywood on four different occasions. (In 1951 fifty eight cooperative witnesses identified over 300 "subversives" in the movie industry alone.)[46] Defiant witnesses, well aware that the First Amendment hadn't worked for the Ten, took recourse in the Fifth, instead. This kept them out of jail but was interpreted, in most circles, as an admission of guilt. Consequently, these too were blacklisted. Given these circumstances, it is easy to understand that the magnet drawing Hollywood exiles into Mexico was the possibility of gainful employment in a more hospitable atmosphere readily accessible to those without passports.

Not all of them were writers. George Pepper, a producer, had originally been a violinist. When his career was brought to an abrupt end by arthritis he organized a musicians' union and threw himself into political activity.

"The Hollywood Ten was a turning point [of sorts]," George's widow, Jeanette Bello, referred to here as Jeanette Pepper, told me. "Everything was in limbo until the final Supreme Court decision. . . . When they [the Hollywood Ten]were sent to jail the whole atmosphere changed and everybody was in danger. . . . There was nothing to be accomplished by sitting in prison, so when a subpoena went out for somebody they said, 'duck it.' And that's why we left."[47]

Today, Jeanette, trained as an economist and statistician, has remarried and lives in Los Angeles. I had put off calling her for an interview remembering, with some apprehension, a bossy woman with an arrogant manner. (This was not the first time my memory deceived me.) When I finally phoned, she was not only receptive, but insisted I come for dinner, despite not having seen me for over thirty years. I was received by an attractive woman of medium stature with dark, gray-flecked

46. Griffin Fariello, *Red Scare*, pp. 258-259.
47. Jeanette Pepper, interview with author, August 2, 1991.

hair, strong, well-defined features and deep-set eyes. She gave me a warm hug and ushered me into her living room. Its cabinet-lined walls displayed a fine collection of primitive art: Mexican, Asian and African. Among the pieces displayed stood a lamp, its base a pre-Columbian vase. She reminded me that my father had made it during his short lived venture into the lamp and curio business.

"There were two reasons for leaving the United States," she told me. "One was that some had [subpoenas going for them] and some . . . were blacklisted . . . could find no work and thought they could find more work somewhere else."

In the Peppers' case, both reasons held true. Since George had headed the Hollywood Democratic Committee, (HDC), a Popular Front organization, credited for its enormous success in electing progressive local and national candidates to office, he was well-known in left-wing circles.[48]

"Well, we were scared to death," Jeanette told me. "There had been a lot of stool pigeons [who] said, I've been to meetings where such and such people were Communists . . . and [George] had obviously been named as a Communist by somebody.[49] A subpoena came out, not from Congress, but from the California equivalent of the HUAC, the Tenney Committee, we heard about it [and] that's when he left. I followed sometime later."

However, even before George was to be subpoenaed, he had been forewarned: "[He] had assembled for production a movie to be filmed in Bali. The screenplay was written. The Indonesian Government agreed to put up half the money for production and he planned to go to Djakarta to complete negotiations. He got a passport but, a couple of days before his trip the FBI arrived and said they wanted it back. So George said, 'What if I refuse to give it to you?'[50]

---

48. It would later become known as the Hollywood Independent Citizens Committee of the Arts, Sciences, and Professions (HICCASP), but as 1946 drew to a close irreconcilable ideological differences within its ranks led to its loss of power and eventual demise. Thus, when the HUAC focused on Hollywood less than a year later they no longer had to contend with the organized opposition such a group could have provided.
49. Eric Bentley, ed. *Thirty Years of Treason: Excerpts from Hearings Before the House Committee on Un-American Activities*, 1938-1968. NY: Viking, 1971, p. 390. Edward Dmytryk testified before the HUAC in April, 1951 that Pepper had attended a communist group meeting held at Ben Margolis's house.
50. David Caute, *The Great Fear*, pp. 245-246. Although the State Department began withholding or withdrawing passports from political dissidents as early as 1947, some individuals still evaded detection and were able to procure them. After 1951 more

"'Well, you can refuse to give it to us, but we can pick you up in Hawaii.' He handed his passport over. The project fell apart. He couldn't go to Indonesia, he couldn't move . . . so when someone said, 'There's somebody in Mexico who is interested in making movies with these blacklisted people, and he'll act as a *front*.[51] You interested?' We were interested."[52]

With those words Jeanette might have been speaking for any of the Hollywood refugees. Ring Lardner Jr., for example. Son of the noted American short story writer and one of the Hollywood Ten, his employment opportunities in films had dried up by 1951 following his release from prison. Furthermore, his wife, actress Frances Chaney, would find that work was unavailable. Unlike the writers, she could not conceal her identity behind a cover name.

When I met Ring and Frances in 1991, Ring was the only one of the Hollywood Ten still alive, and during our time together his phone rang several times with requests for information. He received me at the door and led me into their living room. Its windows offered a glimpse of the New York City skyline and wide patches of sky.

He is a tall, spare man, his eyes intelligent and probing behind his glasses. Although his hairline has receded slightly, his dark brown hair is barely streaked with gray. He is poised, taciturn, somewhat reserved, but cordial. Frances entered a few minutes later, breathless and very beautiful with her short-cropped silver hair, deep-set hooded eyes, porcelain skin. When I commented on her striking good looks she seemed embarrassed, shrugged my compliments aside, and got me back on track.

"You realize," she said, "that one family started it, and we just followed after other people who were very close friends in our particular community."

Ring: "Well, we were close: the Butlers, the Trumbos, the Hunters and us. We had been very close friends in Hollywood."[53]

effective control would be exercised by Ruth Shipley, director of the Passport Office, and by May 1952, Secretary of State Dean Acheson announced that alleged Communists would be denied passports.

51. The term 'front', refers to those people who allowed blacklisted individuals to use their names, often in exchange for a commission.

52. Jeanette Pepper, interview with author, August 2, 1991.

53. Screenwriters Jean and Hugo Butler and their close friends, Hollywood Ten writer Dalton Trumbo and his wife, Cleo, arrived in 1951. Screenwriter Ian McClellan Hunter and his wife Alice, arrived in late '51 or early '52.

Frances: "They [the Hunters] came down after us."

"After we did. But they stayed—"

"Another year or more," said Frances.

"So the main thing was that it was wonderful because there was this extended family. We loved each other, and the kids knew each other, and it was a wonderful experience to get out. . . . Mexico was very nice because it was sort of a respite between the real world and what we might face when we got back."

Suddenly Frances pointed out the window and cried, "Look, a blimp!" By the time I had jumped up, turned around and fumbled for my glasses, it was gone. (Our interview was much the same. Looking back, I recall it as a far too brief, but unexpected, delight.)

"Was your main reason for choosing Mexico its proximity to the States?" I asked.

"No, it was money!" Frances cried.

Ring explained, "The main reason was I think that it was cheaper to live. . . ."

"And because our friends had gone." Frances continued: "We didn't have much alternative.[54] And we could have a lifestyle that was nice, you know. It wasn't expensive then. We could live. I mean suddenly from being terribly poor, black-listed, down-trodden folk, here we were in Mexico with a cook and a maid and Jesus God!"

Ring interjected: "Well, [and] I could do some sort of writing, whether I was to write a movie story as Trumbo did—a couple of them had—and would sell under somebody else's name, or work on a book, which I had started, as Albert Maltz did. . . . The main motive was that we could have more time. You know, the same money that would last us for a year there would last us six months somewhere else. [But] it was tough finding film projects in Mexico . . . the only one of the whole bunch of us who ever did anything there was Hugo Butler. I don't think anyone else [did]. George Pepper maybe?"[55]

Contrary to popularly held belief, the majority of Hollywood refugees who went to Mexico were not rich; many were not

54. Lardner's passport had been seized, and they were unable to go to any country requiring one, England, for example, where work in English was available.
55. Ring Lardner, Jr. and Frances Chaney, interview with author, May 25, 1991. A few others did, among them John Bright.

even solvent.[56] The majority were young and just getting started. Often parents in their mid-thirties or early forties, they had saved little and lacked the safety net provided by pension plans, insurance policies, or job benefits. (The self-employed rarely had them.) When they arrived in Mexico they discovered that its film industry could not provide them with steady employment nor, consequently, with a regular income. However, the country offered respite from the oppressive atmosphere back home.

Some were particularly in need of respite, those targeted by anti-Red investigations for example. These flourished in more than a dozen cities—among them Birmingham, Boston, Los Angeles, Seattle and Miami. During the scores of hearings held to investigate subversive activities in libraries, labor unions, government offices and educational institutions, reputations were destroyed, organizations dismembered, and families forced to leave their homes—generally on hearsay evidence. In addition, many were charged with violating anti-subversion statutes of dubious constitutionality, a number of which were subsequently invalidated by previously existing Federal legislation.[57]

But for sheer viciousness, few investigations would equal Miami's *Little Smith Trials*,[58] which arose out of conflicts with organized labor and a tradition of anti-Semitism and racism in the South.[59] By linking civil rights supporters with a Communist conspiracy, Dade County State Attorney George Brautigam, hoped to discredit integration. In the course of his investigation he subpoenaed more than one hundred people and sent thirty-one witnesses to jail.

Charles Smolikoff, known in Mexico as Charlie Small, and

56. Lester Cole, *Hollywood Red: The Autobiography of Lester Cole*. Palo Alto: Ramparts Press, 1981, p. 301. Of the Hollywood Ten easily five were unable to pay legal expenses and support their families. So when Dalton Trumbo and Lester Cole received a breach of contract settlement from their studio they shared it with the others.
57. David Caute, *The Great Fear*, pp. 70-81.
58. Only four states had their own equivalents to the Smith Act which made it a crime to "knowingly or willfully advocate, abet, advise, or teach the duty, necessity, desirability, or propriety of overthrowing the United States government by force or violence. . . ." However, states lacking Smith Acts did conduct similar trials, availing themselves of other statutes.
59. It is no accident that the trials held in New Orleans and Miami in 1954 coincided with Supreme Court hearings on Brown v. The Board of Education. Ruling that segregation, i.e. the concept of 'separate but equal' was , by its very nature, inherently unequal, Brown vs. the Board of Education would give the Federal government the authority and the responsibility to enforce policies conducive to integration.

his wife Berthe were among them. I heard their story for the first time some fifteen years after Charles' death. I was sitting in his wife's kitchen in New York City, eating a tuna fish sandwich. Berthe, for years my mother's close friend and confidante, is an intense woman, with deep-set eyes, high cheekbones and a dancer's lean body. (In Mexico she studied with Federico Castro, who ran a Ballet Company of the same name.) She is confident and funny, possesses a sharp wit and a penetrating stare, capable of boring holes through anyone foolhardy enough to cross her.

In short, as early as 1941, when Florida was strictly segregated, the unions few, ineffective or mob-controlled, and the Klan a force to be reckoned with, Charles Small brought the Conference of Industrial Unions (CIO) to the south. Unlike the American Federation of Labor, (AFL), the dominant craft union of the period, the CIO was committed to organizing workers of every sort, unskilled as well as skilled, into an industrial union. As his reputation as a key player grew throughout the region, he became the CIO National Representative for the Transport Workers' Union (TWU), their Southern Regional Director and a member of their Executive Board.

He was a force to be reckoned with, until the 1948 TWU Convention, when he, along with eighteen other union officers suspected of ties with the Communist Party, were, with much fanfare, dismissed from their posts. At about the same time, an enemy even more terrifying than the investigating committees or a hostile press singled him out.

The Smalls had just purchased a home in the then isolated community of Coral Gables. Berthe explained: "I [had] put Abbott [who was three years old] to sleep, and I was sitting out on the terrace reading. It must have been nine thirty, ten o'clock at least. And two cars of Klansman drove up—hooded, the whole bit—and they got out of the car maybe eight or ten strong. . . . I'm sitting there! There's not even a latch on the door. I'm paralyzed, paralyzed and then they put gasoline on this thing [a large wooden cross], they light it up and they're screaming epithets about 'Smolikoff' and 'you dirty reds' and 'you dirty Jews', of course. It was a most frightening experience. . . . I never went back [to that house] never, ever. . . . We sold the house . . . everything was left behind. Our clothes [were] packed up and that was all. It didn't matter to me. These [were] horrible, horrible years."

By the time the Little Smith hearings were held in 1954, Berthe and Charles were self-employed, their union activism abruptly brought to an end several years earlier. Despite this, they were both cited for contempt for refusing to give information and jailed.

After being held for seven weeks, Charles was released, but Berthe, who had been apprehended at a later date, was still in jail. Fearing Charles might receive another subpoena in the interim, his attorney recommended he leave the country immediately. (His bail did not stipulate that he remain in the area.) According to Berthe, "He did his own packing and remembered to take the encyclopedia, and not much else."

After calling his brother from a pay phone—his phones were tapped—to let him know where he was going, he drove from Florida to Mexico. Berthe's former college roommate and her husband were living there at the time, and Charles tracked them down. They took him in and nurtured him until Berthe, held for five and a half weeks, was released.

"When I got out," she said, "I weighed ninety pounds, I had two kids and no money. My brother-in-law picked me up at jail in his white Jaguar and told me, 'Charles has gone to Mexico.' The Smith Act was breathing down his neck, and that was the precipitating factor which sent us out."[60]

Charles wasn't the only one who had the Smith Act "breathing down his neck." Building contractor Max Shlafrock and dentist David Prensky also knew what it was like to walk the same road. They too had been called by Brautigam to testify, gone to jail, been smeared in the press and, in Max's case, been deprived of their livelihood. Like Small, they also left Miami for Mexico.

In March of 1954, two months before the Miami hearings, Shlafrock[61] had been called to testify in New Orleans where Senator James Eastland was investigating the Southern Conference Educational Fund (SCEF).[62] At the time, Eastland headed

60. Berthe Small, interview with author, January 17, 1993.
61. Max Shlafrock, letter to author, December 20, 1997.
62. Originally, the Southern Conference on Human Welfare had been established in 1936-1937 on the recommendation of a New Deal agency studying conditions in the South. Its broad aims were the passage of social security and other legislation. In

the Senate Subcommittee on Internal Security, McCarthy's former post, and he was up for reelection. His campaign strategy consisted of exposing the 'Red plot to integrate the south' and uncovering communist collusion.[63]

He also accused the Miami Beach Jewish Cultural Center— Max served on its executive board—of supporting a Communist front. (They had sponsored a concert and donated its profits to the SCEF.) The son of indigent Russian immigrants, Max had arrived in New York as a young boy and became, in turn, a sweet potato peddler,[64] a balloon vendor, a street photographer, a hotel employee, a carpenter, a manual laborer and, finally, a successful building contractor. He had, in fact, been active in several Popular Front organizations and had become a member of the Industrial Workers Order (IWO)[65] which, in turn, led to his joining the Communist Party. "I've been a dues paying member ever since," he wrote me.[66]

At the New Orleans hearings Shlafrock stood on the Fifth Amendment. Back home, while the press looked on, bomb squads ransacked a school he had constructed, searching for explosives. Following the Miami hearings and his release from prison, he was denied building permits, bond, insurance and, as a result, the possibility of continuing to earn a living as a contractor. He told me: "In 1955 I visited my attorney Frank J. Donner, and I told him what had happened. He suggested that I go to Mexico. 'There are a couple of bright fellows there, Charles Small and David Prensky. Perhaps, they can be of help.'"

Dentist David Prensky, the Chairman of the Southeast Florida Area Council of the American Veterans Committee, was denounced

1946 it was allowed to die and was replaced by the Southern Conference Educational Fund which focused on eliminating abuses in the South and abolishing racial segregation and discrimination.
63. Virginia Foster Durr, *Outside the Magic Circle*, Alabama: U of Alabama P, 1985, p. 254.
64. Max Shlafrock, letter to author, November 18, 1997. Max wrote: "A cop arrested me for selling a sweet potato on a restricted street and then made me push my pushcart to 163rd Street. I was afraid I wouldn't be able to hold the pushcart downhill, so I said, 'If you want this pushcart, then you take it downhill.' 'Oh,' he said, 'a Bolshevik.'"
65. The IWO was a multinational, multiracial fraternal order formed by the left in 1930 that offered workers, regardless of occupation, the best possible insurance at the lowest rates and sponsored a wide variety of cultural and athletic activities. The IWO was listed by the House Un-American Activities Committee as a subversive organization in 1947.
66. Max Shlafrock, letter to author, December 20, 1997.

as a "leading communist" by government informers, Paul Crouch and Joseph Mazzei. Despite this, he claimed: "We came to Mexico, not because we risked arrest or unemployment or harassment, but because we didn't like the political climate in the U.S. during the McCarthy period. . . . We also fell in love with Mexico, its dramatic beauty, its fascinating history, and its wonderful people.[67] . . . we didn't come down to stay. We came down to cool off. To decide whether we wanted to go back to Miami. We both disliked Miami Beach anyway."[68]

They stayed for twenty-eight years.

The Miami situation had provided a perfect opportunity to expose the 'Red Menace.' Consequently, during the second half of 1954, the HUAC, under the leadership of Harold H. Velde, a former FBI agent and staunch anti-Communist, held his own hearings there on several occasions. But his investigations led nowhere. Not one of those called to testify was prosecuted for perjury. As a matter of fact, he recognized that, "The situation is not as bad in Florida as in other parts of the country."[69]

In attempting to explain why right wing extremists had been so successful in delaying change and attacking the left-wing community David Prensky summed it up this way: "One of the things that happened was that there was no outrage, really, on the part of the overall community or even in the liberal community. The big thing about the Miami McCarthyite episode was that the most ordinary people, leading the most ordinary lives were singled out. There were no government figures in sensitive positions; no school teachers corrupting the minds of our youngsters, and no people who in any way should have been looked upon as dangerous."[70]

In the course of interviewing them—U.S. resident aliens, Party envoys, the blacklisted Hollywood political activists, espionage suspects and the Little Smith Trial victims—many of them 'ordinary people leading ordinary lives'—I was reminded of something composer Conlon Nancarrow had suggested

67. David Prensky, letter to author, November 30, 1991.
68. David Prensky, interview with author, May 11, 1993.
69. Frank Donner, "The Miami Formula: Grass Roots McCarthyism" *The Nation*, January 22, 1955, p. 71.
70. David Prensky, letter to author, December 18, 1993.

about his music, although not in these exact words: Mine was music without sound. How could we hear it if it was too difficult to perform? Only by writing for the player piano and perforating my own piano rolls could I hear the sound without depending on interpreters.

Many of those who settled in Mexico for any length of time were, like Conlon's music, in the process of becoming. They were, as yet, without sound. True, some began their lives in Mexico at the height of their careers or past their prime, only to leave within a few years or to die shortly after arrival. But for those who were young and willing to give Mexico a chance, the country provided a space where they could develop. It offered them sanctuary and an opportunity for growth. Mexico gave them a voice.

Chapter Three

Bridging the Cultural Gap: Adaptation to Mexico

"When somebody asks why we've moved to Mexico you tell them we're here on business," my mother instructed. No other explanation was forthcoming. My parents never discussed their real reasons for moving to Mexico—certainly not with me—and, as I later learned, not with their friends either. But they weren't the only ones to keep a low profile. Many of the others did too: They varied daily routines, avoided discussing sensitive subjects over the phone and, if they did, used Yiddish or some personalized version of 'pig Latin.' Controversial books were rarely left out in the open. My parents kept theirs in a cardboard box on the upper shelf of their closet. Berthe Small told me that, at one point, the situation in Miami had grown so alarming she drove across the Everglades and dumped hers into the canal alongside the Tamiami Trail. In short, they were always on their guard.

Discretion was essential: The same FBI that had placed us under surveillance in the States, would continue to do so in Mexico. In addition, the American business community could not help but be aware of our presence. Ironically, many of these expatriates shared our same sense of dislocation at having to adapt to life in a foreign country. But, generally speaking, this would not draw us together. On the contrary. In time, we would discover we had run straight into the arms of the very people we were running away from: white, middle class, conservative Republicans. Although they lived in Mexico, they continued to inhabit their own little Americas, Americas far less diversified than the ones we had fled, bringing with them their gift for turning everything they touched into Everywhere, USA. No matter that we shared a common language and a national identity. Our politics set us apart.

Because of our politics, our whereabouts were routinely recorded, our passports withdrawn without notice, and subpoenas delivered to our doorsteps. The local and foreign press publicized our names and political histories, and some of us lost jobs when pressure was placed upon our employers. Deportations, though less common, also occurred along with the occasional detention. Such dangers were real and deprived us of the security planning for the future brings. Indeed, we had little sense of the future, forced as we were to live from one day to the next.

At the beginning, those were the things we shared, and sharing gave us the security of belonging. It drew us together defreakifying the 'I' and making us part of a 'we,' an extended family. What we had in common kept us from standing alone. We could be a part of something, and that masked the pain and isolation. Freaks stand alone, but we didn't. Ergo, we weren't freaks.

With time, we glanced less at our watches and idled a little longer over a heavily spiced meal, learned to roll our tortillas and our 'R's around words like *ferrocarril* and *carretera*, to gesture with our hands, and to kiss casual acquaintances on the cheek, to revel in the warmth of Mexico's people and its climate. We learned to adapt. Time numbed the gnawing sense of unease and diminished—though never completely—our sense of alienation.

Mexico City during the '50s had a decidedly rural flavor, despite its more than a million and a half inhabitants, who referred to it as a *pueblote*, a huge town. Cows grazed, chickens pecked, and corn grew in vacant lots just blocks away from the city center; the surrounding mountains and snow capped volcanoes—Ixtacihuatl and Popocatepetl—were visible most of the year, and on Sunday mornings, *charros*, Mexico's elegantly clad horsemen, cantered down the Paseo de la Reforma, the wide, tree-lined avenue said to resemble the Champs Elysees.

Minor drawbacks, of course, were to be expected: American movies took over a year to arrive; a good malted and shoes in extra large sizes were unavailable; drinking the tap water or eating fruit and vegetables like strawberries, lettuce, grapes and plums was ill-advised; medical and dental care could be careless, and a cloudburst brought the city to a standstill. Such things we took in stride. But reconciling ourselves to wide-spread poverty, the institutionalized corruption, and the casual disregard for punctuality was more difficult.

In an attempt to understand, my father read exhaustively, took notes, and practiced his Spanish on bemused waiters and cab drivers. After a short time, he reconciled himself to the country's shortcomings and summed up Mexico as delightfully *meshugge*—crazy—and consequently, incapable of understanding. Thus, he distanced himself from the place and reduced it to something manageable. (My mother never did. An indefatigable crusader, she would, thirty years after arrival, cast aspersions on anyone who tried to bribe an official, run a red light or break in front of her in line).

Adaptation was easier for the children. My sister Judy and I didn't have to understand the country, just live in it. We could approach it gleefully, which was probably the only sensible way to go about it. I had no trouble with Mexico. My problem was with my parents and the holes in my life. Most likely I would have harbored similar resentments had I remained in the States. Perhaps, if I had been able to keep my old friends and acquire new parents, I would have been happy.

If leaving their homes and coming to terms with life in exile was hard enough for us and others like us, for some, surmounting the initial obstacles—finding a place to live, earning a living, learning the language, helping the children adjust, and making friends—was impossible. A few returned to the United States or went elsewhere after brief stays. While cultural gaps narrowed in time, they were rarely bridged. But there were enormous compensations: A small group, shared the 'one big happy family' security provided by a tightly-knit inner circle.[1] (Not all of us, unfortunately. I, for example, just fantasized about it.) Many made new friends, expanded their interests, developed a growing appreciation for a new culture and language and, sometimes, improved their standard of living.

Although this last would eventually prove true in our case, you

1. For many American Party members the CP provided more than a political reference point. Schools, social activities, literary magazines, insurance programs, legal defense organizations, and so on made it possible to function within a protective sub-culture. In some places, American Communists lived lives almost entirely removed from society at large, so when they arrived in Mexico many were already accustomed to interacting within the protective, mutually dependent framework they had known back home.

would never have guessed it to judge from our first apartment in Mexico City, a decided step down from Parkchester. Located in Polanco, a peaceful residential area in the north of the city, the two-bedroom, second-story walkup was chilly and damp and reeked of gas. My mother described it in her journal:

"It was brand new when we arrived but the rate of deterioration was alarming. Immediately adjacent, another building was going up, and water was constantly poured onto the cement wall to keep it moist. Their walls were moist but ours was soaking wet. What could we do? We tolerated the inconvenience. It reached the breaking point when we heard the noise of a drill making its way through the wall. We stared as the hole grew larger and larger, and finally a startled face appeared. 'Pardon me, *señores*. There must be some mistake.'"

Unlike my parents, many others, George and Mary Oppen for example, settled in the south of the city following their arrival in 1950. A former CP activist, George had attended a Party school and been closely associated with the Workers' Alliance, the King's County Party, and the Farmers' Union milk strike during the '30s. After serving in France during the War, he settled in California and gave up full-time party work but continued to head the Redondo Beach Party Chapter. As a functionary, he was vulnerable to prosecution under the Smith Act, but after he and his family moved to Mexico, the Party expelled him for desertion. Upon their arrival in Mexico, the Oppens installed themselves in the picturesque San Angel area. Subsequently, many later arrivals—particularly those from the west coast—would follow them. During his time in Mexico, George worked as a contractor and built custom-made furniture, but shortly before returning to the United States in 1959, he returned to the calling he had abandoned twenty-four years earlier. In 1969 he won a Pulitzer Prize for poetry.[2]

But that was much later. Upon their arrival, finding a place to live was their primary concern. In her autobiography Mary wrote that casual acquaintances helped her locate an apartment.

"[It] had been built from an old wine storage room in the Monastery of Carmen in San Angel. The plumbing was faulty,

---

2. Oppen kept his identity as a poet a secret from his Mexico City friends who learned of it when they read about his Pulitzer Prize in the newspapers.

so we bathed in the garden in the fountain where water flowed more freely. The garden was the chief reason for living [there]. . . ."

Believing they should "be prepared to receive other political refugees," Mary found a thirteen room colonial house with a patio, ballroom and chapel which shared the premises with the San Angel Post Office and a bank.[3]

Years later, screenwriter Jean Butler recalled, "People kind of got crushes on the Oppens. That crazy life style of theirs and whacky houses, and the way they did everything with such a flair made their impecuniousness seem so fascinating and wonderful."[4]

The Butlers also rented in San Angel, next door to Mexican artist Diego Rivera's studio. The boxy lines of the two story glass and concrete structure were softened by a dusty coat of pinkish paint, and the house was skirted by a stand of cactus on one side, an overgrown garden on the other. A Juan O'Gorman mural covered their dining room wall.

Blacklisted writer Dalton Trumbo, on the other hand, lived briefly in the posh Lomas district in an imposing marble palazzo, a stark contrast to his former quarters in the Ashland federal prison.

Others were taken in by friends: Hollywood writers Bernie and Jean Gordon arrived with their toddler and moved in with the Oppens; artist Philip Stein, forced to leave the San Miguel Allende Art Institute when his wife, Gertrude, contracted a mysterious ailment, lived for a short time with Mexican art expert José Gutierrez and his wife, Ruth.[5] When Spanish Civil War veteran Bart van der Schelling and his wife ran out of money, composer Conlon Nancarrow offered them the gatehouse on his property.[6]

Eventually both the Steins and the van der Schellings found living quarters on Insurgentes or Insurgent Street, a location favored by many refugees. Two buildings, in particular, housed close to a dozen families. (Those interviewed assured me, however, that convenience dictated their choice of address; the street's name had nothing to do with it.)

3. Mary Oppen, *Meaning: A Life,* Oakland, CA: Black Sparrow Press, 1978, p. 195.
4. Jean Butler, interview with author, August 2, 1999.
5. Philip and Gertrude Stein, interview with author, May 15, 1995.
6. Edna Moore van der Schelling, interview with author, August 1, 1991.

When Berthe and Charles Small arrived from Miami in 1954, Albert Maltz, one of the Hollywood Ten, who also lived in San Angel, arranged for them to take over literary agent Maxim Lieber's Insurgentes apartment. After approximately three years the Liebers had given up on Mexico and taken off for Poland. Berthe Small told me: "We simply took over, furniture and all. I remember they gave us a price for the complete apartment, which was some ridiculous thing like $300, but [we didn't have the money] so we paid it out . . . to Albert Maltz [who] had a checking account—we didn't—and could send the money to Poland."[7]

Unlike members of the American community who arrived in Mexico with positions in large American companies or the U.S. Embassy, whose stays were limited to a few years, and who were provided with a reliable support system, most of the political expatriates did not know how they were going to earn a living. Because this was a prime consideration, some chose to settle in small cities like Guadalajara, Oaxaca, Cuernavaca and San Miguel Allende where they could live even more cheaply than in the city and, perhaps, get by on their savings. Furthermore, those few fearing deportation believed living in the provinces made it easier to keep a healthy distance between themselves, the FBI, the press, and the American community. Yet, for those worried about supporting themselves, Mexico City was the most logical place to settle. Some opened small stores and businesses, invested in construction, raised chickens, produced films, wrote, taught at the American School or Mexico City College, or practiced a profession.

Among these were a few who entered Mexico as tourists, exiting every six months. Others, seeking to legitimize their status, had to enter either as 'capitalist investors'—an irony not lost on present or former Communists—or as immigrants. This second option entitled them to work legally in Mexico and was generally preferred by those, who like my parents, intended to find a job or set up a business.

Belle and Mike arrived with their life savings, $1,000. I don't know why they mentioned this to me, but I do remember thinking it a hefty sum and resenting that such imported luxuries as Heinz baked beans (over a dollar a can) were not mine for the

7. Berthe Small, interview with author, January 17, 1993.

asking. (My parents had $1,000, and they were denying me the pleasure of beans?) Within a few weeks my mother found a job—illegally, since she still lacked the proper documents—as a legal secretary in the American law firm of Goodrich, Dalton & Little, where no Spanish was required. Her salary, a pittance compared to what she would have earned in a similar capacity in the United States, allowed her to pay for a maid to take care of us after school and still keep a bit extra.

On weekends we traveled by second-class bus to nearby villages where Mike, previously a salesman for a New York printing company, first saw and fell in love with the hand-crafted pottery, colonial figurines, and occasional pre-Columbian artifacts, not readily available in Mexico City. "A salesman can sell anything," he claimed and rented space in a small flower shop on the Avenida Juarez where he sold lamps made out of curios purchased in the outlying markets. He also stocked *ex-votos* or *milagros* (miracles), crudely painted pieces of tin salvaged from flattened-out cans, thank you notes to God. They hung in churches, manifesting gratitude for the making of such miracles as saving crops, wreaking revenge on one's enemies, and impregnating the sterile. (If my father had been able to make a living at it, it would have been an even greater *milagro* but, alas, the talismans did not work for us.) When the futility of this venture became apparent, my mother's younger brother, Ben, came up with a solution. He suggested my parents set up a sales represen-tation firm to import and distribute electronic components, which he manufactured in the States, in order to capitalize on Mexico's rapidly expanding television industry.

In addition to Ben's assistance, we had something else going for us, the low cost of living. Theatrical technician Asa Zatz, one of the earlier arrivals, summed it up this way: "If you were a drinking man you could get cirrhosis of the liver for practically nothing . . . [Fortunately] I had enough foresight to bring papers along for the G.I. Bill . . . I went to school, and that gave me about a hundred and eighteen dollare a month . . . and I had a U.S. income of maybe one hundred or one hundred and twenty-five dollars, so I had somewhere around two hundred and fifty dollars a month. With two hundred and fifty dollars, I lived regally."

Some, unlike Asa who could depend on a Stateside income,

often chose to invest in Mexico since money was scarce and interest rates high. A few, Vanderbilt heir Fred Field, for example, would live to regret it. Fred wrote in his autobiography: "Looking back, it almost seems as if I had an obsession to lose money. I went into three business ventures and came out with three total losses. Not twenty-five or ten cents on the dollar. No, in two of them it was zero on the dollar, and on the third, less than zero because I assumed responsibility for paying off the losses of a number of people whom I had persuaded to join in the investment. . . ."[8]

Others had similar experiences: When a member of the left-wing community purchased a fleet of soft ice-cream trucks a number of political expatriates enthusiastically raised money to invest with him. Screenwriter Gordon Kahn, one of the Hollywood Nineteen, was so impressed by the venture he insisted on recovering part of his capital, tied up with a local businessman, only to discover that his savings had completely vanished, along with the businessman. Similarly, those who had invested in the ice-cream business also lost their shirts. Victims later claimed to have been taken in by a Ponzi scheme whereby investors initially receive an impressive return on their money because the interest is financed by new money. (Once it is no longer available the schemer leaves town with the principal.) Screenwriter Hugo Butler put it this way, "We were fleeced by one of our own."

However, artist Philip Stein, also an investor, told me, "People weren't ripped off, it's just that the business floundered . . . he did the best he could, and it didn't work out. . . ."

Investors also learned the meaning of the word, 'devaluation.' Since the Mexican peso had been stable for many years, few had considered that possibility. But in the spring of 1954 the dollar rose in value against the peso. Previously worth Mex$8.65 to the dollar, it shot up overnight to Mex$12.50, leaving those who had invested U.S. currency in Mexico, thirty percent poorer in dollars.

Many, regardless of whether they had savings or investments struggled to get by. Former Spanish Civil War nurse Lini Fuhr de Vries, for example, had been identified by Elizabeth Bentley

---

8. Frederick Vanderbilt Field, *From Right to Left*, Westport Connecticut: Lawrence Hill & Company, 1983, pp. 275-276.

as the person who had recruited her for the Communist Party. When Constancia de la Mora, a Spanish refugee who promised to assist her upon her arrival in Mexico, died suddenly, Lini was left homeless and unemployed. She gave English lessons and nursed a few private patients. Eventually, she was able to rent a large property, sublet it and move into the gardener's cottage. But, convinced that her life in Cuernavaca alienated her from a genuinely Mexican experience, she moved to Oaxaca. While teaching English and—despite her broken Spanish—public health and ethnology at the local university, she learned about Mexico's Papaloapan Commission. Engaged in a monumental project to build a dam in southeastern Mexico, which would require the relocation of approximately 200,000 Indians, they hired Lini. Working closely with local school teachers, she developed a program capable of reaching out into the native communities, teaching basic health and nutrition, and helping the inhabitants adapt to change.[9]

Like Lini, many of the expatriates turned to teaching upon arrival: Economist John Menz and Enos Wicher—described as a former Washington union organizer, a physicist and a political scientist, depending on whom you spoke to—taught at Mexico City College; Alan Lane Lewis, a director and producer, worked in the Drama Department of the University of Mexico, and Bart van der Schelling gave a course in German lied at the National Conservatory of Music.[10]

For the U.S. accredited American School, always on the lookout for qualified U.S.-trained personnel willing to work for peso wages, the influx of teachers proved a blessing. They hired former literary agent Maxim Lieber's wife, Minna; Sonia Strand, American poet Mark Strand's mother; Edna van der Schelling; Edith Halperin, Boston University professor Maurice Halperin's wife, and several others. Some, like Gertrude Stein, who with two young children and no household help, was unable to work full-time, gave private English lessons.

At the beginning, few had it easy. When I asked Miami refugee Berthe Small how they supported themselves she replied: "We didn't . . . it took us one year to get our sea-legs, to figure

9. Lini M. DeVries, *Up From the Cellar,* Minneapolis: Vanilla Press, 1979, pp. 355-356.
10. Edna Moore van der Schelling, interview with author, August 1, 1991.

out [what to do], to make contact with people, to get the whole thing set up. Charles' brother, Jerry, supported us . . . the early years were really tough [but] Charles opened a silver shop."[11]

But building up a business, particularly for those unaccustomed to working outside the United States, was no easy matter. Spanish Civil War veteran Eddy Lending, my parents' friend from New York, arranged to represent American manufacturers in Mexico. However, a recently enacted law taxed all but essential imports, and his products hardly qualified. High import duties, which fluctuated with each order, dissuaded potential clients, and Ed, fearing his business was about to collapse, requested an appointment with the Mexican General in charge of processing all merchandise sent through the Mexico City airport.

"'No problem,' the general told me. 'Simply do the importing yourself. All your goods will come in labeled as non-lucrative samples.' The tariff would be about one half of 1 percent of the actual value. He would get a spiff for his trouble. My customers would all get their merchandise. They'd make more. I'd make more. Everybody would be happy. I was back in business. . . ."[12]

For business people like my parents, Eddy Lending, or the Smalls, starting up was difficult, but by no means impossible. However, for professionals like Miami dentist David Prensky, establishing a practice in Mexico was far more challenging. In accordance with Mexican law, David could work as an employee during his first five years in the country but could not command a salary. Once he had completed the five year requirement and attained professional certification by revalidating his U.S. studies, he could open his own office. However, the Mexican statutes governing professionals required he be a Mexican citizen. He therefore, had to file a suit demonstrating that, in spite of his American citizenship, he was, in keeping with the Mexican Constitution, entitled to earn a living in a manner consistent with the training he had received. Although he won the case, the law remained unchanged, and subsequent applicants

11. Berthe Small, interview with author, January 17, 1993.
12. Edward Lending, letter to author, August 5, 1993.

would have to repeat the same procedure.[13]

As a result of such experiences it wouldn't take long to discover that earning a living in Mexico was no picnic for newcomers. Screenwriter Dalton Trumbo wrote, "As for our condition, we are living out an old truism: 'The first time you see Mexico you are struck by the horrible poverty: Within a year you discover it's infectious.'"[14]

Because of the nature of their work, the screenwriters were in a class of their own: In Hollywood they had gained a foothold in the competitive film industry. (The Butlers, for example, discovered upon arrival in Mexico that of twelve English language films being screened in Mexico City, they had worked on four, and they were, by no means, the most successful of the group.) But following the establishment of the blacklist, their names were no longer theirs to use, and they were forced to take on new identities in order to peddle their work. Some were able to acquire *fronts*, individuals, who in exchange for a commission, would loan them their names and stand in for them if the need should arise. On other occasions a pseudonym was adequate. (Writers like Dalton Trumbo, for example, had half a dozen.) Yet, inevitably, as newcomers, they were paid a fraction of what they had earned previously.

In addition, losing one's name could be a traumatic experience. Jean Butler wrote: "That his (Hugo's) name was banished, now and for a long time to come—perhaps for our lifetimes—I had somehow gotten used to. But that my own, my maiden name, the name I'd acted under and continued to use professionally in writing jobs and story sales after my marriage, the name that was my whole identity—the idea that this too was condemned to oblivion, swept over me like a black wave. I felt as though I were losing an arm or a leg."[15]

They lost their names but not their determination to succeed outside the United States. By the beginning of 1952 most of the Hollywood crowd had settled in, placed their children in school, and started to work: Dalton Trumbo wrote an unmarketable screenplay, *The Jean Field Story*; Julian (Hallevy) Zimet wrote for *Oil World* and translated speeches into English for Mexico's

13. David Prensky, letter to author, November 30, 1991.
14. Dalton Trumbo, *Additional Dialogue: Letters of Dalton Trumbo, 1942-1962*, Ed. Helen Manfull. New York, Philadelphia: Evans, 1970, p.278.
15. Jean Butler, *Those Happy Few*, A work in progress, story outline, p. 22.

oil industry manager; Jean Butler worked on a short story set in Mexico, and screenwriters Gordon Kahn, Ring Lardner Jr. and Albert Maltz began to write novels.

HICCASP's former executive secretary, George Pepper, turned to production. He established contact with exiled Spanish director Luis Buñuel and convinced a group of blacklisted musicians to invest in the production of Hugo Butler's version of *Robinson Crusoe*. (Afraid he might be identified during the filming, Hugo was introduced as "Señor Addis," a Canadian investor and wheat rancher who had struck oil. He hung around the set during the day and rewrote the script at night under the name of Hugo Mozo—Mozo means houseboy or butler in Spanish.)[16]

Writer Margaret Larkin had a unique opportunity fall from the sky—literally. Married to Albert Maltz, she had already established a reputation as a journalist, union activist, folk singer and folk song collector by the time she got to Mexico. During a flight to Oaxaca a bomb, planted in the luggage compartment of the plane on which she and her daughter were traveling, exploded. Her subsequent account of the criminal investigation and trial of the man who hoped to collect insurance on seven passengers he had hired to work in a gold mine was published by Simon & Schuster under the title of *Seven Shares in a Gold Mine*.[17]

Although the West Coast émigrés were starting to adapt to life in Mexico, they were barely getting by on their rapidly diminishing savings.

"It's true that the first years were economically very hard . . . [but] we were living as colonizers with all the comforts entailed," Jeanette Pepper told me during an interview. Despite this, life was not easy. She explained: "We were literally eating from each others' borrowings. . . . We would all—the Tumbos, Butlers, Hunters,[18] Lardners, and ourselves—sit around a table and say, 'Who can we borrow money from now?' And somebody would say 'I have a cousin,' and we would hit him up. And at

16. Ibid., pp. 3-4; Patrick McGilligan, and Paul Buhle, *Tender Comrades: A Backstory of the Hollywood Blacklist*, New York: St. Martins Griffin, 1997, p.168.
17. Jean Butler, *Those Happy Few*, A work in progress, story outline, p. 113.
18. Blacklisted screenwriter Ian Hunter and his wife, Alice, a former screen story analyst, who later worked for a Popular Front organization, were in Mexico briefly during the early '50s.

the end of two years, the Trumbos were . . . preparing to return to the States and . . . [they] got some money, maybe $600. The Trumbos were a couple with three kids. The Peppers were just a couple, no kids. The Trumbos took this money . . . split it in half, gave the Peppers half and with half the remaining money took off for Los Angeles. You don't forget things like that."[19]

When times really got tough there was always the pawn-shop. Dalton Trumbo wrote: "I am by now an old customer of the *Monte de Piedad* (Mount of Pity) so called because it is the government pawnshop and charges only 36 percent interest per year. We have at the moment reposing in the vaults of this benign institution a diamond ring, two gold cigarette lighters, a gold cigarette case, my watch, a Leica camera, as well as certain objects of the Butlers. I hocked for them in a moment of need. The appraisers down there regard me as a thief, but apparently one who knows how to stay out of trouble, hence they respect me."[20]

Accordingly, at the beginning, the political expatriates not only established homes, found jobs and, when necessary, hocked the family silver, they did it in Spanish.

For my mother, learning Spanish was a source of such great anxiety that most of her writing about Mexico, adapted years later from early journal entries, dwells on it: "Our bilingual friends assured us that in no time at all we would be speaking fluently. They were not reckoning with my language resistance. Originally, I would try to say some simple thing like, 'Where is Juarez Avenue?' When the response was 'Sorry, I don't speak English,' it was quite a letdown.

"However there were times when I had to accept full responsibility for my lack of comprehension. On one such occasion we were at a resort hotel. We had finished lunch, and it was time for dessert. I noticed a large plate of watermelon at the next table. I called the waiter and, much to his astonishment, asked for a plate of *zanahorias*. I was insistent and added, 'Don't tell me you don't have any because I can see a large plate of *zanahorias* at the next table.' The waiter smiled and diplomatically told me I was asking for carrots.

"I wasn't the only American experiencing these problems. I

19. Jeanette Pepper, interview with author, August 2, 1991.
20. Dalton Trumbo, *Additional Dialogue*, p.278.

was visiting a recently arrived acquaintance when the maid rushed in and pointed to the front of the house where the family car was on fire. My friend dashed to the phone, seized the receiver and stood still. She didn't know the word for fire. Fortunately, the neighbors were able to give the alarm. The fire engine arrived after a lengthy interval, but had to be pushed up the steep hill. When this obstacle was overcome, they discovered there was no water. The car slowly burned to cinders. At the Spanish professor's following visit he was greeted with an account of what had transpired and a request for basic vocabulary. After all, words like fire, water, help, may be mundane but they're infinitely more useful than butterfly, briefcase, or archipelago."[21]

I wish I could report that after decades in Mexico my mother could roll her 'R's with the best of them, but the truth is, even we had difficulty understanding her. Fortunately, Agustina, my mother's cook for over twenty-five years, acquired the uncanny ability to decipher Belle's Spanish and would diligently serve as her intermediary to the outside world for as long as my parents remained in Mexico.

Certainly, learning the language was easier for the children, and by the time they left the country, most were bi-lingual. Shelley, Miami constructor Max Shlafrock's fourteen year old step-daughter, refused to speak Spanish. She told me: "One day my mother confronted me. She said, 'Shelley, if you want someone to iron this skirt you're going to have to learn how to ask for it yourself.' So I learned. But I felt that my life was again being interrupted or destroyed. I guess the word is resentment."[22]

Feelings of resentment, confusion or alienation were not confined to the offspring of political expatriates. (When families, regardless of their motivations, left home, they didn't ask their children for permission.) So, while their parent's politics may have provided one more barrier to adaptation, it was certainly not the only one.

Crawford Kilian, who was son of television technician Mike Kilian, one of the Hollywood refugees, wrote: "Twice an outsider, I was already a *gringuito* in Mexico, a foreigner to be tolerated

21. Belle Zykofsky, "Elephants & Roses" from *Scenes From Our Lives* (Ed. Dennis, John & A.E. Biderman.) San Francisco: University of San Francisco, 1983, p. 18.
22. Shelley Shlafrock, interview with author, January 18, 1993.

but not really accepted by Mexican kids. Now America had receded psychologically as well as geographically. It was another country, hostile to me and my family for reasons I couldn't really understand. . . ."[23]

In reference to that sense of isolation experienced by expatriates, screenwriter Dalton Trumbo's son, Chris, said: "You're separate from the actual country you live in, you're not part of the culture so you're thrown back upon whatever resources exist . . . there was no linkage, for instance, to churches . . . educational institutions. You were absolute foreigners. You were just kind of floating there. There was no connection to the society in general. . . . I didn't find Mexico a happy place particularly. But beautiful, you know."[24]

Like Chris, Mexican playwright Carlos Prieto, a close friend to several political expatriates, also pointed to the community's insularity and its effect on the children: "The persons who . . . really suffered from exile were the sons and daughters because they lived in a never-never world. They were in a vacuum. They [went to] the American School.[25] Their friends were . . . the children of other exiles and the whole thing was hybrid. I told Charles Small, 'Charlie, the least you could have done is send them to a Mexican school. They would have had Mexican friends, they would be living in Mexico. Now they're not living anywhere. They're not living in the United States, and they're not living in Mexico. They're not Mexicans, and they're not Americans. [When they leave] they'll miss a Mexico that didn't exist.'"[26]

Perhaps he was right. Most expatriates, however, would have defended their choice of school: Given the uncertainty of their stays in Mexico, their children's ability to readapt, were they to return to the United States, was of paramount concern.

While attending the American School further isolated us from Mexico, it brought us, and sometimes our parents, into contact with each other. In Jean Butler's words, "the kids discovered each other as if by radar,"[27] because—outside the small circle

23. Crawford Kilian, *Growing up Blacklisted,* an unpublished memoir, second draft, p. 6.
24. Chris Trumbo, interview with author, August 1, 1991.
25. There were certainly exceptions, but the majority of the political expatriate children who resided in Mexico City did attend the American School.
26. Carlos Prieto, interview with author, October 22, 1991.
27. Jean Butler, interview with author, July 22, 1991.

of overlapping friendships—we often had no way of knowing who was whom.

Yet, despite its role in making us aware of each other's presence, we were still, in Crawford Kilian's words, ". . . literally walled off from Mexico." He explained: "The American School sat on fifteen acres behind a high stone and concrete wall in Tacubaya, one of the more wretched slums on the edge of the city. . . . The homes around us were shacks of cardboard and sheet metal, sometimes built in a day, and the children who swarmed the dirt streets would never see the inside of a classroom—least of all in the American School, many of whose students arrived in chauffeured limousines from the wealthy enclaves of Lomas, San Angel and the Pedregal."[28]

Nothing I'd known in the Bronx could have prepared me for the American School. All the girls had names like Lindley, Kay Sandra, Betty Ann, and Letitia, wore crinolines to school, and ate lettuce and tomato sandwiches with the crusts cut off. Their mothers were Pink Ladies at the American British Cowdray Hospital or belonged to the Junior League and the Garden Club. Their fathers worked for the American Embassy, General Electric, General Motors, or the C.I.A. Among them were a select few descended from former plantation owners fleeing the United States—with their slaves—following the Civil War. These had inherited their ancestors' political proclivities and passed them on to the others, who came, for the most part, from Texas, hated Mexico, and couldn't wait until daddy was transferred. The American Legion, the American Society, and the Republicans Abroad, in that order, were the most prestigious community organizations.

Then there were the rest of us, Americans who didn't follow the norm, the politically motivated expatriates, an occasional Jew—outcasts. We read books, visited museums, listened to classical music, traveled throughout Mexico. (Some of us even tried to learn Spanish.)

Let's face it. We children were definitely not your run-of-the-mill American School students. No doubt, our politically attuned parents, recognizing this, did what little they could to prevent unpleasant incidents. Mary Oppen wrote that, prior to registration, one of the political expatriates had visited the

28. Crawford Kilian, *Growing up Blacklisted*, p. 7.

school and asked the principal whether the children might be discriminated against. He was assured that no prejudice would be allowed to continue if any became noted. She added, a bit ingenuously, "We did not, in all the years of our child's education there, hear of any such incident in the school."[29]

Screenwriter Jean Butler's daughter, Mary, remembers her mother's warning on her first day of kindergarten: "'Don't tell anybody what your father does for a living.' Not that I knew anyway, really. But she said, 'Just say that he's a journalist.'"[30]

Emmy Drucker was twelve years old when she arrived in Mexico from New York in 1952 with her mother and her father, David Drucker, counsel for Amtorg, a Russian owned U.S.-based trading corporation: "I was uprooted from Sunnyside, which was a fringe microcosm of things left-wing and Jewish and intellectual. . . . So suddenly I was in this high school which was much more American than anything I would have found in America. . . . [It] was right off the movie screen with sororities and fraternities and football games. I was there for four years; it took me about three years to make friends, and I joined the sorority that took fat girls and people with naturally curly hair and people who weren't beautiful and Jews and Mexicans. I remember my first date was with this guy named Richard Kimrey whose father was definitely in the State Department, and he was this tall, blond, very Anglo guy. I'd never seen anybody like that before in real life. We went to the movies, and I think he liked me, but he never dated me again. I was fresh off the boat and so I didn't realize, but somebody clued him in. . . . He never asked me out again."[31]

Unlike Emmy, I attended the school from fourth grade through graduation and assimilated more thoroughly: I adopted the crinoline, joined the Girl Scouts on Foreign Soil, recited grace before meals in the homes of my church-going friends, and marched in the Girl Scout Honor Guard at Camp Camohmila each year. Still, I never could get my mother to cut the crusts off my sandwiches and resigned myself to joining Emmy Drucker's sorority, the only one that would have me.

In spite of my desire to fit in, I still relished my ability to

29. Mary Oppen, *Meaning: A Life*, p. 198.
30. Mary Butler, interview with author, July 28, 1991.
31. Emmy Drucker, interview with author, May 20, 1991.

occasionally shake the pillars of the American community—no enormous challenge—by delivering a speech in favor of racial integration for the American Legion Oratory Contest or wearing too much lipstick. And, because I was my parents' child, I never lost my contrary side, the one that delighted in shocking others. Consequently, I yearned for the star status reserved for the children of the 'Famous Communists.' (Their parents' names sometimes appeared in the newspapers. Ours never did.) I couldn't even provide a decent excuse for being in Mexico.

But in the end, I think I shared more with the school outcasts than with its insiders because, today, my memories of the things that startled me or set me apart are much the same as theirs: Chris Trumbo recalls that, "At some schools they had cowboys and Indians. Here . . . they divided up into the Confederacy and the Union, and it was considered really chic to be part of the Confederacy."[32]

A few of us remember what Linda Oppen referred to as "a bizarre field trip conducted annually to gape at the man who killed Trotsky. Trotsky was never explained or even talked about and non-leftist kids wouldn't have known who he was."[33] (Neither did many leftist kids.)

I still recall the 1956 Stevenson-Eisenhower mock elections when I was one of only three students in a class of twenty-six supporting Stevenson.

Finally, most of us remember the incidents: Mary Butler was harassed by classmates following her down the hall chanting, "Hi Mary, how's Nikita? How's your uncle, uncle Niki?"[34] Linda Oppen recalls 'fascist-communist' book throwing battles on the San Angel school bus and the playground taunts;[35] and Mike Butler remembered the time when: ". . . somebody threw a rock at me and called me a dirty commie pinko Red or something." But he hastened to downplay it: "It's just one of those things you nurse among your scars and drag out like your Brownie merit badges [because]. . . there wasn't any long term pattern of intimidation or harassment."[36]

32. Chris Trumbo, interview with author, August 1, 1991.
33. In 1940 Ramón Mercader del Rio was sent to Mexico to assassinate Leon Trotsky, was convicted of the murder, and held in Mexico City's Lecumberri Prison, where he remained until his release in 1960.
34. Mary Butler, interview with author, July 28, 1991.
35. Linda Oppen, letter to author, April 27, 1997.
36. Michael Butler, interview with author, July 27, 1991.

Mike is right and, in fact, the younger children who entered school some four or five years after we did, were less likely to be subject to such treatment. They were more readily accepted by their peers, both Mexican and American, often led their classes socially and academically and participated extensively in school activities.

Linda Oppen believes that the ostracism that she and some of the older childeren experienced helped explain why we were such excellent students. (I was the inglorious exception.) "We had no distractions or after-school activities. And we felt a terrible burden to be successful since our parents had fallen so far in their own eyes, and were competing to prove up to the heroics of the leftists, to prove they were best."[37] (Although hers was the highest grade-point average in her graduating class, she was not allowed to give the Valedictory address and was listed, instead, as salutatorian.)[38]

While Linda suggests that we and our time in Mexico were inevitably colored by our parents' reasons for being there, Chris Trumbo claims that the problems "people want to lay upon the politics, I want to lay upon the family. Whatever the marriage was like veers on how the family turned out. And it had nothing to do with all the rest of it."[39]

"For me, politics in Mexico was sort of like sex," Tony Kahn, screenwriter Gordon Kahn's son, told me. "I would hear things, but they weren't grounded in any kind of actuality where I could find out what was true and what wasn't true, and I couldn't discuss it with my parents. So I knew my father had 'performed' politics at some point because there we were in Mexico. In the same way I knew they 'performed' sex because there I was in the family. But I could never figure out why he didn't feel comfortable discussing what he had done. I had to conclude that it was an uncomfortable subject for him for probably a multitude of reasons—[among them] the consequences on the family of what he had done. Perhaps he would have done it differently if he had had a chance. Perhaps it so consumed him with anger and rage he didn't even want to get into it. I don't know. It remains a mystery for me."[40]

37. Linda Oppen, letter to author, April 22, 1995.
38. Linda Oppen, letter to author, January 31, 1992.
39. Chris Trumbo, interview with author, August 1, 1991.
40. Tony Kahn, interview with author, January 21, 1993.

Although Gordon Kahn, author of *Hollywood on Trial,* a definitive work on HUAC's investigation of the film industry, was by no means unknown, his son, Tony, was only five when the family moved to Cuernavaca. Because he was isolated from the bulk of political expatriates in Mexico City, the implications of residing in a foreign country were, no doubt, hidden from him more successfully than from the rest of us.

Chris Trumbo, on the other hand, experienced those years differently: His father was the best known of the Hollywood Ten. "Although the 'odd name' might have something to do with it," he told me. "Dalton Trumbo, you know, is not the same as Mike Wilson,[41] a name of anonymity, and Dalton Trumbo was just one of those catchy little things. You could make rhymes with it: Mumbo Jumbo Dalton Trumbo. Anonymity under those circumstances would have been impossible. When the Un-American Activities Committee hearings were to take place in 1947, my parents spoke with my older sister and me, told us everything that they thought we could possibly understand, which was everything . . . and then we knew [Dalton] would go to jail—probably—and that did happen."[42]

Whatever the circumstances under which we went to Mexico, the country's attractions were undeniable. Crawford Kilian summed it up when he wrote, "We could walk through the ruins of its conquered empires, learn the subtleties of bullfighting, and begin to speak the language. Mexican food had substance and flavor, and light and color were more intense. Even children like us had an odd freedom: We could prowl the Thieves' Market in Tepito, and there, for very little money, purchase a cavalry saber or ancient six-gun. Occasionally, we might have a run-in with a Mexican street gang but, for the most part, we thought nothing of long trips across the city, through its slums and parks and crowds. I look back on those years in Mexico now, and they seemed suffused with a kind of glow. The streets and markets were so beautiful, the people so vivid, the sun so bright, and the air so clear that it seems impossibly romantic."[43]

While Mexicans have no monopoly on romanticism they are

41. A blacklisted screenwriter, Michael Wilson, lived in France during the '50s.
42. Chris Trumbo, interview with author, August 1, 1991.
43. Crawford Kilian, memoir, p. 6, p. 8.

far more comfortable with it than Americans, so perhaps some of us picked it up from them during our years in the country. Whatever the case, Crawf was by no means alone in remembering the Mexican years as "suffused with a kind of glow." Although we were aware of our isolation and, with rare exceptions, never fully assimilated, we romanticized our shared experiences and our relationships with each other. They drew us together into some semblance of belonging.

Whether we believed, along with Jean Butler, who wrote of "a close-knit feeling, as though we and our children were part of a very large family or a very small town;"[44] with her son, Michael, that, "We cut through a lot of bullshit in our need to stick together," or with Chris Trumbo, who never felt a sense of community at all, believing some people "created their own communities, their own fictions, in order to belie their realities,"[45] we were thrown into each others' company frequently enough to share the same experiences. The memories, however, differed. (I sometimes received three or four versions of the same event.)

Perhaps the only thing we could agree on unanimously were the hard facts: We, along with a small group of families from the United States,[46] were drawn together because we shared similar left-wing ideologies and reasons for being in Mexico or were so perceived.

In recalling the early years, Anita Boyer, who arrived with her husband Fred Field in 1953, referred to the group as "the incestuous clique."

"[We were] seeing each other all the time and . . . I didn't mind seeing these people because they were lovely people. But they were certainly a persecuted people when they came here and that's perhaps why they cohered, no? They stuck together because they felt the [need to transplant] their own little world from the United States, and that's what they did . . . they would not assimilate, and I felt that I was in a host country,

44. Jean Butler, *Those Happy Few,* a work in progress, story outline, p. 22. p. 6.
45. Chris Trumbo, telephone conversation with author, August 1991.
46. Although I have identified more than sixty such families I am reluctant to give more precise numbers because it is impossible to determine unequivocally who went to Mexico for political reasons. Sometimes, the individuals themselves are uncertain; a few concealed their motivations from each other; others established no relationships with known political expatriates or lived outside Mexico City, making them more difficult to identify.

and I should learn the language, and I should certainly see people other than Americans."[47]

When Anita spoke of their "seeing each other all the time" she was thinking not only of the evenings spent together in each other's homes, nor the nights out, nor the family excursions to local sites, but of a number of programmed activities involving anywhere from four to a dozen families.

Chief among them were the Sunday-morning musicales at Kurt Odenheim's house, described by one expatriate as memorable "for good pancakes and lousy music." According to a friend, Kurt had conducted a WPA sponsored symphony orchestra in New Jersey.[48] A Communist Party organizer in the late '20s and early '30s, he had left the Party in '37 but his former loyalties would mark him. Berthe Small told me he was a "man without a country."[49] That would have made him particularly vulnerable had he remained in the States.

Shortly after his arrival in Mexico he was joined by his wife and four children and invested in a leather business, which failed. Eventually, he established a company to supply radio and phonograph cabinets to major outlets, work similar to what he had done in the States.

According to Odenheim's daughter, "[On Sunday mornings] my father played the piano, Ralph Norman[50] played the cello, Maur Halperin was a fiddler, and my mom played the violin."[51] Other musicians included David Prensky and Fred Field on the recorder. New Yorkers Frida and Harry Schaeffer, friendly with a number of political expatriates, though not themselves in Mexico for political reasons, claimed during our interview on May 17, 1991: "The largest collection of subversives we ever managed to assemble was at those Sunday-morning *musicales*."

The Schaeffers, obviously, were not the only ones aware of this. The FBI collected information about the *musicales* and other such gatherings—the Butler's Saturday morning softball games, for example—throughout the '50s: "In February, 1954, an unnamed person reported that Hugo and Jean Butler had

47. Anita Boyer, interview with author, February 14, 1992.
48. David Prensky, letter to author, November 30, 1991.
49. Berthe Small, interview with author, January 22, 1992.
50. The Normans were friends of the Smalls but were not in Mexico for political reasons.
51. Lynne Odenheim Kalmar, interview with author, November 7, 1991.

invited a number of their close friends to a picnic and soft ball game at their home on the afternoon of February 13, 1954. According to this person the Butlers arranged the afternoon to give an opportunity for a number of American Communists to get together without arousing suspicion. This person further advised that the following individuals were in attendance at the above-described picnic. (A list of eight names follows.)"[52]

In a somewhat different account, included in his unpublished article "Growing up Blacklisted," Crawford Kilian, today a journalist and science fiction writer, states: "The focus of our week was the Saturday-morning softball game in the big vacant lot next to the Butlers' house on Palmas. By 10:00 A.M. we had a gathering of kids and adults. . . . We would play for a couple of hours, then convene on the Butlers' glassed-in front porch for lunch. The kids were quite welcome in the adults' conversation, but we were just as likely to go into the living room to play records or up to Michael's room to fool around with toy soldiers, or back out into the lot to chuck spears at one another while screaming, 'Dog of an Aztec! Pig of a Toltec!'"[53]

While tending to cling together, particularly at the beginning, political expatriates discovered that, unlike the ordinary American residing in Mexico, they were in a position to meet Mexico's left and its intellectual community. Because Mexican intellectuals sympathetic to their politics and cognizant of the events responsible for their leaving the United States sought them out, they were able to meet such luminaries as artists Diego Rivera, David Alfaro Siqueiros, Francisco Zuñiga, Miguel Covarubias, Pablo O'Higgins and writer Luis Cardoza y Aragón. Socialite Martha Dodd Stern, in Mexico dodging a sub-poena, thought nothing of inviting many of these to her celebrated affairs along with ex-Ambassador Bill O'Dwyer, a couple of second tier Mexican politicians, and a large sprinkling of American leftists. Those parties were famous.

But one party in particular still raises eyebrows. Shortly after his arrival, Dalton Trumbo hosted an affair on the advice of his *coyote*. These well-connected con-artists with legal pretensions earned a living by promising to use their political clout to keep a story out of the press or agents far from ones door. Dalton

52. David Drucker, FBI File NY 100-99497.
53. Crawford Kilian memoir, p. 10.

hired his to steer him clear of potential pitfalls. In order to maintain his legal status in the country, it was important to make an impression, his *coyote* told him, to meet the *influyentes*, the movers and shakers, and toward that end he recommended that Dalton throw a *fiestón* in his marble palazzo.[54]

The guests included a large segment of the exiled community, in particular the Hollywood contingent, along with a number of local big-wigs invited by their Mexican friend, Josefina Fierro de Bright.[55] Dalton's daughter, Nicky, remembered: "At the famous party my father threw shortly after we arrived . . . a young military officer was apparently making a pass at me— a very green just-turned-thirteen year-old—asking me to dance a lot, so Josefina, John Bright's[56] fiery Mexican wife, cut in and danced him to his knees, much to the delight of the assembled."[57]

Frances Chaney, Ring Lardner Jr.'s wife, was there alone: "Well, all of the women in the group were quite attractive, and we were fairly young then. . . . Clio Trumbo was a great beauty, and Jean Butler was pretty lively and . . . there was lots of food and there were drinks and oh, the works. About an hour or two into the party I ran into Clio Trumbo wandering around, and it turned out that we all had had very similar experiences with these guys. And then we began to catch on. This was their off night, and nobody had brought his wife. . . ."

She explained that a few had brought their *casa chica*, or, literally, their small houses, referring to the mistresses who inhabited them. The rest were on the make.

"At the end, all of us were comparing notes and saying, 'What should I do with this goddamn general?' or whatever we had, [when] suddenly, who [should] appear from the States but Herbert Biberman.[58]

---

54. Bruce Cook, *Dalton Trumbo*, New York: Charles Scribner's Sons. 1977, p. 229.
55. Raised in the United States, Josefina was a glamorous left-wing figure admired for her ability to harness much needed moral and financial support within the Hollywood community. She is remembered for her work on behalf of Mexican-Americans during the '30s and '40s. Accused of subversion by California's Tenney Committee, she settled in Mexico in 1948.
56. John Bright was a blacklisted Hollywood screenwriter, actively involved in the Screen Writer's Guild and a founding member of the Motion Picture Democratic Committee, a Popular Front organization. (He and Josefina were subsequently divorced.)
57. Nikola Trumbo, letter to author, November 21, 1994.
58. Director and screenwriter Herbert Biberman was one of the 'Hollywood Ten.'

"'Isn't this the most wonderful, glorious thing that ever happened?' [he asked].

"And I asked, 'Why Herbert?'

"'Well, just think, you know, all these marvelous people from Mexico, the cultural elite meeting in this great rapport. . . .'

"And as he spoke of this wonderful meeting between the cream of the left culture in Mexico, I knew I would never be able to set him straight."[59]

Sometimes, such occasions provided the newly arrived political expatriates with an opportunity to witness events generally closed to outsiders. María Asúnsolo's party, attended by the Maltzes, artist Philip Stein and his wife, and by *Daily Worker* correspondent, A.B. Magil and his wife, was one of these.

On February 17, 1952 María Asúnsolo, known for her antifascist political activism during the '30s and '40s, her beauty, and her intimate relationships with Mexico's intellectual community, invited close to one hundred people to commemorate Siqueiros's and Rivera's reconciliation. Their antagonism dated from 1937 when Rivera had enraged local Communists and been expelled from the Mexican Communist Party (PCM) after persuading Mexican president Lázaro Cárdenas to provide sanctuary for Leon Trotsky. Some three years later, Siqueiros and a small band of followers had attempted, unsuccessfully, to assassinate the Russian revolutionary. So their burying the hatchet after all these years was indeed a historic event.

Held in the garden of Mária's Pedregal home, it was attended by prominent left-wing figures including the Mexican Revolutionary general, Heriberto Jara; former cabinet Minister Marte R. Gómez, Alfonso Caso, the archeologist, composer Blas Galindo, and writer José Mancisidor.

Siqueiros and Rivera were seated next to each other in the middle of a long table flanked on either side by two additional tables set at right angles. A large banner extolling both men hung above them. Following the meal, after left-over food had been cleared, speeches delivered and the guests of honor toasted, both artists leaped to their feet, whipped out their handguns, and, aiming above their heads, fired gaily into the air. All around them, the assembled guests rose from their seats and cheered them on.

59. Ring Lardner and Frances Chaney Lardner, interview with author, May 25, 1991.

All except Harriet Magil. She remembered, "[When] Siqueiros and Rivera . . . started shooting their guns into the air— I [was petrified] and wanted to scream. And that was their idea of a big joke!"[60]

As she and countless others would discover, Mexico bears as little resemblance to the United States as Alice's Wonderland does to a convenience store. Even something as basic as the country's names convey the difference: 'The United States of America' is self-descriptive, curt, and lends itself to easy abbreviation. Its name means business. 'Mexico,' or—as it is pronounced in Spanish—'Meheeco,' is cadence and rhythm, a lullaby of a name which gives away nothing about itself.

Moving to Mexico required more than just packing a suitcase and changing your address. It required changing your points of reference, learning to feel out a situation rather than think it out, and conditioning yourself to living with uncertainty. This was unavoidable when one lived in a country where expectations bore little resemblance to reality, where customs, values and mores were at odds with one's own, and where personal security could never be taken for granted.

According to Berthe Small: "Because of Charles' always precarious position in Mexico—some of it real, some of it imagined—every day was an anxiety. He refused, for his own crazy reasons, to have a telephone in the shop for twenty-five years, so I couldn't reach him. If he was ten minutes late, or what I perceived to be late, as he always was, I'd figure that either he had dropped dead on a street corner from a cardiac problem or he had been picked up and was being harassed or deported. . . ."[61]

True, personal safety, could never be taken for granted by political dissidents no matter where they lived, but it appeared all the more elusive in a country bristling with unknown dangers. Equally elusive was the issue of moral integrity because security, or at the very least, adaptation, could hinge on compromising one's principles. Jeanette Pepper summed it up when she said: "The people who came down were socially conscious so they were the [ones] who would be most aware. . . . People asked me, 'How can you live in a country like this that's so poor?'

60. Abe and Harriet Magil, interview with the author, January 20, 1993; Joel Gardner, *The Citizen Writer in Retrospect: Oral History of Albert Maltz,* Los Angeles, California: UCLA Oral History Program, Regents of the University of California, 1983, p. 835.
61. Berthe Small, interview with author, January 17, 1993.

and I said, 'Well, after a while you learn how to ignore it.' That's not admirable. . . . I can answer only for myself, of course, but it wasn't only a case of becoming inured to it, although that was part of it. It also meant, that in our case, we gave money to every beggar who crossed our path, paid our help more than the going wage, and that sort of thing, but we lived as 'Colonials,' the way people did in 'Indjah'. . . . I don't think we liked being 'Colonials' but it was very easy to fall into that pattern [which] . . . is corruptive both to the colonizer and the colonized, and [at the time] I didn't realize the extent to which I'd been corrupted."[62]

Even as a child I was incapable of ignoring the contradictions between what my parents said and the way we lived. On one occasion, shortly after our arrival, my father and his employee, Calixto, were driving down the Paseo de la Reforma when my father lost control of his car striking a pedestrian. When the police arrived, Calixto took the rap and, since he had no driver's license, spent the next few nights in jail while my father arranged for his release. My mother told me, that as a foreigner, my father would have been far more vulnerable to prosecution than a Mexican citizen. I didn't buy that. Only now does it occur to me that, as political dissidents, my parents dreaded the possibility that Mexican officialdom—or, God forbid, the American Embassy—might intervene. (Upon mentioning this to Tony Kahn he recalled having heard of a similar incident involving one of the Hollywood writers.)

On another occasion, my parents fired an employee for attempting to negotiate a contract with a labor union. At the time this shocked me even more than the traffic incident, perhaps because it was contrary to their espoused political principles. (Labor unions were good, weren't they?) Years later, however, my parents' lawyer, Harry Schaeffer, assured me that the man in question had been a con-artist using the threat of a union as a way to extort money from my parents. (Although such incidents certainly occurred elsewhere, Mexico's judicial flexibility increased the likelihood of their taking place. On the other hand, negotiating a speedy solution was far easier there than elsewhere.)

62. Jeanette Pepper, letter to author, March 5, 1992. Jeanette Pepper, interview with author, August, 1991.

In spite of cultural differences and gaps in understanding, an occasional quirky incident could jolt us into recognizing our similarities. In some ways we political dissidents were not so unlike our Mexican hosts: When Nicky, Dalton Trumbo's daughter, confessed to her Mexican boyfriend that her father had been in prison he responded, "So? Whose father hasn't?"[63]

For some, fear of incarceration, unemployment or harassment were the only reasons for remaining in Mexico. Playwright Carlos Prieto observed that the best way to recognize who was in the country involuntarily was to identify the people who openly disliked Mexico but refused to leave.[64]

Others, well-known American novelist Howard Fast, for example, liked the country and certainly had sufficient reason for maintaining some distance between himself and his government. Following his imprisonment in the United States, he considered the possibility of moving to Mexico, and he and his family spent the summer of 1954 there. He wrote: "Yet this was not life, not any kind of life for us. I couldn't write, and Bette couldn't paint. Days drifted by without meaning. We could not make a life here as other American Communists, writers, artists, film people had done. We were bored to distraction."[65]

In addition, there were a few who appeared to have settled down in Mexico and then suddenly disappeared. Robert Rossen, the talented, well-regarded writer-director of films like *All the King's Men* (1947) and *Body and Soul* (1949) and one of the 'Hollywood Nineteen,' was one of those. At the beginning of 1953 he was living in Mexico and working on *The Brave Bulls* with Anthony Quinn.

During the course of his work he became friendly with Gabriel Figueroa, a highly respected film photographer. Figueroa remembers that Rossen visited him at his Coyoacan home during the spring of 1953. Bursting into tears he told the Mexican film maker he had been summoned to testify in Washington and begged for his assistance. Figueroa approached international legal expert, Don Luis Cabrera, a former Cabinet minister and writer, and introduced him to Rossen. Cabrera assured the American he could request political asylum for

63. Jeanette Pepper, interview with author, August 2, 1991. Nikola Trumbo, letter to author, May 5, 1997.
64. Carlos Prieto, interview with author, September 19, 1991.
65. Howard Fast, *Being Red*, New York: A Laurel Trade Paperback, 1990, p.333.

him in Mexico and volunteered his services in preparing a case against the U.S. government.

Figueroa claimed that, following the meeting with Cabrera, "Rossen embraced me, wept for joy and kissed me. I took him home to his Colonia Roma apartment. We said good-bye, agreeing to see each other the next day at four o'clock to go to Cabrera's office. When I knocked at his door the next day, there was no answer. I asked the janitor about it, and he told me Rossen had left that morning with all his luggage and had left no message. . . .Three months later Rossen wrote to me from Spain where he was working and later from the United States. I never wrote back."[66]

Figueroa wasn't the only person Rossen had approached. John Bright, blacklisted after 1951, had written the scripts for *The Public Enemy*, *Blonde Crazy*, and a documentary, *We Accuse*. According to Asa Zatz, after Rossen received a second subpoena from HUAC he often visited Bright in his Mexico City apartment: "He would pace the floor, hashing it over with John as he tried to make up his mind what to do about testifying. Finally one night he declared himself: He had made up his mind. He was going to face up to the Committee and tell them off. The answer was to hit back, and he was going to do it. 'What we need right now is someone to [pull] a Dimitrov.'" (Dimitrov was the Bulgarian Prime Minister who heroically challenged the Nazis at the Reichstag fire trial.)

Following this decision, he dropped from view, and Bright finally decided to check up on him only to discover he had precipitously fled the country. Sometime in May, John Bright opened the newspaper and read of his appearance before HUAC—as an informer. He named fifty individuals, including many of his friends. John wired him: "Did you say Dimitrov or Dmytryk?" (Dmytryk was the 'Hollywood Ten' writer who, after serving a prison sentence, turned informer.)[67]

So while many, like Robert Rossen, returned to the States after a couple of months, those who remained—sometimes for only a year or two—became absorbed in their new lives. The

66. Margarita de Orellana, "El arte de Gabriel Figueroa, palabras sobre imagenes: Una entrevista con Gabriel Figueroa," *Artes de Mexico*, Numero 2, Invierno, 1988, p. 90.
67. Asa Zatz, letter to author, November 20, 1995. Victor S. Navasky, *Naming Names*. New York: The Viking Press, 1990, note p. 303; Navasky reported a slightly different version: "Bright sent him a wire: 'How do you spell Dimitroff?'"

process of finding a place to live, earning a livelihood, learning the language, placing the children in school and establishing a social life required they extend their reach beyond the tight-knit expatriate community and, in so doing, they invariably became aware of the vast cultural opportunities offered by a country like Mexico: Berthe Small studied dance with a national ballet company and anthropology and Latin American literature at the University of Mexico, earning an honorary Master's degree; Brynna, David Prensky's wife, attracted by the country's art scene would eventually open a leading art gallery in Mexico City; Cleo Trumbo, an accomplished photographer, recorded her new surroundings and turned a room in her house into a darkroom; Hollywood couple Ian and Alice Hunter traveled through Mexico following up a newly ac-quired interest in Mexican folk art, and my father and Bart van der Schelling began to paint; George Oppen studied art and took up wood carving, Asa Zatz worked on a doctorate in an-thropology; the Trumbos, Smalls, Hunters, Peppers and my parents began collecting pre-Hispanic artifacts; Fred Field turned his interest in the field into a serious pursuit, studying archeology and becoming an authority in pre-Columbian seals; Anita Boyer immersed herself in the local theater and later opened a combination bookstore-art gallery; and David Prensky and Fred Field met others sharing their enthusiasm for re-corder music and formed *La Sociedad de la Flauta Barroca*.

Assimilation is generally regarded as an absorption process, and in time absorption did take place: Mexico never fully ab-sorbed us, but we absorbed Mexico—gradually. We laced our hot dogs with salsa and our conversations with Spanish colloquial-isms. We practiced the language on newly acquired Mexican friends, and they their English. We started off by shaking hands and, as we acquired *confianza*, greeted them—and our Ameri-can friends too—with a firm hug and a kiss on the cheek.

For those who stayed on, adaptation to Mexico as a foreigner and, in particular, as a political expatriate, signified transcend-ing distances—not only geographical but spiritual ones, as well. It meant taking mind leaps, traveling from a place in the brain to a place in the heart and, like the bread boy I'd spotted my first day in Mexico City, learning how to dodge danger and keep on pedaling.

Chapter Four

Lying Low:
Living with Surveillance and the Media

My parents were running scared when we left New York at the end of 1950. No doubt about that.

"Why?" I asked my uncle Benny.

"Because they were communists, that's why." He may not have sympathized with their politics, but he helped them anyway by providing a reason for them to leave: "The purpose of Meyer Zykofsky's trip is to survey the possibilities of investment in Mexico," read the letters my mother typed below my uncle's business letterhead. If my father were employed by an American firm, obtaining a passport might be easier and, possibly, deflect any interest the FBI might have in him.

My uncle must have been right. Why else would they leave home, family, and jobs, procure passports under false pretenses and, with two small children, flee to a country they knew nothing about ? They must have had a good reason, but I sometimes think they panicked, overestimating, perhaps, their personal importance in the larger scheme of things and, consequently, the danger of remaining in New York. (On the other hand, it's possible they merely overestimated the competence of the FBI.) Given the times, would their absence have gone undetected if their activities in New York had aroused suspicion? In fact, more than two years elapsed before the FBI became aware of their departure.

At approximately 1:00 P.M. on March 21, 1953, during what was probably one of several exploratory trips that Alfred Stern made to Mexico before moving there permanently, an FBI operative in Cuernavaca spotted a 1952 Ford Sedan with Mexico City license plates 33-159 parked in front of Stern's hotel. Since he and his wife had long been suspected of espionage,

Stern's visit to Mexico had naturally aroused the FBI's interest. The owner of the car was apparently photographed. Once again on June 5, 1953, the same individual was observed leaving Stern's office in Mexico City. According to an FBI report, "He proceeded in the car from the office to the residence at Calle de Lafontaine No. 225, Colonia Chapultepec Polanco, Mexico, D.F. Investigation of the latter address reflected that the individual was one Meyer Zykofsky."[1]

The presence in Mexico of a group of politically suspect individuals would not go unnoticed: A number of U.S. and local agencies, the media, and a handful of smalltime operators kept track of their movements. In fact, they may well have been one of the most closely scrutinized American communities abroad. Thus, in addition to coping with the challenges confronting all newly arrived families, political expatriates would learn to deal with surveillance, media coverage, and phone taps. (Many already had in the United States.) But not knowing how Mexico would react was, inevitably, a source of great anxiety.

Things in Mexico are seldom what they seem. One situation may have an infinity of outcomes depending on who the president is, who your lawyer knows, or on what day of the week you are arrested. Dealing with this required the acquisition of a whole new set of survival skills, and that took time. Political expatriates learned to recognize the dangers, to distinguish between a sticky situation with a solution, a threatening situation requiring more drastic tactics, and a hopeless one fraught with danger.

Such uncertainties could prove menacing, but it was a menace laced with farce: The middle aged lawyer clambering over his back fence in his pajamas to elude police, the professor who carried around a vial of chili powder to fling in his adversary's eyes in case of arrest, or the government agent who loaned his vacation home to American dissidents fleeing government agents.

Those were the kinds of things the political expatriates could tell me about, but there was a great deal they didn't know, and I had to go elsewhere for information. They were aware, of course, that the American Government continued to keep an eye on them in Mexico, but I think the extent of the surveillance far

---

1. Federal Bureau of Investigation, Alfred Stern, September 17, 1953, NY 100-57453-906.

surpassed all but their wildest speculations. Even today it's difficult to grasp without some understanding of the political mentality which reigned during the '50s.

The United States justified its presence, not only in Mexico, but throughout Latin America, by citing the dangers inherent in the Cold War stand-off between the United States and the Soviet Union. Communist activities—espionage in particular—socialist movements and popular uprisings needed to be vigorously suppressed. If not, capitalism, democratic government, and religion as we knew it, would cease to exist. This ideology was embraced by national leaders throughout the hemisphere. In Mexico, President Miguel Alemán, (1946-1952) and, to a greater or lesser extent, his successors, joined forces with the United States in the belief strong ties with that country would prove mutually beneficial.[2]

While President Cárdenas (1934-1940) had legitimized workers' aspirations and imposed revolutionary reforms, Alemán's strategy emphasized capitalism and economic modernization. In his eyes, Cárdenas's goals[3] were incompatible with his own. Toward this end, he and his followers openly attacked and incarcerated union leaders and well known radicals, curtailed trade unionization, rolled back union gains, and encouraged manifestations of anti-communism. Through an Alemán advisor formerly with U.S. intelligence, Colonel Applegate, the Mexican government made it known they would be open to U.S. suggestions regarding Communists in Mexico.[4]

The irony is obvious: American leftists like my parents turned to Mexico for refuge at a time when Mexico, under Alemán, was growing increasingly unsympathetic toward the left. In 1947, a year after he assumed office, Alemán consulted the FBI and, with their assistance, created the Mexican Security

2. Barry Carr, *Marxism in Twentieth Century Mexico,* Lincoln & London: University of Nebraska Press, 1992, p. 191.
3. Manuel Avila Camacho, President of Mexico from 1940-1946, had already changed political direction, moving significantly to the right of his predecessor, Lazaro Cardenas (1934-1940).
4. Barry Carr, *Marxism in Twentieth Century Mexico,* p. 191. The American government was involved in other ways as well. For example, under its Four Point program, the U.S. Embassy's labor attaché sent twenty-three members of Mexico's Petroleum Industry Union (STPRM) to the United States to participate in a program aimed against communist indoctrination.

Police, the *Dirección Federal de Seguridad*, (DFS).[5] According to their calculations, there were approximately 150 American Communists living throughout the country in the early '50s. Some avoided Mexico City, gravitating toward towns like Cuernavaca and San Miguel de Allende. However, the DFS estimated that many returned to the States once the more virulent anti-Red attacks had subsided. Within a few years they were estimated at less than one hundred.[6]

The agency most responsible for keeping track of U.S. dissidents in Mexico was the FBI. Under restrictions imposed by a new 1947 charter, its jurisdiction had been limited to "international aspects of domestic cases," but its Mexico City office would remain one of the few in operation overseas. Therefore, the FBI, rather than the CIA, would coordinate procedures concerning American political expatriates in Mexico.[7] They collected and disseminated information and maintained close relationships with the DFS, the CIA, the Department of the Interior, referred to here as *Gobernación*, the American Embassy, and the media. In addition, cordial ties with the Ministry of Communications and Public Works facilitated intelligence gathering through telephone taps and cable interception.[8]

Unfortunately, much information regarding surveillance and, more specifically, the role of the FBI in Mexico during the '50s, is not readily available. Though more than forty years have passed, I found few published sources and no well informed individual willing to speak to me, with one exception: "You can call me a highly reliable, non-attributable source." (I will refer to him here as 'Keith'.) Our interview took place in the garden of the Maria Cristina Hotel, and Keith's wife was present. She positioned herself with a view toward the hotel, while he faced the opposite direction. Whenever he sensed someone's approach he flinched, then lowered his voice. Though not allowed to use

5. Barry Carr, *Marxism in Twentieth Century Mexico*, p. 145. Sergio Aguayo y John Bailey, "Servicios de inteligencia en México antes de 1985," *Reforma* Enfoque, January 26, 1998, pp. 11-14. In theory, the *Dirección Federal de Seguridad* or National Security Directorate, was a dependency of Mexico's *Gobernación*, i.e. the Department of the Interior. In reality, it remained an instrument of the executive, free from congressional control, and was employed primarily, for coercive purposes rather than for the purpose of collecting intelligence.
6. Karl M. Schmitt, *Communism in Mexico: A Study in Political Frustration*, Austin: University of Texas Press, 1965, pp. 217-18.
7. Barry Carr, *Marxism in Twentieth Century Mexico*, p. 364.
8. Ibid., p. 145.

a tape recorder, I was permitted to take notes, which he reviewed to his satisfaction on a later occasion. Despite the cloak and dagger touches surrounding our meeting, my informant provided invaluable insight into procedure and the mentality governing the intelligence community at the time.

After the CIA was created in 1948, Keith told me, the FBI continued its jurisdiction over suspect Americans in Mexico. But if an individual under surveillance proceeded to another country, the CIA took over. When there was any overlapping, the two organizations worked closely together. In Mexico, for example, the CIA and the FBI communicated with each other every day, and somewhere between five to ten written accounts plus an additional three to four operations reports concerning the ACGM, reached CIA desks weekly. These would be "officially denominated," i.e. given a name whereby they could be traced, and disseminated within the Embassy.[9]

Former CIA agent, Philip Agee, who achieved notoriety with his defection and subsequent exposé of the CIA,[10] confirmed this. He recalled writing occasional memoranda during 1966 and 1967 containing information he had picked up on left-wing U.S. expatriates in Mexico, including, in particular, possible connections with Communist country missions. These were forwarded to the FBI.[11]

In addition, the CIA fed misinformation to the local press,[12] routinely tapped all Soviet phones in Mexico, and relayed pertinent intelligence to the FBI.[13] Information relating to the license-plate numbers of U.S. vehicles together with photographs of their occupants, snapped by observers posted in close proximity to the Soviet, Soviet satellite and Cuban embassies, was also transmitted to the FBI.[14]

9. Keith, telephone conversation with author, January 19, 1993; Ellen Schrecker, *Many are the Crimes. McCarthyism in America*, Boston, New York, Toronto and London: Little Brown and Company, 1998, pp. 204-205. Ms. Schrecker notes that Hoover's attitude toward the newly formed agency was hostile and that cooperation with the CIA was discouraged. (For example, the FBI began decoding the Venona Decrypts as early as 1948, if not earlier, however, Hoover neglected to inform the CIA until the end of 1952.)
10. Philip Agee, *Inside the Company: CIA Diary*, Toronto, New York & London: Bantam Books, 1975.
11. Philip Agee, letter to author, April 24, 1996.
12. Jorge Luis Sierra, "Entrevista con Philip Agee," *Reforma*, September 18, 1997, p.20A.
13. Philip Agee, *Inside the Company: CIA Diary*, p. 542-543.
14. Ibid.

Furthermore, according to Keith's information, FBI surveillance activities were conducted by "more than two but certainly less than a dozen indigenous teams," each composed of from four to six persons hired locally. "The basic nature of the Bureau's business was criminal, and . . . the Mexican police, working in a normal liaison capacity, would handle most of their surveillances (sic.) for them."

The Mexican Security Police, the DFS, was most certainly involved in these procedures as poet turned furniture maker George Oppen and his wife, Mary, soon discovered. Shortly after moving into their new home above the San Angel post office, they were accosted by two Mexican plainclothesmen. Living with them at the time was a Chilean citizen, Rafael Baraona, who as a U.S. resident, had been cited for perjury, but was free on a bail bond. Fearing he might be called to testify, he panicked and fled to Mexico with his wife and baby. While the two agents questioned George and Mary in their patio, Rafael was poised on the roof prepared to bolt should either of the Oppens give a prearranged hand signal.

What most impressed them during that and subsequent encounters with the investigators was that background information—much of it erroneous—was the same the California FBI had confronted them with. Mary Oppen wrote, "But these were Mexican men, supplied with dossiers that the CIA and the FBI had compiled. . . ."

When they consulted their lawyer, Carmen Gama Otero, she assured them they had nothing to worry about: "That's not done in Mexico, we don't have an FBI or a CIA; you must be mistaken."

They continued to insist that they were obviously under surveillance, so she accompanied them to *Gobernación* and, with the cooperation of the secretaries, who greeted her warmly, pulled one photograph after another from the files. But the Oppens were unable to identify their surveillants.

As a result, Carmen concluded the matter must be more serious than she had supposed: "They must be from the presidential secret police. We will go outside and look for them on the steps of the palace, where they congregate in the mornings."

Mary Oppen explained: "As we walked toward the steps we saw our men and pointed them out to Carmen, who walked directly up to one of them. 'My clients tell me that you are bothering them,' she said. '*Es muy feo.* . . . (This is very ugly.) If there is something you want to know, please come to me. I will confer with my clients. I will speak for them.' We never saw the men again."[15]

Most surveillance subjects, however, were denied the Oppens' satisfaction of confronting their enemy. Maggie, Abe and Harriet Magil's daughter, was barely seven when *The Daily Worker* sent her father to Mexico. According to her parents, she was playing outside their apartment building on Insurgentes with friends when a man approached and questioned her about her family, offering her toys in exchange for information. The Magils chose to leave Mexico shortly after.[16]

Both the Oppens and Maggie Magil were harassed by Mexican agents who may have been working for the Americans. Whether they were employed by the FBI without official cognizance or provided to them by the Mexican government probably varied from president to president and depended, to some extent, on the head of *Gobernación* and the prevailing political climate.

According to Keith, the Mexican government did accommodate U.S. requests for police assistance, and in much the same way, Americans honored Mexican Embassy requests for FBI support in criminal matters affecting both countries. Keith claims that Bureau jurisdiction includes stolen cars, flights from justice, and draft evasion, in addition to crimes touching on international bank robbery; fraud and forgery; Interpol cases and, of course, matters relating to the ACGM. This, in turn, implied direct and routine contact between the Bureau, the Mexican government and the police, although the extent of such contact might vary from one Bureau chief to another.

In relation to the ACGM, Keith reconfirmed rumors which had circulated periodically throughout the '50s and early '60s: The FBI had sent down at least one infiltrator and possibly more, an individual or individuals who appeared to have been persecuted, with backgrounds similar to others already in residence. When I asked him to describe the average ACGMer he told me that approximately sixty to seventy percent were 'doctrinaire Communists.'

15. Mary Oppen, *Meaning: A Life*, p. 199.
16. A. B. Magil, interview with author, January 20, 1993.

He further explained: "[Of those] thirty percent . . . [had] aided and abetted the Soviets. This aid may have been only financial, showing up at parties and demonstrations to help give the appearance of a protest by the masses, or it could have been more operational in nature. Since ACGMers had no information of value, their worth lay in being able to help in the establishment of contacts in the United States with others who could give support, provide fronts, and so on.

"My general impression is that [they usually] kept to themselves. As a matter of fact most of them wanted to distance themselves from the PCM [the Mexican Communist Party] or anything having to do with the ultra-left. Some of the expatriates who were dyed-in the wool communists received invitations from the Soviet Embassy for their soirees but, after one or two parties, very few of this group continued to frequent the Embassy functions."[17]

In concluding, he assured me that: "Most ACGM'ers had overactive imaginations and saw FBI and CIA spies behind every bush and a microphone in every wall and telephone. They were unaware of the jurisdictional distinction between the two organizations and since the Agency was new and fashionable, they liked to think [it] was after them in Mexico. It was due to this paranoia that the individual members of the ACGM (probably those with the most to feel guilty about) developed basic survival tactics to evade surveillance. They also adopted outlandish hand signals to warn others that there were imagined microphone plants in a room. For those few of the ACGM who were genuinely part of the Soviet apparatus, it would be only a normal precautionary measure for the Soviets to school them in counter-surveillance techniques."[18]

To the above I can only add the following: I am convinced, based on my own investigation, that, if a handful were involved in espionage or in anything remotely connected to local politics during their time in Mexico, I found no evidence.

I did, however, find evidence of FBI involvement in Mexico: In an October 10, 1951 communiqué from the Ambassador's counselor to the Department of State the following suggestion

17. Keith, letter to author, July 16, 1992.
18. Keith, letter to author, December 5, 1994. Keith, interview with author, November 12, 1993.

was advanced: "As I informed Director Hoover one possibility might be for our Embassy informally to furnish a list of such known American Communists in Mexico to the Mexican police authorities with a hint that if action of some kind were taken against them the Embassy would not interest itself particularly in their defense. This would be done on the theory that it might be better to keep them in the United States where, as Mr. Hoover has pointed out, the police powers of our government are so much more complete and effective."[19]

Backstage maneuvers, such as the above, make it all the more difficult to analyze the complex roles assumed by each of the agencies involved—the FBI, CIA, DFS, and *Gobernación.* In addition, there was the ubiquitous presence of the media. Since stories dealing with suspect Americans, particularly those tainted by rumors of sabotage, conspiracy or treason sold copy, journalists made it their business to keep a close watch over the political expatriate community. At the same time, the FBI through the Embassy and the other local agencies, disseminated misinformation on a regular basis, identified cooperative journalists, and occasionally made it worth their while. In effect, by focusing on the political expatriates, the press, either on its own or manipulated by outside entities, could also limit their freedom of movement, in much the same way the official agencies did.[20]

With the influx of American political expatriates during the latter half of Alemán's administration, news items touching on the Red menace and the presence of foreign radicals throughout Mexico, were published with troubling regularity.[21] These are

19. Federal Bureau of Investigation, Gordon Kahn, October 10, 1951 as reported in "Blacklisted," Segment three, Tony Kahn's docu-drama of the blacklist broadcast on public radio.
20. Ellen W. Schrecker, *No Ivory Tower: McCarthyism & the Universities,* New York, Oxford: Oxford University Press, 1988, p. 257. The FBI divulged secret material to political allies and the press. Since these never identified their sources victims had no recourse. Once they were identified as subversives, their reputations were generally damaged beyond repair.
21. After the Spanish Civil War and, again, following WWII, Mexico's liberal immigration policies allowed significant numbers of European refugees to enter the country. These too were sometimes targeted by the press. Among their numbers was a small group of prominent communist intellectuals, some of whom had been denied entry into the United States and a few of whom were in contact with the political expatriates. These included Germans Anna Seghers, Gertrude Duby, Bruno Frei, Bodo Uhse, and Ludwig Renn; Czecks Egon Erwin Kisch and Otto Katz (aka. André Simone); Hungarian Lazlo Radvanji, and Spaniards Constancia de la Mora and Margarita Nelkin.

striking, not only for their inaccuracies, but because, seen in perspective, they illustrate how the media operated and the role it played.

For a while, the expatriate groups residing outside Mexico City in towns like Cuernavaca and San Miguel Allende were of particular interest to both the local and foreign press. San Miguel Allende with its winding, cobble-stoned streets, lush vegetation and colonial ambiance housed a small privately owned art school, the *Escuela de Bellas Artes*. During the late '40s, over a hundred American students, their tuition covered by the U.S. government under the G.I. Bill, moved there, attracted by its low cost of living and its proximity to the internationally acclaimed Mexican art movement. Among its foremost practitioners, known both for his skill and his radical politics, was painter David Alfaro Siqueiros. During a visit to the art institute in 1949, he was shown a vast hall in the former *Convento de la Concepción* owned by the government's *Instituto Nacional de Bellas Artes*. Inspired by the possibilities for artistic expression and encouraged by Alfredo Campanella, the *Escuela de Bellas Artes's* owner, he agreed to paint a mural on the site in collaboration with the institute's students. Thus, an understanding was reached, permission granted, and work begun.

Although the Siqueiros mural got off to a good start, subsequent disputes flared up periodically: Painting materials were not forthcoming, and former agreements were ignored. A *Time* magazine article explained: "Increasingly excited over the project, Siqueiros wanted to work full time to complete it. Campanella, anxious to preserve the publicity the Maestro's presence was bringing to his school, balked. Finally, three weeks ago, Lawyer Campanella drew up a contract to let Siqueiros do the job. The painter took one look at its provisions, pronounced them insulting and shoved Campanella and his brother down a flight of stairs."[22]

Included in the body of the same article was an account of a crime committed by a drunken student infuriated by his wife's infidelity. It ended on a threatening note, "The U.S. Embassy is quietly looking into both the Siqueiros affair and the Zurnis death; if it is to recommend a revocation of the G.I. accreditation, San Miguel would be finished."

22. "School for Scandal," *Time* magazine, August 1, 1949.

When I contacted the former art institute director, Stirling Dickinson, to check out the *Time* story, he replied, "The article did bring back some unpleasant memories. In my own personal case this is basically what happened: About 1945 the original *Escuela de Bellas Artes,* of which I was director, was sold almost overnight. . . . Without going into details, getting along with Campanella, [the new owner], was virtually impossible; at one point I resigned, but our students insisted that I be recalled, threatening to close the school. I did return."

In reference to the Siqueiros incident, he wrote that the contract Campanella had drawn up was ridiculous: "[Siqueiros] tore it up and dropped the project.[23] This was the proverbial straw that broke the camel's back. Of 132 students and our faculty all but two left, and we set up a new school under the auspices of *Bellas Artes* [The government-sponsored Institute of Fine Arts headquartered in Mexico City]. I remained as active director. . . . Naturally, this infuriated our lawyer-owner of the now defunct school, so he and the two students left with him sailed off to Mexico City and gave out a vile interview to some underling in the Embassy, calling us all Communists, etc. The Third Secretary of the Embassy . . . who knew us well, told the underling secretary . . . he had been told a pack of lies and slander, but, evidently, the material got into some Embassy file."

A year went by without incident. The newly established institute was, not surprisingly, denied G.I. sponsorship, but continued to operate normally. Then one morning in August, Dickinson and eight other foreign employees were rounded up and taken away.[24] When students and friends opened their newspapers the next day they read: "They Entered as Tourists and They Broke the Law." According to the article, *Gobernación* had expelled eight American and Canadian painters,[25] who had

---

23. When I asked Dickinson whether Siqueiros had pushed the Campanella brothers down the stairs, he replied, "I simply don't know. I wouldn't be the least bit surprised if he at least shoved them, but I wasn't present and Siqueiros, being a rather fiery individual, might easily have gotten very upset over the insulting contract he was offered."

24. Aside from Dickinson these included Canadians Leonard and Reva Brooks and Americans James and Ruska Pinto, Judy Martin, Howard Jackson, and Jack and Bunny Baldwin.

25. "Entraron como turistas y violaron la ley," *Excélsior* Section 1, August 16, 1950, p. 3.

entered the country as tourists but, contrary to the law, had remained and were gainfully employed.[26]

According to Dickinson: "The shyster lawyer, [the school's former owner] bribed someone in *Gobernación* to take us out of the country under the guise of giving us working papers of a different kind. I was certain, from the beginning, that this was strictly a deportation. Otherwise, someone from *Bellas Artes* would surely have been with these men to assure us that we were to get new documents.

"Various *Gobernación* people got into the act: One man waved his pistol wildly as we were escorted to the railway station, herded up like people about to be deported. He was shouting: '*Yo soy el FBI* (I am the FBI).' When we finally boarded the train for Nuevo Laredo there was just a single one-legged man along with us. He was one of several *Gobernación* people sent out to help us get deported, but for some reason he was chosen to be our guard on the train ride to Laredo. He had a crutch, but seemed a mild sort who couldn't possibly have done much if we had tried to escape. Obviously, one or more of us could have jumped off the train at a way station, and actually I did contemplate doing this myself. . . . We all went out together and roomed in a ramshackle hotel in Laredo pending our return to Mexico."[27]

They did return, thanks to powerful friends: Siqueiros, a handful of Mexican generals, and several highly placed government officials intervened on their behalf. But the incident, little more than a contractual dispute between a well known Communist painter and the owner of an art school, began to acquire a life of its own.

A year after the deportations the *Saturday Evening Post* ran a story about Mexico's attempt to cope with communist subversion: "A few American communists also appeared briefly at San Miguel Allende's School of Fine Arts. They were among the same 125 American painters that Siqueiros taught there,

---

26. "Pueden volver los profesores que fueron expulsados" *Excélsior* Sección Uno, August 20, 1950, p. 1. Dickinson explained how those detained had entered Mexico on tourist and student visas. The Secretary of Education, however, had been apprised of their status in the country. While illegal employment was a convenient motive for expulsion, it is unlikely to have been the principal one.
27. Stirling Dickinson, letters to the author, July 23, 1993, August 12, 1993, September 25, 1993.

and most of them attended the school under their GI rights. When Siqueiros fell out with the school owners, so great was his influence that almost all the Americans walked out with him, and through cutting classes, the veterans lost their GI aid."

The same article included a remark made by an unidentified DFS spokesman: "Siqueiros and [the artist Diego] Rivera are the most dangerous [intellectuals] because of their great fame. This is particularly so with North American boys who come here to study under them and believe in these men almost as gods. You have here also the problem of your GI students who may become indoctrinated in certain schools and then go back to your country as communists, having learned this at your government's expense."[28]

Any attempt to dispute such allegations was futile, as political expatriates discovered on numerous occasions. Jean Butler remembers one incident in particular: Shortly after their arrival, they were lunching with the Trumbos in *El Círculo del Sureste*, a crowded restaurant well-known for its Yucatecan delicacies, when the conversation turned to bullfighting, always a sore spot between the two men. (Butler defended it, while Trumbo considered it barbaric.) The conversation grew heated. When a Hollywood newspaper ran an account of how they had come to blows, they were furious.

Jean Butler explained: "[But] when you're in a situation like ours . . . you can't really sue for libel because your reputation's already so damaged by your own actions. . . . We sent it to Boudin, [our lawyer], and asked him whether he thought a libel suit could be sustained. He said if we wanted him to he would, but he didn't think it was a very good idea."[29]

During Alemán's term in office the media regularly stirred up public opinion in an attempt to create a climate favorable to Cold War policy. Just as the San Miguel Allende incident had been distorted by the press, "The Battle of Cuernavaca," as it was later referred to by one journalist, was also misrepresented.

By 1951 an assortment of artists, writers and Hollywood

28. Richard English, "Mexico Clamps Down on Stalin", *Saturday Evening Post*, August 30, 1952, p. 14.
29. Jean Butler, interview with author, August, 2, 1991.

characters had gravitated to Cuernavaca. Among their numbers was Willard Motley, the author of such well respected books as *Knock on Any Door* and *We Fished All Night*. According to literary authority Alan Wald, "Politically, he was known as a Henry Wallace supporter, although it is not impossible that he passed through the CP at some point."[30] While he was known to harbor a progressive outlook, his reasons for being in Mexico do not appear to have been primarily political.

Apparently, Motley and some friends were having a drink on the terrace of the Bella Vista Hotel when a Texan, irked by the presence of what he referred to as "those dirty niggers", complained to the hotel's owner who promptly informed him that if he didn't like it he could leave. The Texan and his companion stomped out, and Motley and his friends, overjoyed by the proprietor's response, proceeded to overindulge until they were tipsy and burst into song. Apparently, one of the many selections with which they regaled their audience was the *Internationale*, the anthem of the Socialist and Communist Parties.

Shortly after, a series of articles highly critical of the political expatriates and of Mexico's tolerant policies regarding them appeared in the local press. Among these was *Excélsior's* "Cuernavaca, Refuge for Runaway American Reds."[31] Without mentioning names, it referred to a group of communists who chose to sing the *Internationale* on the Hotel Bellavista terrace thereby antagonizing a group of tourists who proceeded to walk out in protest. The same article mentioned a party hosted by Willard Motley, "a man of color," and attended by prominent communist screenwriters. In addition, thirteen individuals were identified as Cuernava Reds, among them "screenwriters Albert Maltz and George Khan (sic.)." According to the article, this last had not only been imprisoned in the United States, which was untrue, but also headed Cuernavaca's Red community.

The Willard Motley saga was reported in the American press a year later, but this time, seated on a hotel terrace singing revolutionary songs and getting plastered on "planter's punch" was "the Hollywood group." The *Saturday Evening Post* article explained: "Parading into the dining room singing the Internationale they

30. Alan Wald, letter to author, March 7, 1992.
31. "Cuernavaca convertida en nido de rojos prófugos de EEUU," *Excélsior*, October 8, 1951.

caused a small riot. A few Texans started to take them apart, and only the frantic pleas of the manager saved the room from becoming a shambles. The Texans grimly stalked out, and the Hollywood communists then promptly complained to the management about this discrimination."[32]

People with few sanctuaries at their disposal learned to take the surveillance and the occasional media exposure in stride. They knew that the tapped phone or the muddled newspaper account was the inevitable outcome of political dissidence and a life in exile.

Nevertheless, between 1950 and 1951, a time when politically motivated migrations to Mexico were at their height, two isolated but potentially terrifying events, the Morton Sobell and Gus Hall abductions, drove home a singular fact: Only exiles could be deported or forcefully returned to their country of origin. It reminded them that not everyone seeking sanctuary in Mexico would find it.

Morton Sobell, an electrical engineer, had been a member of the Communist Party from 1939 to 1941. Given the fervor of anti-Red sentiment, his departure from the United States on June 20, 1950 was unremarkable: He and his wife had perjured themselves when they signed loyalty oaths at their place of employment, the Reeves Instrument Company in New York City. In view of the times, this was incentive enough for leaving the country.

However, on June 16, just four days prior to Sobell's departure to Mexico, David Greenglass, a mechanic who had worked at a wartime facility devoted to atomic development, was arrested and accused his brother-in-law, Julius Rosenberg, of having been the ringleader in an atomic espionage plot. Rosenberg, Sobell's friend and New York City College classmate, was seized on July 18. That same day Sobell, already in Mexico, began searching for a way to travel to Europe without a passport. According to Sobell, "Since [Rosenberg] was a good friend of mine, this intensified my fear of being indicted for perjury. I could not imagine that he was an atom spy as the newspapers asserted, and felt that I too might be arrested on a similar charge."[33]

32. Richard English, "Mexico Clamps Down on Stalin," p.11.
33. "Re. Sobell on Venona and the Rosenbergs," September 12, 1997, Internet, H-DIPLO, http://h-net2.msu.edu/~diplo/essays.htm.

From July 18 through August 16, 1950 Sobell made the rounds of Mexico City travel agencies and visited the ports of Veracruz and Tampico under an alias hoping to procure passage out of the country. When this proved impossible, he approached a newspaper editor, whose progressive stance had impressed him, as well as the prominent left-wing labor leader Vicente Lombardo Toledano. Both claimed they were unable to help him.[34]

On the evening of August 16, 1950, scarcely two months after he arrived, Sobell was eating dinner with his wife and children when there was a knock on the door. Upon answering, three men with drawn guns made their way into the vestibule and told him they were looking for the bank robber, Johnny Jones. They identified themselves as Mexican Secret Police, (DFS), and started searching the apartment. When he asked permission to call the American Embassy, they reacted violently and pushed him out the door. He resisted. They carried him down the stairs and out the building.

"They dragged me down the street, and I was yelling, 'Police, police!' They hit me over the head and shoved me into the car. They took my wife and the children in another car. They took us to their headquarters where they made arrangements with the FBI. Then they drove us straight to the border, seventeen hours, where they handed us over to the customs people."

For political expatriates living in Mexico, this was the stuff of nightmares. Early accounts gave the impression the Mexican Government had ordered the kidnapping, and if this were true, it might signal an official change in policy. A prominently displayed news item, "Mexican Campaign Against the Fifth Column in Moscow's Employ," run less than a week after the Sobell incident, informed of a vigorous effort on behalf of Mexico and the United States to combat Red interests on the continent. According to "extra-official but reliable sources" the FBI, the DFS, and principal police organizations throughout the country had already initiated the first step in this collaboration with *Gobernación's* expulsion of Morton Sobell. The article claimed that upon returning voluntarily to the United States, Sobell had been nabbed by American agents.

In effect, however, there was no deportation through official

34. Morton Sobell, *On Doing Time*, N.Y.: Scribner's, 1975, pp. 71-73.

channels nor does *Gobernación* appear to have been officially involved. The FBI, using Mexicans in the employ of the DFS to carry out the operation, probably engineered the abduction. Upon reaching the border, American law enforcement officers took over. (It is also possible that President Alemán was apprised of this maneuver.) While the kidnapping theory is generally accepted, it has never been confirmed.

During an interview, Arnoldo Martínez Verdugo, who became the Secretary General of the Mexican Communist Party from 1963-1981, told me the following: "At the time [Sobell was trying to leave Mexico] I was friendly with the caretaker of our offices in *Colonia Roma*. Following Sobell's abduction on August 16 the watchman became most agitated telling us that the previous day—a Sunday, I believe—someone had knocked desperately at the door. (The office was closed.)[35] So he went out to open the door and . . . this person asked to be taken in, claiming the Americans were after him. Naturally the watch-man's first thought was, 'How am I to know whether this guy is really being persecuted?' So he asked him for a reference or a letter. At the time there were a lot of problems between the Parties and with the media. So he tried to get someone on the phone to authorize his allowing the man to stay—he was obviously in great difficulty—but he couldn't get a hold of anyone so he told him he was very sorry but he would have to return. Well, when he read in the paper that this same man had been seized, he fell into a depression."[36]

When I asked Sobell whether he recalled having contacted the Mexican Party he replied, "I have no recollection, and I doubt that I would have done so at that time."[37] Did the caretaker make the story up? Was Sobell lying? We will probably never know, but regardless of whether it occurred or not, and it might have—to someone else—it was one of many such stories making the rounds at the time. Such accounts were often accepted at face value if only because they *seemed* plausible and allowed those fearing deportation to express their own apprehensions.

35. August 16, 1950, the day Sobell was abducted, fell on a Wednesday so the previous day could not have been Sunday. The first press reports appeared in Mexico City papers on Saturday, August 19, 1950.
36. Arnoldo Martinez Verdugo, interview with the author, August 28, 1991.
37. Morton Sobell, letter to author, April 8, 1996.

One can't help but ask why, if Sobell had indeed spied for the Soviet Union, some help was not forthcoming as it was for others who were accused of espionage or had been affiliated with the Party.[38] As far as we know, he was never assisted by any of the Eastern European Embassies in Mexico nor by political expatriates already living there. Despite his former affiliation with the Communists, Sobell appears to have known no one in the country and to have been unaware of the presence of an American Party underground. (It is possible, however, that this apparatus had yet to be activated.)

Following the Sobell incident, what little confidence the community had vested in Mexico's ability to defend its interests eroded rapidly. Strident attacks against the Mexican left continued unabated: Mexican Communists and union leaders were routinely kidnapped or jailed, and private and state industry, encouraged by government example, discharged *troublemakers*. Thus, when a second abduction occurred a little over a year later, Mexico's political expatriates would not rest any easier.

Gus Hall, the former General Secretary of the Party, one of eleven Party leaders found guilty under the Smith Act, was escorted across the border to Mexico City by the CPUSA underground, assisted by the Mexican Party, in an attempt to jump bail and avoid imprisonment. After less than twenty-four hours, he was seized by Mexican agents, escorted in the opposite direction, and delivered into the arms of U.S. law enforcement officials. (The Americans blamed the Mexicans for the disastrous outcome, and the Mexicans blamed the Americans.)[39] As a result, members of the CPUSA underground, went into hiding for six months, and further plans to use Mexico as an escape route were abandoned.[40]

According to information released the following day, *Gobernación's* Secret Police had apprehended and deported Hall.[41] However a subsequent article, printed by the same paper twenty four hours later, claimed Mexican migration officials

---

38. Among those who came through Mexico and received outside assistance were Abraham Chapman and Morris and Lona Cohen. (The Cohens were accused of atomic espionage.)

39. Arnoldo Martinez Verdugo, interview with author, August 14, 1992.

40. Peter Steinberg, *The Great 'Red Menace'* p. 405.

41. "El principal cabecilla comunista. Arresto en México tratase de Gus Hall convicto de conjura," *Excélsior*, October 10, 1951, p. 1.

had recognized him when he entered Mexico City, followed him to his hotel, and returned him to the United States.[42] In either case, the CPUSA underground's attempt to send Hall to the Soviet Union via Mexico was a fiasco and resulted in an additional three year sentence for Hall.[43]

Obviously, the Sobell and Hall incidents were cause for concern: Both were shrouded in secrecy, little official information was forthcoming, no one assumed blame, and no one was held accountable. In addition, as foreigners, ACGMers were not given equal protection under the law. According to Article 33 of the Mexican Constitution, originally adopted to protect Mexicans from foreign exploitation, the President could deport non-citizens without a hearing if they were accused of meddling in internal affairs. (During times of unrest this provision could come in handy.)

Thus, while the knowledge that the FBI, DFS, *Gobernación* and the media could operate with impunity was worrisome, the possibility, of being "thirty-threed out of the country," or kidnapped, as Sobell and Hall had been, was downright alarming. According to DFS sources, some American dissidents left Mexico around this time.[44] Perhaps they were afraid that if they remained, Mexico would be unable or unwilling to protect them.

The Americans who did stay on were, in the words of Hollywood refugee Jeanette Pepper: ". . . [afraid] of being tossed out of the country . . . [we] saw shadows where there weren't any. The famous incident [concerned] Gus Hall . . . he was just picked up and sent back to the United States. I don't remember if it was the FBI or Mexican agents. But the point I'm making is that there was no extradition, no nothing. He was just lifted. And you know, that put the fear of death into us. So when anything happened, people could take advantage very easily. There were always incidents that came up, that reinforced this fear. . . ."[45]

Such fear made the political expatriates vulnerable to blackmail and the prey of independent con-artists who, for a fee, promised to use their influence to protect them from harassment

42. "Está ya en la prisión el que soñó derrocar a Harry Truman," *Excélsior*, October 11, 1951, p. 1.
43. Peter Steinberg, *The Great 'Red Menace,'* p. 486.
44. Karl M. Schmitt, *Communism in Mexico*, pp. 217-18.
45. Jeanette Pepper, interview with author, August 2, 1991.

or worse. Keith, my source for such matters, explained it this way: "In those days [you had] the *Jefatura*, i.e., the police headquarters, and the judicial police and the *Dirección Federal de Seguridad*, the Federal agents . . . and, frankly, anyone [with] a credential and a badge could impose himself on a situation in hopes of a *mordida*."[46]

Medical translator Asa Zatz remembered that with the arrival of the first dissidents in the late '40s and early '50s, the U.S. Embassy had informants reporting on the Americans. "Then when it heated up, the Mexican *coyotes* branched out on their own to make themselves a bundle from the victims. There were a lot of shady individuals who lived on the periphery of the group . . . [and were generally] connected with *Gobernación*. They tried to exploit the presence . . . of many people who were there possibly in an endangered species role. These were shaken down very often. That was also part of the scene. Well, there were informers all over the place. You could pick up $10 or $25 by giving somebody's name to the Embassy. So . . . that was a lot of money at the time. That's how they got these huge lists of . . . people who really had nothing to do with anything, but found themselves blacklisted and in trouble."[47]

The most vulnerable to blackmail were the well known figures whose names appeared frequently in print or those who attended events associated with the left. Friends remember the swindler who appeared on Dalton Trumbo's doorstep occasionally demanding a payoff "to keep something terrible from happening." Trumbo refused to give him a dime, and he eventually vanished. (The anticipated retributions never occurred.)[48] In an unrelated incident, Spanish Civil War veteran, Bart van der Schelling, attended the funeral of a Spanish Republican general and, according to his wife, was identified by an individual who offered him protection in exchange for cash. Soon after, Bart contacted a well-placed friend who was able to end the harassment.[49]

The drama of exile was played out against a background of

46. Keith, letter to author, February 11, 1992. *Mordida* refers to a bribe, but is, literally, the Spanish word for "bite."
47. Asa Zatz, interview with author, May 20, 1991. Asa Zatz, letter to the author, November 20, 1995.
48. Jean Butler, interview with author, August 2, 1991.
49. Edna Moore Van der Schelling, interview with author, August 1, 1991.

mistrust and fear, its actors politically suspect foreigners subject to surveillance, occasional harassment and the possibility of a shake-down or arrest. As a result, political disengagement was the norm. According to former Amtorg counsel David Drucker, "[It] was accepted by all of us that any connection with the Mexican Communist Party was out of the question, since the Mexican government would not countenance it."[50]

Berthe Small concurred: "We all kept away from any inference of political activity. And that was the wisest and the best path to follow. It was the only path. We were denied that by the Mexican government, and nobody wanted to risk that even if we had had the inclination . . .because we didn't want to be thirty-three out of the country."[51]

Consequently, former political activists were stripped of their identity: "I think what most of us resented," Jeanette Pepper told me, "was that we really had been forced out of battle . . . we [became] *hors de combat*."[52]

Because their behavior in Mexico was ruled by extreme caution, those on the look-out for conspiracies would, in the long run, be disappointed. Almost without exception, the bulk of political expatriates kept away from politics once they left the States. This had not always been true: An earlier generation— the militant anarchists, socialists and other radicals arriving in Mexico during World War I and well into the '40s—often remained politically active.[53]

In May of 1940, for example, when a group of artists, led by painter David Alfaro Siqueiros, tried, unsuccessfully, to assassinate Leon Trotsky, the Russian revolutionary exiled in Mexico, Americans were said to have been in on the planning. Rumor had it that members of the American Friends of the Mexican People, a group of Lincoln Brigade veterans who moved between Mexico and New York raising funds for the Spanish Republicans, had arrived in Mexico a few weeks earlier. But, by the time the attempt was made, they had scattered.[54]

---

50. David Drucker, letter to author, May 2, 1993
51. Berthe Small, interview, January 17, 1993.
52. Jeanette Pepper, letter to author, September 30, 1997.
53. Among their numbers were Americans Frank Shipman, (also known as Charles Francis Philips), Linn A.E. Gale, Roberto Haberman, Bertram Wolfe, Michael Gold, Carleton Beals, Tina Modotti and others.
54. Betty Kirk, *Covering the Mexican Front*, Oklahoma: U of Oklahoma P, 1942.

After hearing that Spanish Civil War vet, William Colfax Miller, still resident in Mexico, had participated in the assassination attempt, I set out to find him. He had arrived in 1939, easily ten years prior to most of the other expatriates, but he was closely associated with the ACGM. "He's an old-timer, tells everyone he fought in Spain and left the States because he was a Marxist," people told me.

Despite his lack of discretion, finding him was not easy. I tracked him down shortly before his death in 1994. He and his wife, Virginia, had moved to Ajijic, a small town alongside Lake Chapala, some years earlier, and he was in the process of installing a phone. The phone lines were unreliable, but he wasn't. He turned out to be an admirable correspondent. Shortly after establishing contact with him, I received a letter: "I was involved in the [first] Trotsky episode in Mexico, and later became a very good friend of Jacques Mornard (aka. Ramon Mercader del Rio), who did kill him [in August, 1940]. The Secretary of the penitentiary, Pepe Farah was an old friend of friends of mine, and he was a Marxist too. He's dead now, but he introduced Jacques Mornard to me, and we spent much time together."[55]

I picked up the phone and called Miller immediately. Well, no, he replied in answer to my question. He had never actually participated in the attempt but, yes, he had known about it and later became friendly with Mercader.

I persisted: "Well, did you belong to The American Friends of the Mexican People?" He evaded my question, so I repeated it in a letter.

He replied: "I belonged to the Friends of Mexico. It was an organization that got top liberal people . . . to give us speeches on their particular specialty. We usually met at some member's home. The admission was free, and we served coffee and *pan dulce* (sweet rolls)."[56]

So much for my attempts at sleuthing. However, another early arrival, John 'Brick' Menz, the economist and academic who was in Mexico on two occasions, first as a student in 1946-1948, and again as a political refugee from 1951-1956, had participated openly in Mexican politics. He provided a

---

55. William Colfax Miller, letter to author, June 30, 1993.
56. William Colfax Miller, letter to author, November 6, 1993.

link between two generations: the early arrivals, who involved themselves in local politics, and the vast bulk of political expatriates, who kept their distance.

'Brick,' so called because of his red hair, told me he and his wife, Billie, originally moved to Mexico when he enrolled as a student in Mexico City College, a haven for former enlisted men wanting to continue their education under the G.I. Bill. During that time he was one of the Amigos de Wallace (Friends of Wallace) founders. The group supported Henry Wallace's 1948 presidential bid on the Progressive Party ticket, a coalition of New Deal Democrats, the Communist Party, some labor unions, and other progressive interests throughout the United States.[57] (I later asked John Menz whether he remembered Bill Miller. It had occurred to me that Miller might have been involved with The Friends of Wallace, rather than The American Friends of the Mexican People. But Menz could not remember.)

He did, however, remember Mexico City's 1948 May Day Parade, when he marched, arms linked with Diego Rivera and David Alfaro Siqueiros: "I was only in the damn parade because the two refused to have anything to do with one another. Mine was a salvage operation. . . ." American participation in an event supported by the Mexican Communist Party and other left-wing organizations received wide-spread press coverage in both Mexico and the United States. "When my good, conservative father-in-law saw my photo in the paper he blew his stack and had some nasty things to say about my values."[58]

In fact, Miller and Menz were rare exceptions. Despite this, throughout the '50s and early '60s some viewed the entire left-wing expatriate community as a hot-bed of radical activity. So successful were the security agencies and the media in distorting their image, even the political expatriates themselves were confused. This situation, in turn, was compounded by a generalized reluctance to divulge one's own political history. Thus, many questions went begging for answers as the gaps between reality and perception were filled with speculation, gossip and intrigue.

Blacklisted screenwriter Gordon Kahn's son, Tony, observed of Cuernavaca's expatriate community—although the same applied

57. John Menz, letter to author, November 11, 1993.
58. John Menz, letter to author, January 8, 1994.

to political expatriates throughout Mexico: "In Cuernavaca people tended to hang out either in front of the Bella Vista Hotel or a place called the Pigalle, and tables were very close to each other, but the people sitting at them were miles apart in terms of how they felt . . . and you knew that this gossiping would be going back and forth, and every once in a while somebody would accuse somebody else of being a spy or what not, and maybe with cause and maybe not . . . [but] you sort of had the feeling that really nothing was happening. Most of these people were just sitting there in neutral, in terms of where their lives were going. They were licking their wounds, they were in exile, and they knew they'd better be careful if they wanted not to soil their nests. Maybe that's what made the gossiping so intense, that it wasn't . . . connected with a hell of a lot of political activity. There was partying. and there was talking but . . . I don't remember any meetings."[59]

There were meetings, of course. While local politics were taboo, this would not prevent a few ACGMers from addressing more general political concerns.[60] "It was in our bones and backgrounds, as well," May Brooks told me.

During the early '50s one small group met on a fairly regular basis. According to Philip Stein: "We had our little political meetings with a handful of people . . . we had political friends in the city, all Americans, and we would often, for a while, have little discussion groups because we needed that kind of activity for ourselves, for our stimulation. [We] were always concerned about the political situation so we were brought together regularly for a good while and felt that we were doing something. . . . So we had five, six or seven of those people who we would see on a regular basis. That was it. We would never [become politically involved.]. . . . You couldn't do that in Mexico."[61]

However, this would not prevent those living in exile from supporting a wide variety of non-political causes: an earthquake in Guatemala, a famine in Africa, a flood in Mexico.[62]

59. Tony Kahn, interview with author, January 21, 1993.
60. Martha Dodd Stern Correspondence, Library of Congress Archives, Box 7, Folder 7: Albert Maltz, letter to Martha Stern, June 14, 1956; Box 5, Folder 19: Martha Stern, letter to Paul Jarrico, August 29, 1955.
61. Philip and Gertrude Stein, interview with author, May 15, 1995.
62. David Prensky, telephone conversation with author, May 14, 1993. In 1957 or 1958, following a devastating flood in Tamaulipas, Albert Maltz organized a collection of relief supplies with a drop-off point at his home.

David Prensky recalled helping organize a Citizens Committee to Control Smog. "We had a good committee," he told me, "but I'm afraid that if you look out your window today you'll realize we were not very effective."[63]

So, if Mexican politics were definitely off limits, American or international politics were not. These activities kept the surveillants busy, swelled individual FBI dossiers and, no doubt, contributed to the high incidence of ulcers, gastritis and stress within ACGM ranks, but it did not dampen their spirits. Throughout the 50s, the community united around such issues as restoring civil liberties lost during the McCarthy years, saving the Rosenbergs, and protesting Gus Hall's 1951 abduction from his Mexico City hotel room.

Within hours of Hall's capture, the Mexican Communist Party had been alerted. They, in turn, hoping to whip up public outrage against what they claimed to have been "disgraceful U.S. intervention in our lives, flagrantly violating our right of asylum,"[64] sent a delegation to *Gobernación*. But agents had whisked Hall back across the border so swiftly any legal attempts to impede his deportation would have been in vain. Three weeks later, an offshoot of the Mexican Communist Party calling themselves the "Organizing Commission for the Defense Committee of Human Rights" published a pamphlet protesting Mexico's role in the kidnapping and held a large rally. A few Americans are rumored to have been involved in writing the pamphlet and helping organize the public meeting but, of course, none attended the event. Meanwhile, the CPUSA gave up plans to smuggle Party members out via the Mexican route, and its local operatives vanished for six months.[65]

Although Mexicans protested their government's role in the Gus Hall affair, ACGMers were reluctant to openly censure their hosts. However, when Morton Sobell appealed the thirty year prison sentence imposed for conspiracy to commit espionage they participated on his behalf because the legal transactions took place in the United States, not in Mexico. The appeal hinged, in part, on Sobell's forceful removal from Mexican soil and the role played by Mexican agents. Therefore, his attorney,

63. David Prensky, interview with author, November 30, 1991.
64. "El principal cabecilla comunista—arresto en México tratase de Gus Hall convicto de conjura," *Excélsior*, p.1, October 10, 1951.
65. Peter Steinberg, *The Great 'Red Menace,'* p. 486.

Marshall Perlin, visited Mexico on several occasions. A small group of political expatriates met with him during his visits and eased his way through the intricate process of obtaining information. They also raised money for Sobell's appeal.

Their attempts did not go unnoticed. One FBI file reads: "In late March, 1956, (Deleted) advised that Asa Zatz, a leader of the ACGM, was raising money among the associates of the ACGM for the Morton Sobell fund. According to (Deleted) Zatz explained that the money would be used to assist in reopening the Sobell case in the United States. (Deleted) added that Zatz indicated that David Drucker was among those who had contributed to this fund."[66]

Other steps were taken to assist the Sobells, although few community members were aware of them at the time. Screenwriter, Jean Butler, for example, received an early morning phone call from Albert Maltz's secretary, Carmen Carrasco. According to Jean Butler: "Albert was out of town and Carmen said she needed a loan for an out-of-town guest. I asked if I knew her and she said, 'No, but you'd sure like to.' When I arrived, the house was surrounded by *pistoleros*—well, under surveillance. I was furious of course, because they got my license plates."[67]

Although Jean didn't know it at the time, the "mystery guest" was Morton Sobell's wife, Helen.

While most American dissidents significantly curtailed their political participation during their stays in Mexico, it is possible, had they remained in the United States, some might have done the same. Yet, despite diminished activity, few lost their interest in reform. During the '60s and '70s their efforts were directed toward ending segregation in the United States and war in Vietnam, securing the absentee ballot for Americans residing abroad and, once they had obtained it, supporting McGovern's candidacy.

When I asked Berthe Small who had guided those efforts and others she responded, "Probably Charles."[68]

Their friend, Asa Zatz, agreed: "Charles [never reconciled himself to political disengagement. He] kept on with his activities. . . . He was constantly writing letters all over the place

66. Federal Bureau of Investigation, David Drucker, July 31, 1956, NY 105-12761-57.
67. Jean Butler, interview with author, January 22, 1992.
68. Berthe Small, interview with author, January 17, 1993.

and . . . [exerting] pressure . . . wherever he could. . . ."[69]

His wife, Berthe, put it this way: "Charles was the political pivot of the expatriate community. However, his activities were all focused toward the States. People used to come in to visit [the silver shop] and say, 'Hey Charles, tell us what's going on in the States. . . .' He knew what was going on in every city and he supported—because of reading material, because of personal contacts—endless activities. . . . And so—anyone who came in was fair game. You could not buy a pair of earrings if he knew vaguely who you were, unless you also ponied up a little something for the kitty."

Furthermore, he was among the first to openly support the anti-Vietnam War movement after the first intimations of discontent started surfacing through the coffee house newsletters in the mid '60s. These were written by small groups of disillusioned servicemen stationed in Vietnam and circulated clandestinely by, it is believed, returning soldiers. After reading a number of these, Charles realized that the only way to influence public opinion was to make anti-War information more readily available. He began raising money, some of which was used to purchase typewriters, and made contact with sympathizers who took charge of channeling the money to the dissidents via Canada.[70]

During the 1972 U.S. elections, American opponents to the Vietnam War in Mexico campaigned vigorously for McGovern over Nixon believing Democrats would be more likely to bring the war to an end. Lynne Kalmar, daughter of former Party organizer Kurt Odenheim, told me: "The only political act I ever engaged in when I lived in Mexico was campaigning for McGovern, and that only after my parents had died and were no longer at risk from my actions." After McGovern's defeat, Lynn, a co-chair of the American Democrats for McGovern Committee, and a few others decided to stage an anti-Vietnam demonstration in downtown Mexico City. Upon applying for a permit, subsequently denied, Mexican officials questioned her at length, asking, among other things, if she was a Communist (*comunista*) or a *normalista*, (teacher trainee). (Communists and teacher trainees were protesting that winter.) Shortly after, her phone was tapped, she was placed under surveillance, and

69. Asa Zatz, interview with the author, May 20, 1991.
70. Berthe Small, interview with author, January 17, 1993.

attempts were made to apprehend her. In response to her friends' advice she chose to "disappear" until the affair blew over.[71]

So, for some, the Mexican experience was encapsulated in the bitter coating of menace. Generally, however, political expatriates discovered that the consequences of living under surveillance depended more on the whims of local functionaries than on any official policy, U.S. or otherwise. No matter how much influence the American government and its agencies wielded, there was, undeniably, another half to the equation, the Mexican half. Americans were, after all, operating on foreign soil. If push came to shove, Mexico's Executive, *Gobernación*, and of course, the vagaries inherent in the system, determined the outcome.

Understandably, ACGMers never completely overcame their fears. Surveillance is a form of intimidation, and as long as U.S. and Mexican agencies kept an eye on them, their personal freedom was restricted. Yet, when viewed as a whole, their experiences in Mexico were, more often than not, pleasant ones. My parents, for example, considered themselves fortunate to have found a secure refuge and learned to adapt to life under surveillance and cope with the occasional scare.

Certainly, one way Belle and Mike tried to cope was by distancing themselves from their ACGM friends during the second half of the '50s. "After all, we knew there were informers in the group," my mother told my sister many years later. They also knew that by 1954 the FBI had placed them under surveillance, linked them to the ACGM, and labeled them subversives.

The procedure reminded me of a documentary I'd seen on the American bald eagle, threatened, at the time, with extinction. After the birds were captured and secured, scientists meticulously fastened a metal identification band to each bird's talon. This allowed them to keep records of their diets, life spans and migrations. I felt sorry for the birds, but in their case, their long-term welfare, if not improved, would remain the same. For political expatriates, however, similarly labeled for life, the outcome could be disastrous.

71. Lynn Kalmar, telephone conversation with author, August 22, 1992.

The author—1950. (Courtesy of Diana Anhalt)

The author, her father Meyer (Mike) Zykofsky, Eddy Lending, her mother, Belle Zykofsky, and sister, Judy. (Courtesy of Diana Anhalt)

The author, her mother, Belle, and sister, Judy. (Courtesy of Diana Anhalt)

Jean and Hugo Butler. (Courtesy of Jean Butler)

George Oppen, Linda Oppen and Conlon Nancarrow
(Courtesy of Linda Oppen)

Dalton and Cleo Trumbo. (Courtesy of Mitzi Trumbo)

Charles and Berthe Small. (Courtesy of Berthe Small)

Jeanette and George Pepper. (Photo by Cleo Trumbo)

Chapter Five

The Temperature Rises:
Official Policies, Sanctions and Incidents
1950-1957

Within days of having identified my father as the driver of
the car parked in front of spy suspect Alfred Stern's home, the
FBI initiated an investigation, which would continue for
eighteen years. On the front page of his file alongside the
words, 'Character of Case,' someone had typed, 'Espionage,'
along with, "According to (deleted), Meyer Zykofsky aka.
Michael Foster aka. Meyer Dvorchansky has a history of active
participation in the Communist Party in the United States."[1]

A separate file indicated that the FBI had speculated on the
possibility that ". . . the above-mentioned individuals" (Zykofsky,
Stern, Drucker and two unidentified sources) had come to
Mexico with some type of pre-arrangement. It was noted that
they contacted one another upon their arrival and utilized similar
channels in getting their residence documentation arranged. It
was further noted that, although setting up ostensibly separate
businesses, there were a large number of interlocking financial
arrangements between the various companies.

Two pages of this file are missing, followed by: ". . . one or
more Soviet espionage parallels. On the basis of the activities in
which these Subjects have thus far engaged, it would appear that
their chief interest at the present time is in getting themselves
firmly established in Mexico. In view of the backgrounds of
Drucker, Stern, (Deleted) and (Deleted) the definite possibility
exists that one or more may be presently involved in espionage
activities or, if not so involved at present, they will become so."[2]

1. Federal Bureau of Investigation, Meyer Zykofsky, August 16, 1954, Bufile 100-411142.
2. Federal Bureau of Investigation, David Drucker, December 13, 1954, Bufile 105-
12761-57. Through the diligence of Washington D.C. lawyer Kathy Meyer who
filed my suit, Civil Action No. 96-CV-02384 TFH against the FBI, I was able to
procure many of the documents referred to here.

Although my father, David Drucker and Alfred Stern no longer lived in the United States, the FBI monitored their movements anyway. We knew this, of course, but at the time were less likely to understand why the intensity of the campaigns directed against ACGMers fluctuated so widely between 1947 and 1965. After reaching their peak during the tail end of Alemán's administration (1950-1952), they tapered off, and Ruiz Cortines's first four and a half years in office, while marked by occasional incidents, were, for the most part, uneventful. No doubt, his independent stance in dealing with the U.S. agenda in Mexico was responsible for that. But after Mexican-American relations suffered a severe setback during the summer of 1957, official policy, as regarded Mexico's far left and the political expatriates, hardened.

While some measures could be taken by American agencies working independently, others relied on the willing cooperation of the Mexican Government. (It was often impossible to determine which country had instigated a specific action.) Both kept an eye on suspects, intimidated them, and as a last resort, pressured them into leaving Mexico. Using methods similar to those employed against radicals in the United States, American officials and those acting on their behalf were in a position to withhold jobs and legal documents, restrict travel, and curtail the participation of the politically suspect in a multitude of activities.

Newly arrived political expatriates soon discovered that all foreigners, regardless of nationality, depend on their embassies to renew a passport, register a newborn child, or notarize official documents and affidavits. For Americans, the U.S. presence in Mexico was, and still is, further strengthened by a complex maze of community institutions—businesses, schools, hospitals, cemeteries, libraries, newspapers, churches and clubs—radiating from one common core, the American Embassy.

We therefore held it responsible, occasionally without reason, for just about everything which affected us adversely: If a school administrator was investigated for having defended a suspect teacher, if a phone was tapped, or if a child was barred from the Boy Scouts, the Embassy was to blame. As the most visible symbol of the U.S. presence in Mexico it became a metaphor for the underside of the political expatriate experience.

In addition to its image as the repository of U.S. culture, influence and power abroad, the word 'Embassy,' loosely applied, also referred to the FBI, the CIA, the U.S. controlled media and all community institutions. In our minds, the 'Embassy' represented the U.S. capacity to obtain, coordinate and utilize information gathered by its informants.

Such information, in turn, was used to influence community leaders, potential or present employers and clients, and Mexican and U.S. government officials. It could determine one's chances of engaging in educational or cultural pursuits, earning a living and remaining in the country. As a result, ACGM lore is filled with 'Embassy Stories,' shared memories of deportations, official chicanery, positions or jobs lost or, in rare cases, retained against all odds. I heard scores of them.

Fred Field had a particularly large collection. (Given his notoriety as the Vanderbilt family black sheep, this is not surprising.) When a fellow trustee on the board of his stepson's small, private school asked for his resignation for political reasons, the remaining board members, all of whom were Mexican, rebelled. They demanded that the dissenting trustee give up his seat, deplored what they believed was the Embassy's attempt to interfere in the workings of a Mexican institution, and refused to accept Field's resignation.[3]

Mexican playwright Carlos Prieto, taught economics at Mexico City College, a U.S. run institution. Prieto told me: "I was denounced by two of my students for teaching, among other things, Marxism, and I was called in by the head of the economics department, [John] Menz. He called me in [and] said, 'Students of yours have said this [and that] about you. . . .' And he said, 'Don't look so angry. I'm a Marxist too. Unfortunately, Paul Murray, [the President of the college], can't even spell economics.'"[4]

Menz also had problems. After a student who had repeated his class twice in a row aroused his suspicions, he confronted him and accused him of being planted in his classroom in order to spy on him. The student invited him for a drink. Menz

3. Fred Vanderbilt Field, *From Right to Left*, p. 290.
4. Carlos Prieto, interview with author, October 22, 1991. When I asked economist John Menz about the incident he claimed that Prieto's name, although not the specific incident, rang a bell. He wrote, "At the time I was not too keen on identifying my own preferences to anyone on campus."

explained: "I am not a good drinker as I tend to get pie-eyed, but I knew that this time I would have to drink him under the table. And I did. Before we parted, he was crying. He told me he didn't want to do it, but he had to. [He explained that] as a baby his folks left Russia, first to China then to South America, eventually ending up in the States. The chilling thing about this is that neither I nor anyone I know ever saw him from that day on."[5]

While the outcome was heartening for Field, who retained his board seat, and for Prieto and Menz, who held on to their positions, others were not so fortunate: Jeanette Pepper, who taught statistics at Mexico City College from 1955-1957,[6] and American School teachers Sonia Strand[7] and Edna Moore van der Schelling[8] were fired for political reasons.

So was former Boston University professor Maurice Halperin's wife, Edith: According to a U.S. Foreign Service telegram: "The Embassy learned today that [the] wife of Maurice Halperin, known United States Communist, was discharged [on the] fifth from position as teacher at American School in Mexico City. This action was taken by School Director on own responsibility, information concerning Mrs. Halperin having been available to School many months ago."[9]

It is no accident that those who lost jobs generally worked for American institutions. Since Mexican firms were not as likely to be swayed by Embassy pressure, their employees were less vulnerable. There were exceptions, however: In one case, photographer and film maker Bill Miller was fired from a Mexican production when the U.S. Ambassador pressured a local company into releasing him.[10] However, the vast majority of political expatriates were nearly all self employed and had nothing to fear from the Embassy on that score.

But the U.S. government exercised its authority over us in other ways. The most effective were those related to its official

5. John Menz, letter to author, December 16, 1992.
6. Jeanette Pepper, interview with author, August 2, 1992; Jeanette Pepper, telephone conversation with author, August 7, 1992.
7. Ruth Wright, interview with author, June 29, 1991.
8. Rosalind Beimler, interview with author, September 19, 1991.
9. Foreign Service Telegram signed Raymond G. Leddy, September 7, 1957. Control Number 824.
10. Tim Hogan, "The US Film Maker Who Wanted to be a Mexican General Isn't Finished Yet," *Ajiic Colony Reporter*, July 2-8, 1994.

role as the U.S. representative in Mexico. Only then was it free to exert complete control, unhampered by recalcitrant Mexican officials, cumbersome bureaucratic procedures or the directors of assorted institutions. It was in charge. It could deny services and passports, cancel valid travel documents and cease to extend protection and recognition to those nationals whose proof of citizenship it had removed.

However, I doubt my parents were aware of just how much power the Embassy wielded until my brother Paul was born in August, 1954. They had been in Mexico for nearly four years and renewed their passports without incident in the fall of 1952. Most likely they were completely unaware of FBI surveillance and the measures the Embassy could employ against them. (I certainly was and would have continued in ignorance had I not requested my parents' FBI dossiers under the Freedom of Information Act when I was preparing this book.)

One of the early reports indicated that: "Mr. Zykofsky, a neighbor of the [Embassy] drafting officer, stated yesterday that he planned to come to the Embassy to execute a report of a birth of a child, which was recently born to them in Mexico City. He was told to bring his and his wife's passport to the office when he called." [11]

Just four days later, the Embassy was instructed to seize their passports should they appear.[12] When they didn't, the Embassy proceeded to contact them. By then, my parents must have known there was a problem because they managed to dodge several summonses until December 13, 1954 when an Embassy officer visited their home and told them he had been instructed to collect their passports. According to the agent, my father claimed he had misplaced them, but had not reported the loss because he considered the matter unimportant.

Eventually, after my parents failed to show up, the Embassy reached the conclusion that they could no longer afford the Zykofskys official protection or registration facilities unless they surrendered their, by then, expired passports and prepared affidavits explaining their alleged Communist activities.

11. Foreign Service Dispatch from the American Embassy, Mexico D.F. to Department of State, August 16, 1954, Control Number 284.
12. Department of State instruction to the American Embassy, Mexico D. F., August 20, 1954, Control Number #A-238.

Furthermore, the Mexican Foreign Office was to be notified that those documents with which they had entered the country and procured resident status were no longer valid.[13] In other words, they were advising Mexico that in withdrawing the documentary evidence which had allowed my parents to legalize their status in the country, the Embassy was giving Mexican authorities grounds for deporting them, should they decide to do so.

Nearly every political expatriate I interviewed had, in addition to their 'Embassy Stories,' a 'Passport' or 'Non-Passport Story,' as the case might be. (Many, including the Butlers, Peppers, Lardners, and Oppens had either lost theirs while still residing in the United States or had been unable to obtain them prior to leaving.) Others were stripped of theirs after moving to Mexico. Crawford Kilian's father, Mike, fired from his job with a Mexican television network in 1954, lost his passport a few months later, and returned to the States.[14] Another couple, closely associated with a well-known Mexican Communist, gave up theirs in 1953; John Menz's passport was removed while he was in the process of acquiring his Mexican working papers, in 1951. (Shortly after, the Embassy refused to acknowledge the birth of his daughter.)[15]

In effect, the U.S. government's reach defied borders. Political expatriates, a number of whom had fled to Mexico to dodge subpoenas, learned that distance would not discourage authorities from summoning them to appear for questioning at trials held in the United States. Maurice Halperin was asked to return as a government witness in connection with an investigation held on November 1, 1954. (It is unlikely he did.)[16] The Senate's McCarran Committee summoned Albert Maltz in 1955 or 1956 but he refused to go.[17]

Fred Field received two subpoenas while living in Mexico. On the first occasion, he was told to present himself at Owen Lattimer's second trial to be held in Washington D.C. in October,

---

13. Foreign Service Despatch from Amembassy (sic.), Mexico, D.F. to Department of State December 21, 1954, Control Number 964.
14. Crawford Kilian, *Growing up Blacklisted*. An unpublished memoir, p. 13 A.
15. John Menz, letter to author, November 11, 1993.
16. Letter from the Department of Justice, Washington, to the Secretary of State, Attn: Office of Special Consular Service, October 15, 1985, Microfilm DNA RG 59.
17. Joel Gardner, *The Citizen Writer in Retrospect. Oral History of Albert Maltz*, p. 888. Apparently, a foreign resident does not have to honor a subpoena from a congressional committee, but is bound to reply to one served by a grand jury.

1954. Billed by Joseph McCarthy as the "the top espionage agent in the United States," Lattimer was a celebrated Sinologist and former editor of the Institute of Pacific Relation's journal, *Pacific Affairs*, which Field had helped finance. While questioning the subpoena's validity because he no longer resided in the States, Field agreed to attend and requested a train ticket since he disliked flying. (His request was ignored because, he later learned, it is easier to tail a man on a plane than a man on a train.) After citing the Fifth Amendment, he was threatened with a contempt citation and barraged with personal questions, none of which were related to the Lattimer case. However, no attempt was made to detain him, and he returned without incident to Mexico.[18]

The second subpoena was for an appearance before Eastland's Senate Internal Security Committee for a September 1956 trial in connection with Republican Jacob Javits, who was then running for the Senate. Apparently Eastland believed he could hurt Javits' chances by connecting him with the *Red Menace*, in other words, with Fred. (The two had been observed speaking to each other on a San Francisco ferry in 1945. All either of them recalled of the incident was a remark one made to the other about the view.) This time Field didn't even bother to reply to Eastland's summons. (Javits won the election anyway.)[19]

If the U.S. government could reach into Mexico and into the lives of American nationals residing there, the opposite, arresting a political expatriate during a sporadic incursion into the United States, was even more feasible. After all, seizing U.S. citizens on Mexican territory, while not impossible, was problematic because it required some degree of cooperation by local authorities. Thus, the more vulnerable, particularly those with Party ties, often avoided returning to the States during their first few years in Mexico.

Then, as memories of their former problems with the authorities receded, some ventured across the border. Nevertheless, their visits to the States, however brief, did not go undetected. *Masses and Mainstream* editor Charles Humboldt and Sam Brooks, who had left the States on Party instructions in 1951, returned for a short trip.

18. Fred Vanderbilt Field, *From Right to Left*, p. 263.
19. Ibid., p. 288.

They borrowed a New York City apartment from a political friend, and, according to Sam's wife, May: ". . . they get into this apartment and the phone rings. Sam picks it up, and it's this creepy voice: 'Is Mr. Sam Brooks there?' [Sam answers.] 'This is Sam Brooks.' [Voice continues.] 'This is the Latin American Travel Agency. We're offering special discounts to blah blah blah blah blah.' It was a very phony call. Well, Sam says to Charley, 'Charley, we've got to get out of here.' Upon leaving the apartment Sam dropped by the office of a lawyer friend but stopped first at the concession stand in the lobby below. The man who ran the stand was known to Sam from years back, and Sam mentioned that he was there to see a lawyer, a man to whom the stand owner was devoted.

"Sam . . . wasn't there [in the lawyer's office] ten minutes before this guy [the stand operator] called up and said, 'Listen, there are three men here. They are coming up to your office . . .and I think you ought to know this.' So the lawyer looks at Sam and says, 'Sam, I think you'd better go.' So Sam gets out of the building—God knows how.[Sometime later] he had to meet some people at a restaurant, and he's getting off the bus, and the restaurant was close to the corner. . . . He could see his two friends standing in the doorway, and they go like this, [makes a hand sign.] So, he gets back on the bus. . . ."

Sam immediately decided to return to Mexico. People who were in political trouble used KLM airlines because it didn't land in the States. Sam left New York, took a train to Canada and flew KLM back to Mexico.[20]

In another incident, sculptor Elizabeth Catlett, desperate to return to the United States upon learning her mother had been diagnosed with a possible malignancy, was denied a visa. By the late '50s she had become a naturalized Mexican citizen and could not enter the United States without one.

She explained: ". . . a man called me in . . . and he said that I was a member of the Mexican Communist Party, and I started to say, 'I don't know where you got your information but it's not true,' and he cut me off and he said, 'We're not allowed to reveal our sources of information.' And I said, 'I hope your mother is never in danger of dying because somebody told a lie on you,' and he said 'You should of thought of that

20. May Brooks, interview with author, July 19, 1994.

before.' And I said, 'Before what?' And so he mumbled around a little bit, and I went home.

"There was a friend of mine, a tourist, and she said "Take my tourist card and go." I was very worried. I thought maybe I'd never see my mother again. So I was packing a little bag and Pancho [Elizabeth's husband], came in and said, 'Where are you going?' and I said, 'Going to Washington.' He said 'Don't you know provocation when you see it? You're not going anywhere.'"

Convinced government officials had denied her a visa in the hope she would attempt to enter the United States illegally, he persuaded her to remain in Mexico. A few days later her sister called.

"She said, 'Immigration is looking for you.' And I said, 'Really?' and she said, 'Yes. They went to my house, they went to my aunt's house, and they came to the hospital, and I don't know where else, but they were always asking for you. In any case, they put off mother's operation.'

"It seems the doctor took another X-ray, and the spot was gone. I used to kid and say my mother was on very good terms with the Lord. She said a word to the Lord, and he cleared up whatever it was."[21]

Of course, by this time, Elizabeth was no longer a U.S. citizen, but this had not stopped American officials: Mexicans with radical backgrounds, among them several with ties to ACGMers, were routinely blacklisted, intimidated, and refused entry visas. Over a cup of coffee at his Cuernavaca home, former economics instructor and playwright Carlos Prieto told me he had been denied a U.S. visa for fifteen years. "But everyone [I knew] was denied a visa. If you weren't on that list you were suspect."

He and his wife, Evelyn, recalled driving to the border and attempting to cross into the United States on foot. (Evelyn is an American citizen.) When he was asked to present his passport he did so, only to be told, "I'm sorry but you'll have to make your peace with the State Department." He was stunned. According to Evelyn his passport had been marked and this allowed inspectors to identify him. "I didn't believe her," he told me. "I didn't believe that the Embassy, the American Embassy,

21. Elizabeth Catlett, interview with the author, January 17, 1991.

would have the effrontery to place a signal, a mark, on a Mexican's passport."

On another occasion, a play Prieto had written about an oil strike and the Mexican expropriation of the oil fields . . . opened in Mexico City. The French Cultural Attaché, Javier Pomeret, who had attended the opening, approached Prieto and offered to translate it for presentation in Paris. Prieto agreed, but while the two of them were at work on the translation, the play was closed down.

In Prieto's words: "The motorcycle cops came up, and they put up their chains and their seals and everything else on the theater . . . and I remember Pomeret asked me, 'Why did they shut down your play? There's nothing here that offends Mexico or the Mexican government.' And I said: 'It's the Embassy.' And he asked, 'Which Embassy?' I said: 'You don't ask that question in Mexico.'"[22]

As Mexican writer and intellectual Alfonso Aguilar explained to me: "McCarthyism was not produced in the United States alone. Its reach and projection were international."[23] He was in a position to know. Denied a U.S. visa from 1956 until 1990, it is likely he aroused suspicion for his many publications and his participation in a variety of organizations, but primarily, because of his role as the General Coordinator of the *Movimiento de Liberación Nacional,* (National Liberation Movement). Committed to uniting the members of Mexico's fragmented left, the group was high on the Embassy list of 'subversive organizations.' Of course, Prieto and Aguilar were just two out of hundreds of Mexican citizens who were barred from entering the United States, sometimes for decades, for a multitude of reasons.

However, while U.S. agencies could restrict entry of non-Americans into the United States, some things were impossible even for them. True, they could refuse passports, cancel documents and deny protection to U.S. dissidents but other initiatives could not be taken independently. In these cases, they could either approach their counterparts in the Mexican government and request their cooperation or find ways to circumvent official channels.

22. Carlos Prieto, interview with author, October 22, 1991.
23. Alonso Aguilar, interview with author, July 9, 1991.

Although both methods were employed, some requests—those for information regarding ACGMers' whereabouts and their status in Mexico, for example—were, as a general rule, likely to be carried out on a routine basis. Others presented greater obstacles. We knew, for example, that Embassy attempts to influence *Gobernación* and the Foreign Relations Secretariat in matters relating to working papers, automatic re-entry into Mexico, or deportation proceedings against dissidents were sometimes ignored or 'forgotten.' (No doubt, stepping on *Tio Sam's* toes—occasionally at least—provided a certain perverse satisfaction.)

When the Embassy decided to deny a certificate of U.S. citizenship to Hollywood Ten writer Albert Maltz, they apparently assumed that without it *Gobernación* would refuse him his *inmigrante* (Mexican resident) status. (Maltz, as was the case with most political expatriates, had originally entered Mexico on a tourist card valid for six months. He was required to exit and re-enter the country before it expired.)[24] In the fall of 1951, shortly after the "Cuernavaca-Willard Motely" scandal hit the front pages, Maltz dropped by the Embassy and requested his certificate of U.S. citizenship. When the consul turned him down he lost his temper and cried, "Do you mean to tell me I'm not an American citizen?" The Consul informed him that the State Department was not interested in facilitating his residence in a foreign country and asked him to surrender his passport. He lied, claimed he had neglected to bring it, and proceeded directly to his lawyer's office. The lawyer insisted they arrive at *Gobernación* the next morning at 8:00 A.M. sharp. They were too late. Pinned to the wall above the front desk was a memo: "Notify U.S. Embassy when Albert Maltz arrives."

The lawyer was not discouraged. He asked Maltz to write a statement explaining his current predicament and his reasons for being in Mexico and took him around to meet several local big-shots. To each, Maltz presented an autographed translation of his book, *The Cross and the Arrow* (he received his *inmigrante* papers shortly afterward.)[25]

24. Since some political expatriates feared they might be seized should they return to the United States, they preferred to legalize their status thus avoiding the necessity of having to leave every six months.
25. Joel Gardner, *The Citizen Writer in Retrospect: Oral History of Albert Maltz*, pp. 844-846.

David Drucker, whose reputation as "probably the only person in the United States to be registered as a foreign agent of both the Soviet Union and China," had proceeded him, found himself in a predicament similar to Maltz's, but with one additional handicap: He had written no books to present to local *influyentes*. Thus, rather than approach the Embassy, as Maltz had some six months earlier, he went directly to *Gobernación* when he wanted to legalize his status in Mexico. He explained to the official behind the desk that he would be unable to procure the required Certificate of Citizenship because the U.S. government disapproved of his politics. In its stead, he produced a March 28, 1952 letter from the State Department refusing him his passport and signed by Ruth Shipley, Chief of the Passport Division. The *Gobernación* employee responded by agreeing to waive U.S. Embassy proof of citizenship. Across the bottom of David's letter, he wrote: "The Applicant, David Drucker, is exempt from presenting Consular Proof by virtue of having shown and proved that he has no relations with the Consular Representative of the country of his origin. Mexico, D.F. February 3, 1953, signed Lic. Gilberto Suárez Aroizu, Chief of the Department of Demographics."

Periodically, a visa, proof of his *inmigrante* status, was stamped onto the back of the letter, in order to expedite his entering or leaving the country.[26]

After living in the country for a few years, we generally learned the ropes. Bureaucratic red tape or official intransigence, whether on the part of the Mexican government or the American Embassy, was something we could cope with. More frightening, by far, was living with the knowledge that, because we were foreigners we could, at any time, be subject to deportation[27] or detention. In the case of the second, an individual would simply be seized at home or on the street and vanish for a few days. After being locked up, usually over the weekend, the detainee was sent back to the United States. (Occasionally he would 'agree' to leave under his own volition.)

When Ralph Roeder, a highly regarded historian and long time resident of Mexico, was apprehended during the early

26. A copy of this letter is in possession of the author.
27. The term deportation implies a legal process. These "deportations" were far from legal.

'50s, *Gobernación* held him incommunicado for over a week. Once his well placed friends at the Ministry of Culture learned of his plight they informed *Gobernación* of its mistake—it had incarcerated a national hero—and demanded his immediate release. But after the incident, Ralph, "a very fragile gent, was visibly shaken and never quite the same."[28]

Born into an aristocratic southern family, he had originally visited Mexico in 1911 during the Revolution, shared a box car with legendary Communist hero, John Reed, fought with Pancho Villa, and barely escaped execution.[29] After returning to the States he worked briefly as a Shakespearean actor and was then hired by the *Chicago Daily News* as its Rome correspondent during the '20s.

But not until the publication of his elegant books on Italian history, among them *Savonarola* (1931), *The Men of the Renaissance* (1933), and *Catherine de Medici and the Lost Revolution* (1937), did he earn his reputation as a leading historian. By the time he returned to Mexico in 1942 he was married to Fania Mindell. (Her brother, Jacob *Pop* Mindell, headed the CPUSA Marxist cadre school and was subsequently imprisoned under the Smith Act.)[30]

In 1952, after translating his two volume history, *Juarez and his Mexico*, into Spanish he was awarded the highest honor accorded a foreigner, Mexico's Aztec Eagle, and a pension from the Mexican Government.[31]

Although I never met him, I remember hearing about his tragic death in 1969. At the time, he was working on his Spanish translation of *Hacia el México Moderno (Toward the Modern Mexico)*, which picked up where *Juarez* left off. His wife Fania had died shortly before. "She was a horror," Jean Butler, told me, "but he was a saint [and] the saint depended utterly on her to keep the distractions away. So when she died, he committed suicide."[32]

The manuscript was never found. His old friend and former head of the League of American Writers, Franklin Folsom, wrote,

28. Jean Butler, interview with author, August 2, 1991.
29. Franklin Folsom, *Days of Anger, Days of Hope: A Memoir of the League of American Writers, 1937-1942*, Niwot, CO.: University Press of Colorado, pp. 255-56.
30. A dentist by profession, Mindel was prominently known for his role in the Party schools and was a director of their national school commission.
31. Alan Wald, letter to author, March 8, 1992.
32. Jean Butler, interview with author, August 2, 1991.

years later, that during a visit to Mexico Roeder had asked him to deliver his manuscript to a U.S. publisher. Folsom refused because he had previously agreed to carry Albert Maltz's papers out of the country and feared he might run into problems.[33]

Fifteen years earlier, when Roeder had been detained, he had been spared deportation, not over concern for his civil rights, but because he was regarded as a valued friend by Mexico. Had he been subsequently deported, U.S. agents would have been placed in an embarrassing position, particularly if there was any suspicion of FBI participation in his detention. For that reason, Americans were reluctant to engage in any action which might anger their neighbors, be construed as a threat to national sovereignty, or result in an international incident. On the contrary, they proceeded with extreme caution when engaged in unauthorized seizures of U.S. citizens on Mexican soil or 'unofficial extraditions,' as they were referred to in police jargon.[34] Although they collaborated closely with their Mexican counterparts, the Americans kept a low profile until a deportee had been delivered across the border.

Ironically, *Daily Worker* and Telepress correspondent A.B. Magil's deportation took place after he no longer resided in Mexico. He and his wife Harriet had left in 1952, but Abe was sent back two years later. "To cover the Party Convention," he told me. "At the time, I was in charge of the Party's Latin American work."[35]

In a letter following our interview he wrote: "I was held from Friday evening till the following Tuesday morning. I was abducted by agents and held incommunicado for several days . . . [at the] detention center for foreigners in Mexico City. . . . Before my release, a group of intellectuals was being formed to protest my disappearance to *Gobernación*."[36]

During his detention one of his interrogators asked about his daughter, Maggie:

"Well, you have a daughter, Maggie?"

"Yes."

33. Franklin Folsom, *Days of Anger, Days of Hope*, p. 158.
34. Harry Thayer Mahoney, Marjorie Locke Mahoney, *The Saga of Leon Trotsky: His Clandestine Operations and His Assassination*, San Francisco, London, Bethesda: Austin & Winfield Publishers, p. 511. The best known unofficial extradition was Morton Sobell's.
35. A.B. Magil, interview with author, January 20, 1993.
36. A. B. Magil, letter to author, May 5, 1994.

"She goes to the American School?"

"Yes."

"And she sometimes plays outside the building in which you live?"

And suddenly Abe remembered how, prior to their leaving Mexico, Maggie had been accosted on the street in front of their building. "Well, I got enraged," Abe told me "and [I said] 'You mean to tell me that you spied on this seven year old girl?' And the man said: 'I refuse to answer.'"

Magil was released four days later, and three agents drove him to his hotel to pick up his things, call his wife, and escort him onto a plane. Prior to take-off, he signed a statement to the effect that he was aware he would be prohibited re-entry into the country. "This was in 1954. Three years later [I] returned to Mexico without any difficulty."[37]

John Menz was luckier. During his second stint in Mexico, he was, in his own words: ". . . picked up and taken to *Gobernación*, and I guess they were going to ship me out on the next plane. Fortunately, I was able to get to a phone and call Jorge Espinosa de los Reyes, who, together with Gustavo Kolbeck, was an economic advisor to the then president of the country. Jorge was in—most fortunate—and he came from the presidential palace to *Gobernacion* like a bat out of hell waving his presidential badge, and that was that. Never bothered again—at least not by Mexicans. . . ."[38]

When I asked Menz when the deportation attempt had taken place, he knew only that it had occurred sometime during his second stay in Mexico. Most likely, however, it occurred prior to December, 1952 while Alemán was still in office. Once Cortines took over, he distanced himself from his predecessor's administration and announced his return to the original values of the Mexican Revolution. Diplomatic strategy was aimed at counteracting powerful U.S. interests in the hemisphere, and the Department of Foreign Relations became more openly hostile to American interests. Despite this, there were other government agencies where a more conservative, anti-communist orientation continued to dominate.[39]

37. A.B. Magil, interview with author, January 20, 1993.
38. John Menz, letter to author, February 11, 1994.
39. Enrique Krauze, *La Presidencia Imperial: Ascenso y Caída del Sistema Politico Mexicano (1940-1996)*, Mexico D.F.: Tusquets Editores, 1997, p. 206.

Rumor has it, that upon taking office in 1952 President Adolfo Ruiz Cortinez received an official state visit from the then Vice President Richard Nixon. At the time, U.S. pressure on Mexico to combat communism continued unabated. The Mexican president ordered his chauffeur to drive them through Mexico City's worst slums and then commented, "This, Mr. Nixon, is the most widely diffused 'ism' in Mexico, 'hungerism,' and this is the one I wish to eradicate so we don't catch the *isms* that are worrying you."[40]

Although Cold War politics and the U.S. posture regarding the political expatriates did not change appreciably throughout the '50s, overt antagonism on the part of the Mexican government was less palpable than it had been during the Alemán administration. This did not mean, however, that Mexico ignored American concerns in this area. In the confidential report "People who should not receive documentation in any migratory status," dated December 3, 1955, the then sub-secretary of Foreign Relations, José Gorostiza, expressed his concern with the process employed in granting migratory permits to *Extranjeros Indeseables*, (Undesirable Foreigners). He informed members of the Mexican Foreign Service that, in the future: ". . . the names of people to whom our competent authorities have decided to deny documentation in any migratory status, will be transmitted to you periodically. . . . All subsequent communications related to this matter will be preceeded by the letter, 'Omega' in order to avoid having to repeat these instructions."[41]

Ruiz Cortines's more tolerant policies remained in effect from the end of 1952 to the middle of 1957. In the end, the fact that a group of politically controversial individuals, some of whom were accused of conspiracy or worse, were living unmolested right across the border, was simply unacceptable. Inevitably, the situation would explode. The Stern Affair ignited the fuse.

In December, 1953 following columnist Leonard Lyons' disclosure that 'the daughter of a former ambassador to Germany during Roosevelt's regime was being summoned to testify before the HUAC,' Martha Dodd and Alfred Stern had left precipitously for Mexico. Once there, the Sterns traveled

40. Ibid., p. 207.
41. Relaciones Exteriores, Confidential Circular, General Management of the Consular Service Department of Migration, Mexico D.F., December 3, 1955, Air Mail IV-17-27, IV/550 (016) (S-1)/18185.

within the country, added to their impressive art collection, entertained regally and divided their time between Mexico City and Cuernavaca, where they were constructing a weekend residence.

After a little more than three years, in January 1957, their tranquil existence was shattered when information provided to the FBI by double agent Boris Morros resulted in three indictments: Jack Soble, his wife Myra, and Jacob Albam were charged with handing over U.S. defense intelligence to the Soviet Union.[42] Morros had also implicated the Sterns, and on February 27, 1957 subpoenas were delivered to them in Mexico summoning them to appear before a New York Federal Grand Jury. At the time, they accepted $468 each to defray travel costs, but never showed up in court.

The Federal Grand Jury convened on March 14 and issued a three count indictment. The Sterns were accused of conspiracy to commit espionage, the same charge that had sent the Rosenbergs to their deaths. They were subsequently indicted in absentia and were charged with collaborating in a music-publishing business which had served as a cover for espionage activities. Since the Sterns had failed to appear for the hearing they were cited for contempt and fined $25,000 each.[43]

Given the outcome, the U.S. Justice Department decided that questioning the Sterns was a matter of great urgency. In the last instance, American authorities could always resort to an 'unofficial extradition,' as they had done with Morton Sobell or Gus Hall, but there were plenty of reasons not to: Mexico shared a border with the United States, and relations between the two countries, while occasionally strained, had generally been amiable; President Ruiz Cortines exercised greater autonomy in foreign affairs than had his predecessor, Alemán, and was less likely to be mollified if the Sterns were seized without his consent; the Sterns, given their economic means and social position, would be able to generate unwelcome public protest if they were seized illegally. Consequently, in April

42. Katrina Vanden Heuvel, "Grand Illusions," *Vanity Fair*, September 1991, Vol. 54, No. 7, pp. 223-248.
43. Ibid., pp. 223-248, p 252. The grand jury handed down an indictment which presented no concrete evidence of espionage activity. However, when a grand jury believes there is enough evidence against the accused to warrant their standing trial, it has the power to indict even if it isn't convinced of guilt beyond a reasonable doubt.

1957, the American government instructed Ambassador Francis White to initiate high level, behind the scenes negotiations.

He began by consulting Finance Minister, Antonio Carrillo Flores, whom he considered his "most reliable contact" in the Mexican government. Carrillo Flores suggested he approach the Minister of the Interior, ie. *Gobernación*, Angel Carvajal Bernal, but upon doing so Carvajal referred him to Roman Lugo, *Gobernación's* Administrative Officer. In the meantime, the Ambassador heard, from an unnamed source, that the Stern's lawyer, William O'Dwyer, had already contacted Roman Lugo, and the Administrative Officer had promised the Sterns they would be permitted to remain in Mexico in exchange for "an unspecified gratuity." Despite this information, the Ambassador did meet with him. But Mr. Lugo denied knowledge of the case, and the meeting proved unfruitful.[44]

Nevertheless, it wasn't until several months later that the Ambassador, discouraged by his failure to negotiate through normal channels, decided to appeal to the highest authority: "I called on President Ruiz Cortines on the evening of Friday, June 7, and discussed with him the case of Alfred and Martha Stern. . . . I reminded him of his statements to me in the past. That if we want American communists shipped back to the United States he would be glad to do so, and that, on that basis, President Eisenhower had instructed me to ask President Ruiz Cortines to return these two people to the United States. I said that President Eisenhower did this on the basis of the security of the United States."

Before taking leave, the Ambassador also referred to recent Soviet inspired disturbances in Guadalajara and, possibly, Ciudad Juarez. He then reminded the President of some "twenty one important things which the United States had done for Mexico" in the past few years. At the same time he reported that his earlier meetings with Roman Lugo and Carvajal had been unproductive. Ruiz Cortines promised to intervene immediately.[45]

44. National Archives, DNA, RG 59, Box 2816, "Summary of developments in the case of Alfred and Martha Stern," Office Memorandum, United States Government, May 13, 1957, State Department Document #05613657.
45. National Archives, DNA RG 59 Box 2816, "Ambassador's Conversation with President Ruiz Cortines regarding Stern Case," June 10, 1957, State Department Document, #F790009-2071, #F790009-2072.

On June 25, 1957 White visited President Ruiz Cortines in order to bid him good-bye prior to leaving his post as Ambassador. During their meeting, he mentioned President Eisenhower's disappointment at Mexico's failure to deport the Sterns. The President emphasized that he was willing to do so providing the procedure was legal.

According to the Ambassador: ". . . twice I reminded him that he had full authority under Article 33 of the Constitution to get these communists out of here. President Ruiz Cortines mentioned, in the course of the conversation, that he had once told me that any time we wanted communists returned to the United States he would do so, and I had replied it was preferable to leave them here where it was easier to watch them. I replied that that was correct and that here was the case of two communists we would like to have sent back, and we would be very appreciative if he would send them back as he had said he would do."[46]

In spite of the Ambassador's insistence, Ruiz Cortines refused to commit himself. He promised to ask Carvajal to call the Ambassador and arrange to meet him the following day. Whether such a meeting took place is unknown. What we do know is that the Sterns were never deported. Most likely, someone tipped them off.

At 1:00 A.M. on July 21, 1957 Martha, Alfred and Bobby, their twelve year old son, boarded a KLM flight to Montreal and gave Switzerland as their final destination. Although they used their *inmigrante*, ie. resident, visas to exit Mexico as American citizens, they presented Paraguayan passports upon their arrival in Amsterdam. These had been issued on July 13, 1957 to the 'Escamilla family' by the Consul General of that country in Mexico City and bore a Czech Legation visa.[47]

---

46. National Archives, DNA RG 59 Box 2816, "Conversation with President Ruiz Cortines regarding Stern Case," June 25, 1957, State Department Document, #901027 , #901027-9, #901027-10.

47. National Archives, DNA RG 59 Box 2816, "Foreign Service Dispatch from Mexico City to Department of State," September 9, 1957, State Department Document #F790009-2036. See also: National Archives, DNA RG 59 Box 2816, "Department of State incoming telegram from Mexico City to Secretary of State," July 23, 1957, State Department Document, #F790009-2039. The telegram reads as follows: "Alfred and Martha Stern and adopted son left Mexico City 1:00 A.M., July 21, KLM plane to Montreal. Final destination on passenger list shown as Switzerland, believed to be Bern. Gray."

Given the secrecy surrounding their departure from Mexico, it is not surprising that several contradictory accounts exist. One possibility is that upon reaching Amsterdam they were met by Czech officials who gave them airline tickets to Prague.[48] However, engraver and sculptor Elizabeth Catlett told me that their reservations for Prague were for the next day, and they would have had to spend the night in Amsterdam. By sheer coincidence, Mexican engravers Arturo García Bustos, Rina Lazo, and several other members of the *Taller de Grafica Popular*, were on their way to a youth congress in Prague. The artists agreed to cede their reservations to the Sterns who, in exchange, insisted on compensating them for remaining an extra day in Amsterdam.

While it is now known that they traveled on Paraguayan passports issued in Mexico City, there are questions relating to their acquisition of the documents. (An early report stated that they had originally obtained Paraguayan nationality in Chicago in 1956.)[49] However, at least a half dozen individuals who had known the Sterns in Mexico, insisted that former Boston University Professor Maurice Halperin, also wanted for questioning in the United States, was instrumental in negotiating the Stern's exit.

Within six weeks of their departure, an article accusing him of playing a major role in their get-away and announcing his imminent apprehension appeared in the local papers.[50] Although this article was undoubtedly written with the purpose of discrediting Halperin, it is also possible that it was responsible for the generally held opinion that he had assisted them.

A subsequent article, published more than two years after the fact, gave an account of secret meetings between the Sterns and Soviet officials, who designated Halperin to negotiate with local influence peddlers on the Stern's behalf.[51]

Others insist that the Soviet Embassy in Mexico City furnished the passports. Their former Cultural Attaché (1953-1957),

48. Allen Weinstein, *The Haunted Wood*, p. 70.
49. National Archives, DNA RG 59 Box 2816, "Department of State Outgoing Telegram Sent to American Embassy Asunción & Amembassy Mexico DF," August 2, 1957, State Department Document #F790009-2047.
50. "Expulsara Mexico al espia rojo Helpering (sic.) Facilito la huida de los esposos Stern a Europa," *Ultimas Noticias*, Segunda Edición, September 2, 1957.
51. "Underground Railway for Reds begins at U.S. Border," *U.S. News & World Report*, Nov. 7, 1960, pp. 82-83.

Yuri Paparov,[52] an attractive man in his early seventies who possesses old world charm and a youthful smile, told me he remembered hearing that Martha Dodd had visited the Embassy. "She insisted on seeing the consul. When she heard he was out she decided to wait and stressed that it was important that she speak to him."[53]

Then, there are researchers who claim the Sterns met with Soviet Embassy personnel. One records a June 18, 1956 meeting with the Mexico City KGB station chief, code named *Ostap*. However, this same source claims the family left the country on July 20, 1956, a year earlier than the actual date.[54] A second source credits "Boris Kolomyakov, the second Secretary of the Soviet Embassy and a ranking NKVD officer in Mexico" with having obtained their passports.[55]

Almost immediately after the Sterns fled Mexico, the FBI discovered that the Paraguayan Consul General in Mexico City, Mr. Garcete, had furnished their documents. Rumors were rampant. The general consensus was that the going price for each passport had been $10,000. Surprisingly, however, telegrams between the State Department and the U.S. Embassy in Paraguay reveal that the Under Secretary of the Foreign Office believed that Garcete's actions resulted largely from his naiveté. A contrite Paraguayan government promised to invalidate the Stern passports, publicly inform their consulates and missions of this decision and permit Garcete to "resign." Futhermore, investigation would proceed in order to determine whether there were grounds for criminal prosecution against the former Consul.[56] Howerver, by the middle of November, the State Department learned that the Paraguayans had yet to invalidate and retrieve the Sterns' passports and had,

52. Elena Tamargo, "Yuri Paparov: En Mexico he vivido los años mas dichosos de mi vida," *La Cronica Cultural*, December 15, 1993, p. 18. Paparov, according to his own admission, was involved in undercover work directed, for the most part, against the Americans. Upon leaving Mexico in 1957 he broke ties with the KGB, devoted himself to journalism and literature, and, in addition, translated a number of books from Spanish into Russian. He returned to Mexico in 1990, was employed by the Trotsky Museum, and continues to write articles and books.
53. Yuri Paparov, interview with author, July 22, 1993.
54. Allen Weinstein, *The Haunted Wood*, p. 70.
55. Harry Thayer Mahoney, *The Saga of Leon Trotsky*, p. 352, note 559.
56. National Archives, DNA RG 59 Box 2816, "Summary of Telegram from Asuncion to Secretary of State," September 15, 1957, State Department Document #F790009-2101.

quite possibly, failed to inform the Mexican authorities of the invalidation.[57]

When information surfaced to the effect that the Sterns were planning to return to Mexico a few months after they had fled, the State Department fired off the following telegram to the American Embassy in Mexico City: "When Sterns departed Mexico, GOM [Government of Mexico] took position this was 'voluntary' action and avoided giving any explanation failure return Sterns to US despite our high level effort. . . . US would view their return negatively unless Mexico is prepared to effect their return [The word 'deportation' is crossed out] to US. Otherwise presence of Sterns in Mexico would constitute serious irritant to our relation with possible far-reaching consequences detrimental to best interests both governments."[58]

As it turned out the Americans never proceeded with their threats. The Sterns did not return to Mexico, although their son Bobby did. When he began to hallucinate and exhibit schizophrenic symptoms as an adolescent, his parents sent him to Mexico for psychiatric treatment. He moved next door to Ralph Scott, a long time family employee who had originally followed the Sterns into exile. (Bobby is believed to still live in Mexico City, where he works as a mechanic.)

After spending a half a dozen years in Prague, the Sterns migrated to Cuba. They remained there from 1963 to 1968 only to return to Czechoslovakia disappointed by what they had seen. By 1977, when the Czechs rebelled against USSR domination, they supported Czech dissidents involved in the human rights movement. During this time they fought to have the espionage indictment against them dismissed, and in 1979 the U.S. Government dropped charges because once the prosecution witnesses had died no evidence against them remained. Their American passports were reinstated, and they traveled to London and Geneva, but never returned to the States. Four years after Alfred's death in Prague in June, 1986,

57. National Archives, DNA RG 59 Box 2816, "Summary of Telegram from Asuncion to Secretary of State," November 15, 1957, State Department Document #F790009-2092.
58. National Archives, DNA RG 59 Box 2816, "Summary of Telegram from State Department to American Embassy Mexico City," November 1, 1957, State Department Document #F790009-2106.

Martha considered returning to New York but, dissuaded by the high cost of living, remained in Prague.[59] She died in August, 1990.[60]

One thing is certain. Despite the flurry of high level appeals reaching all the way to the Mexican presidency, Mexico had refused to deport the Sterns, thus facilitating their flight, and the Americans would not easily forgive this affront. The Sterns had eluded them, and they were furious. In a telegram signed by the newly instated Ambassador Hill, mention is made of a meeting he held with the Mexican Foreign Minister in the company of Dr. Milton Eisenhower, the President's brother, and a U.S. government official. During the meeting, they expressed their disappointment and dismay: How could Mexico have permitted the Sterns to depart for Europe? Why hadn't they returned them to the United States? "The Foreign Minister lamely disclaimed responsibility," Ambassador Hill wrote, "passing the buck to [the] Minister [of] *Gobernación*. He stated that Mexico was glad to be rid of Sterns."[61]

After all, Mexico had been placed in an embarrassing position. Its loss of face confirmed for some Mexican officials close to the United States what the *gringos* had been saying for years.: "What can you expect from a banana republic?"

In a front page article published within weeks of the Stern's flight, the *New York Herald Tribune* quoted an unidentified American Embassy official: ". . . the Sterns' departure was no blow to the American movement there. . . . [The American Communists here don't constitute a threat to Mexico . . . but they do to the United States.] Despite the intense activity of the Communists, however, there is little American agents can do because of their hesitancy to impinge upon Mexican sovereignty."[62]

The Stern affair accomplished one thing: If the United States had been hesitant "to impinge upon Mexican sovereignty," the Americans could now thank the Sterns for removing all restraints. Their flight handed the United States a moral

---

59. Katrina Vanden Heuvel, "Grand Illusions," *Vanity Fair*, pp. 254-256.
60. Katrina Vanden Heuvel, "Martha Dodd Stern," *The Nation,* September 24, 1990, p. 197.
61. National Archives, DNA RG 59 Box 2816, "Telegram from Mexico City to Secretary of State," August 12, 1957, State Department Document #F790009-2107.
62. "Red Haven in Mexico," *New York Herald Tribune*, August, 1957, p. 1.

victory, provided additional leverage, and gave them virtual carte blanche to forge on. They could begin to take matters into their own hands. The Stern's escape had humiliated the Mexicans and revindicated the Americans, placing them in the camp of the righteous. It was time, once and for all, to eliminate the ACGM menace.

Chapter Six

Surviving the Heat:
Official Policies, Sanctions and Incidents
1957-1965

My life changed the year I turned fifteen. By then I'd stopped missing snow—but not Hershey bars—and had developed a taste for tuna fish tacos, a family favorite. Mexico was good to us and many of the others. We established businesses or found work, learned Spanish, made friends and, for the most part, were living fairly well. We even started feeling safe. True, an alarming report in the newspapers or the occasional rumor of a government crackdown could set off a momentary panic, but in general, the Ruiz Cortines years had been tranquil ones. Not until the Sterns fled to Czechoslovakia in August of 1957, did things start heating up. That's when we began to question whether Mexico would continue providing us with sanctuary.

Although I have forgotten most of the details, I remember feeling troubled and impatient, much as I did before taking a test I hadn't studied for. At some level I was probably responding to rumors and to my parents' uneasiness: My mother, ordinarily voluble, grew silent and morose. My father no longer listened to me and lost his temper at things he'd formerly laughed at, like my sister's imitations of the radio commercials. (One of our stations never transmitted anything other than the time: A rapid string of advertisements would be abruptly interrupted every minute on the minute by an announcer giving the exact time. My sister memorized the entire sequence and could repeat it at lightening speed.)

Previously, my mother rarely answered the phone. Now, every time it rang, she lunged ahead of me and grabbed the receiver. I think, at some level, I sensed danger, like birds sense earthquakes, and braced myself for change. I eavesdropped on my parents' conversations, read the newspapers more carefully and, though ordinarily unobservant, drank in even the most insignificant details. I think that was my way of dealing with uncertainty. It gave me a sense of control. Even today, many years later, some events still stand out sharply.

The phone woke me early one Saturday morning. I heard my mother answer and then the sound of my parents' voices, engaged in rapid conversation. I got out of bed and walked down the hall to their bedroom. They were starting to dress.

"We've decided to leave town for a day or two," my father explained. "If anyone should ask, just say you don't know where we went." (We didn't.) They left some extra cash and the phone number of a Mexican friend. "Just in case."

I remember asking, "In case of what?"

They didn't say.

A few days later my mother and I were eating breakfast together. I was reading the comics; she the news. "Oh boy, just listen to this: Bernard Blasenheim, Millionaire Businessman, Arrested and Deported." She sighed. "Poor Bernie, he always wanted to be a millionaire."

Upon reaching home one afternoon the Butlers learned that an unidentified man in a black trench coat had come looking for them. Several people they knew had already been detained or deported so, thinking the worst, they packed up the kids and drove to Taxco. From there, they proceeded to Acapulco, returning to Mexico City a few days later.

Shortly after, Jean bumped into one of her daughter's friends, a young man who looked older than his years because of his thick glasses and heavy beard. He mentioned having dropped by to say hello.

"Tell me," Jean asked, "do you, by any chance, own a black trench coat?"

He did.

Almost immediately after the Stern's get-away in August 1957, the press, both foreign and national, was on the offensive: They touted Mexico's tough stance against radical elements, attacked the Soviet presence in Mexico, and identified politically controversial foreign residents. By the end of that year, Mexican agents, working independently or with the FBI, had engineered a number of arbitrary detentions and deportations directed at foreigners, among them a handful of Americans. (These actions were probably organized by *Gobernación* with the tacit approval of the Presidency.) But it wasn't until September 1958 that the arrests and deportations of foreigners reached their height. These coincided with widespread labor unrest and political agitation. The government retaliated with a vigorous campaign aimed at debilitating radical opposition.

According to Keith, my source for information related to intelligence matters in Mexico: "There's no question that the Mexican campaign against the ACGM was stepped up . . . after the Sterns fled. The Mexican government was chagrined, and Ruiz [Cortines] himself felt personally remiss in not having cooperated with the United States when he was asked. . . . He felt he had to do something to make amends with the U[nited] S[tates], so he cracked down on the ACGM, which the Bureau had probably been asking him to do for years."[1]

Although I agree with Keith's assessment I also believe that following the Stern's escape, the United States seized the opportunity to carry out previously frustrated activities with renewed vigor.

Just days after the Sterns fled the country, the community in exile, always sensitive to any change in the prevailing political winds, realized that the media was becoming increasingly hostile toward the left. The shift was a fitting tribute to the Mexican proverb, *Tapan el pozo después de que se ahoga el niño.* ("They cover the well after the child has drowned.")

Under the headline "Anti-Spy Network Along the Border: 500 Men on Watch to Prevent their Escape via Mexico" was a report claiming that the FBI had thrown a "safety cordon" across the border stretching from McAllen to Brownsville in an attempt to stymie Russian spies trying to elude prosecution by escaping to Mexico. (The relative ease with which the undocumented could cross the border had long been a bone of contention between the two countries.) According to the article, Rudolph Abel, a colonel in the Soviet secret police posing as a New York photographer, had been detained by the U.S. Immigration and Naturalization Service in McAllen, Texas as

1. Keith, letter to author, August 9, 1997.

he was crossing into Mexico only eighteen days earlier.[2] In fact, Abel had been detained nearly two months before, on June 21, 1957. He was subsequently indicted and charged for conspiracy in transmitting military information to the Soviet Union.[3]

Other articles were aimed at demonstrating Mexico's willingness to "right wrongs." A self-congratulatory item in *Excelsior* touted Mexico's deportation, not only of Americans, but of undesirable aliens in general. According to the report three foreigners, a Salvadoran, a Nicaraguan and an American, had been deported by *Gobernación* bringing the total of those expelled in the past two months to fifty-eight. It reported that within the next seventy-two hours an additional twenty individuals, in particular Central Americans and West Indians, would be expelled in the hope that by the month's end the country would be rid of all undesirables currently detained in migratory holding stations. Reasons for expulsion included involvement in illicit activities or remaining in Mexico after the expiration of migratory documents.[4]

In an obvious allusion to the Stern Affair, a newspaper editorial decried Mexico's insistence on deporting undesirables solely on the grounds of improper documentation, illegal entry, or the pursuit of illegal activities. Instead, the writer stated: "The Union's executive, [which] has the exclusive authority of ordering every foreigner he judges inconvenient to abandon national territory immediately without trial, [should apply] Article 33 of the Constitution. . . . The doors of Mexico, open to well meaning men, should be closed to thieves."[5]

Articles of another stripe were also printed with increasing frequency in both the local and Stateside press. These dealt with the Soviet presence in Mexico, the influence it wielded in

2. "Red contra espías a lo largo de la frontera – 500 hombres vigilan para evitar que aquellos escapan a México," *Excélsior,* August 31, 1957.
3. Oscar Jeffers Broadwater, *The Search for Security: Dwight D. Eisenhower and Anti-Communism in America, 1952-1961,* Ann Arbor, MI: University Microfilms International, 1989, p 410. Joseph Albright and Marcia Kunstel, *Bombshell: The Secret Story of America's Unknown Atomic Spy Conspiracy,* Nebraska: U of Nebraska P, 1992, pp. 244-245.
4. "58 expulsados de México en 2 meses – Ayer se aplico a 3 indeseables mas el articulo 33," *Excélsior,* August 24, 1957, p. 1.
5. "Extranjeros Indeseables," *Excélsior,* August 26, 1957, p. 6A. At a time when a journalistic reference to a Presidential omission, no matter how indirect, was interpreted as criticism such a suggestion was unusual.

the country's radical movements, and its role in fomenting espionage and political unrest. According to a long story in the *Universal*, Mexico's vast and, for the most part, unpatrolled territories were particularly well suited to Communist intrigue. Such operations were difficult to identify because many were directed by American spies and other Soviet supported elements. In addition, individuals like Myra and Jack Soble, the Sterns and David Greenglass[6] were smuggled out of the United States through Mexico, often with the complicity of the Soviet Embassy, which, with its staff of more than ninety secretaries and aides played a major role in fomenting international espionage.[7] Reports of this nature were misrepresented and embroidered: An item with a similar slant, published shortly after, reported that Robert Morris, Senate Internal Security Sub-Committee counsel, claimed 900 Russians were working out of the Soviet Embassy in Mexico.[8]

The press also repeated each others' allegations against specific individuals. Among those singled out for attack was the Russian Cultural Attaché, Yuri Paparov, in Mexico from 1953 through 1957. On occasion, Paparov was linked to the ACGM, accused of inciting student agitation,[9] conspiring with known Communists,[10] and heading a complex operation, *Operación México*, aimed at promoting Soviet interests abroad.[11]

Although he admitted, years later, to having been involved in undercover work,[12] Paparov told me he was targeted because of his high visibility in the diplomatic community and his success in fomenting closer relations with other diplomatic missions. He claimed that during the 1958 presidential campaign, which culminated with López Mateos's inauguration in December of that year, the American Embassy funded the *Frente*

6. Jack and Myra Soble were implicated, along with the Sterns, in passing U.S. defense intelligence to Russia; David Greenglass was Julius Rosenberg's brother-in-law and the leading prosecution witness against him. He pleaded guilty and was sentenced to fifteen years in jail. With the exception of the Sterns, none of the above left the United States via Mexico.
7. Lic Alfonso Luis Galan, "Cuartel Soviético en Tacubaya," *El Universal*, Sept. 4, 1957, p. 2.
8. Bert Quint, "United States Reds Have Haven In Mexico, Draft Strategy, Live Amid Luxury," *New York Herald Tribune*, September 2, 1957.
9. Lic. Alfonso Luis Galán, "Cuartel Soviético en Tacubaya."
10. "Red Haven," *Time* magazine, September 9, 1957, p. 46.
11. "Paparov: El titiritero de nuestros comunistoides," *Universal*, July 13, 1957, p. 2.
12. Elena Tamargo, "Yuri Paparov—En México he vivido los años mas dichosos de mi vida" *La Crónica Cultural*, December 15, 1993, p. 18.

Popular Anticomunista de México, (Popular Anti-Communist Front of Mexico.)[13] The Front and other right-wing organizations attacked Paparov, demanded his deportation from Mexico under Article 33, and attempted to weaken left-wing opposition.[14]

For those who remembered the Alemán years, such media coverage, not only locally but in the States, as well, foreshadowed difficult times to come. When political expatriates read, for example, that the counsel for the Senate Internal Security Sub-Committee had told the *Herald Tribune* that the ACGM was making important strategic plans in Mexico, and that ". . . something is going on but we don't know what. . . ."[15] they automatically assumed the worst: Mexico's tolerance toward them was bound to decline. A week later, *Time* magazine, citing the U.S. Embassy in Mexico City as a source, identified a group of American Communists who "operate businesses in travel, real estate, even eggs, clip coupons or live on fat inheritances. Some are reportedly involved in genuine cloak-and-dagger plotting. . . ."[16]

Not surprisingly, those named would subsequently be targeted for detention and, in a few cases, deportation. Furthermore, to the astonishment of the entire left-wing community, the press identified "mystery man," Stirling Dickinson, director of San Miguel Allende's art institute, as an ACGM leader. One of those who had been deported and later returned to Mexico following the 1949 Siqueiros imbroglio, he was now accused of keeping "open house for Communists and fellow travelers."[17]

Within weeks the *Herald Tribune, Time* magazine, an August 30, 1957 edition of the *Washington Post,* a September edition of the

13. My records, however, indicate that the attacks against him began slightly earlier, in July, 1957, about a week before the Sterns left Mexico.
14. Elena Tamargo, "Yuri Paparov—En México he vivido los años mas dichosos de mi vida."
15. Bert Quint, "Communist Expatriates Abroad," New York Herald Tribune, August 30, 1957.
16. "Red Haven," *Time* magazine. They identified Hollywood Ten screenwriter, Albert Maltz; Fred Field, former treasurer of the Civil Rights Bail Fund; his ex-wife, Anita Boyer; Amtorg's U.S. legal representative, David Drucker, referred to as "Field's business agent;" former Boston University professor Maurice Halperin; Asa Zatz, who, according to the article, had served with the Office of Strategic Services during World War II and had left the United States to escape congressional committees; Samuel (Sam) Novick, associated with the United Electrical, Radio and Machine Workers of America, a powerful left-wing union, and Max Shlafrock, the former Miami builder, who had been called before the Eastland committee in 1954.
17. Bert Quint, "Communist Expatriates Abroad." and "Red Haven," *Time* magazine, September 9, 1957, p. 46.

Chicago Sun Times, and Guenther Reinhardt's book, *Crime without Punishment*,[18] had libeled him. In reality, Dickinson was politically conservative, the member of an eminent Chicago family, a pious Catholic, and the Mexican archbishop's close friend. In addition, the native and foreign population of San Miguel Allende, where he had resided for over twenty years, held him in the highest esteem.

When Stirling died at the end of 1998, *Atención*, the San Miguel Allende English language paper, published a long obituary. No mention was made of this chapter in his life, but he described it to me in a sporadic correspondence lasting several years: ". . . one day in the mid-50's I got a letter from a former student, an editor at *The Reader's Digest*, asking if I had seen an article which she enclosed. It was a clipping from the first page of the *New York Herald Tribune* entitled 'Communist Expatriates Abroad.' The writer of the article . . . seemed to think that San Miguel Allende was a sort of nest of pseudo-Communists. Then, about two weeks later, *Time* ran a prominent story along the same lines, but I now appeared to be giving cocktail parties and such in my home here, naturally for my Communist buddies. . . . Obviously something had to be done."

Dickinson was fortunate. His first cousin and an uncle headed Wilson and McIlvaine, a prestigious Chicago law firm. They agreed to handle the case and, in an early communication with *Time* magazine, stated: "Regardless of how it came about . . . the publication of the article is terribly unfortunate since, as you know, calling a man a Communist in this day and age is one of the most damaging things that it is possible to do, especially when the assertion is made in a magazine with your circulation and reputation."[19]

Dickinson's attorneys then arranged for him to travel to Washington, D.C. Accompanied by one of the firm's junior partners, he met with the counsel for the House Un-American Activities Committee, who recognized that a mistake had been committed and agreed to read a statement to that effect into the Committee's minutes. His name officially cleared,

18. Guenther Reinhardt, *Crime without Punishment*, The New American Library of World Literature, Inc., 1957, p. 90.
19. Wilson & McIlvaine, letter to Roy E. Larsen, President of *Time* magazine, Inc., Oct. 30, 1957.

Stirling's attorneys now proceeded to advise *Time* and the *Herald Tribune* of their client's clean bill of health.

According to Dickinson, the upshot was: "The *Herald Tribune* . . . agreed immediately to write a full page story on the school, myself, etc. including an apology for their error. They were broke and this was the best they could do. True to their word, when I got back to San Miguel they sent Joe Hyams, one of their top reporters, to San Miguel, where he did a rather overblown story with a picture of myself, calling our institute the Sorbonne of Mexico."

His attorneys, in an out-of-court settlement with *Time*, agreed to a small compensation, one sufficient to cover the expenses their client had incurred in litigating the case, and extracted a promise to publish Dickinson's letter of protest along with a briefly worded statement.

A few years prior to his death, Dickinson wrote me: "But what has always bothered me is the realization that if I had not been lucky enough to have [had] relatives and partners in one of the country's most respected law firms, I would never have come out unscathed. One can only wonder how many poor souls had their lives virtually ruined by false accusations, whether from McCarthy or from a powerful publication such as *Time*."[20]

Only today, years after the fact, is it possible to piece together fragments of information unavailable in 1957. Dickinson always believed that following the Siqueiros incident former art institute owner, Alfredo Campanella, accused him and others of being Communists and passed this information on to a U.S. Embassy official causing the school's loss of G.I. benefits in 1949 and the deportations of Dickinson and other institute personnel a year later. This material, he believed, had found its way into the Embassy's archives where, most probably, it would have remained buried had reporters not solicited information on U.S. Communists residing in Mexico following the Stern Affair.[21]

This assumption is, of course, extremely plausible: An affidavit signed by J. Paul Phillips, the USIS Research Officer who gave the *Time* and *Tribune* reporters the information they

20. Stirling Dickinson, letter to author, July 23, 1993.
21. Ibid.

used in their articles, lists the data he made available to them. (It is worth noting that the *Tribune* piece includes several extracts lifted verbatim from information Philips had selected from the files.) In his defense, he claimed he had handed over the same material which his superior, Joseph Ravotto, had released on "an unattributed basis" several weeks earlier to a number of American correspondents. Excluded from the affidavit, however, is any mention of Dickinson. While Philips admitted to meeting with *Tribune* journalist Bert Quint he swore, under oath, that he had not released material about Dickinson, a man he denied having heard of at the time.[22]

Bert Quint's statement is more ambiguous. In his apology to the U.S. Embassy the journalist wrote, "I know this is going to sound like some high-type buck passing, but permit me to say that when I wrote the story, the information was attributed to Robert Morris and to official sources, reliable sources and what-have you, without a word about the Embassy."

Quint continues: "The powers-that-be later decided that 'American Embassy' should be substituted for 'official sources' so as to pin down the story more. That, by the way, is how the American Embassy got into the Stirling Dickinson act. He had been lumped with others attributed to official sources."[23]

Unlike Philips, who swore he had never heard of Dickinson, Quint, the journalist, simply apologized for allowing the Embassy to be used as a source. In any case, I believe it possible that the Dickinson material either originated elsewhere or was given to Quint by another Embassy official.

In the end, Dickinson emerged triumphant: "Evidently the Embassy did have some second thoughts, especially after . . . I settled out of court with *Time*. With the arrival of Ambassador Hill, things improved a great deal, and one of my most satisfactory moments, in a small way, was when Hill insisted that I ride in his top-down limousine during the big annual *fiesta* parade here in San Miguel. . . . Whether or not this constituted some sort of indirect apology on the Embassy's part, I can't say."[24]

22. This information is contained in a U.S. Embassy affidavit dated September 10, 1957, witnessed by Marc L. Severe, U.S. Consul, and signed by J. Paul Phillips USIS Research Officer, Service No. 08045, Tariff Item No. 58.
23. Copy of September 18, 1957 letter by Bert Quint addressed to Joseph Ravotto, Deputy Public Affairs Officer of the U.S.I.S.
24. Stirling Dickinson, letters to author, July 30, 1995 and October 15, 1996.

What appears to have been a campaign directed against radical elements, in general, and radical foreigners, in particular, was just warming up. People, like my parents, who had been in Mexico long enough to recognize the symptoms: adverse press coverage, an increase in detentions and deportations, and stepped-up vigilance and harassment, remembered similar episodes and hoped it would blow over within a few weeks. (My father used to joke that the political climate in Mexico, like the weather during rainy season, changed every time he opened his umbrella.) But he hadn't bargained for what nearly became another international incident: On December 18, 1957, within four months of the Sterns' departure, three American political expatriates were detained by DFS agents representing the Department of the Interior, ie. *Gobernación*, presumably, on grounds of having entered and remained in Mexico on false pretenses.

The three, Enos Wicher, a researcher formerly with Columbia University; Sam Novick, a one-time president of the Electronics Corporation of America, and Miami contractor Max Shlafrock, had weathered considerable controversy in the United States prior to moving to Mexico. All had resided there for more than two years and were reasonably well-known to most of the political expatriates.

Although originally a Wisconsin Party organizer, Enos Regent Wicher was working for the Wave Propagation Group in Columbia University's Division of War Research before moving to Mexico, where he taught an engineering course at Mexico City College. (I have been unable to determine the date of his arrival, but he was here by 1955.) According to KGB communiqués and the Venona Decrypts, the intercepted and partially deciphered Soviet war-time telegrams, Wicher provided information on U.S. military electronics to the Soviets. His wife, María, was also an intelligence source. However, Flora Don Wovschin, María's daughter from a previous marriage, was, by far, the most active of the three.[25]

From 1943 to 1945 as an employee of the Office of War Information and, subsequently, the State Department, Wovschin

---

25. John Earl Haynes and Harvey Klehr, *Venona: Decoding Soviet Espionage in America*, New Haven & London: Yale University Press, 1999, p. 198, p. 370.

recruited several agents including Judith Coplon,[26] who was subjected to two investigations on espionage charges, and Marion Davis, a long-time friend and former U.S. government employee.[27] The FBI apparently became aware of Flora's activities in 1949. However, when they tried to track her down, they learned of her move to the Soviet Union in 1946 or 1947. Years later, intelligence sources surmised that her leaving the United States was due either to Elizabeth Bentley's defection or to having received information regarding the decryption of the Venona cable codes.[28] She renounced her American citizenship, married a Russian, and was working as a nurse in North Korea when she died.[29]

According to Jean Butler: "Enos, [Flora's father,] went over with somebody else to try to find some trail of the daughter, and they never did. . . . Flora had . . . fallen in love with somebody in the Russian Embassy, and she apparently had given him some sort of American documents of some nature, I don't know what. . . . She went over to the Soviet Union then. Did she stand trial? I don't know. I never knew her. Marion [Davis] used to talk about her. They had been friends in school. And she [Flora] had been an observer in the Korean War."[30]

The second man seized by Mexican agents, Sam Novick, arrived in Mexico in 1951, following his well-publicized appearance before the House Un-American Activities Committee in the summer of 1949. At the time of his detention he was running the Super Winchester battery factory. According to his step-daughter, Johanna Friedman, he left the United

---

26. Coplon worked in the Foreign Agents Registration section of the Justice Department, was tried twice on espionage charges, and was released on technicalities.

27. John Earl Haynes and Harvey Klehr, *Venona*, p. 198. Davis was an American Embassy employee for the Office of Naval Intelligence in Mexico City and for the Office of the Coordinator of Inter-American Affairs in Washington D.C. during the '40s. She married Bolivian painter Roberto Berdecio, and resided in Mexico City for many years.

28. The FBI kept Venona so hushed, that for some time, neither President Truman nor, after its establishment, the CIA was aware of it. To reveal its existence, even during the highly publicized spy trials of the late '40s and early '50s, would, so the reasoning went, make the Soviets aware that their codes had been cracked. Ironically, in the mid-'50s the Americans discovered that the Russians had already learned that their codes had been broken. Despite this, American security officials did not take the lid off Venona until 1995, figuring that the less said about the percentage and nature of the information obtained the better.

29. John Earl Haynes and Harvey Klehr, *Venona*, pp. 198-201.

30. Jean Butler, interview with author, August 2, 1991.

States because, "[He] got a lot of flak from business associates after his appearance before the HUAC."[31]

As secretary of the Electronics Manufacturers Association, a business concern closely connected to the United Electrical, Radio and Machine Workers of America (UERMWA), a communist dominated union, he was a well-known figure on the left: His company had sponsored liberal broadcaster Johannes Steele's war-time radio programs and he, reportedly, had contributed generously to Popular Front organizations.[32]

During the HUAC hearings he was accused of using his company, the Electronic Corporation of America, which manufactured radar systems for the Navy, to provide Arthur Adams, a Soviet spy, with a business identity. Information contained in FBI files[33] indicates that Novick expedited Adam's illegal entrance into the United States via Canada when he signed his immigration papers. He claimed Adams had been employed by him ten years prior to his actual date of entry.[34]

I now believe that FBI personnel stationed in Mexico City were behind the detentions. Eager to apprehend espionage or conspiracy suspects to compensate for their loss of the Sterns, they set their sights on Enos Wicher and Sam Novick. (If they were returned to the United States by Mexican agents, American authorities could arrest them there and thus avoid the diplomatic complications implicit in a legal extradition.) If this is true, however, it fails to explain why construction contractor Max Shlafrock, called to testify in Miami and New Orleans, but never accused of anything remotely connected to espionage, was one of the three detained. (He was Enos Wicher's partner in a chicken farm located on the outskirts of Mexico City and socialized, occasionally, with both men.)

I first contacted Max, who now lives in Miami, in 1991 and requested information about what expatriates later referred to as "the kidnapping." In response, he sent me a seven page, single-spaced, typed document written during and shortly after the event:[35] "On Wednesday, December 18, 1957 at 9:15

31. Johanna Friedman, letter to author, March 18, 1999.
32. Congressional Record, United States House of Representatives Committee on Un-American Activities, August 9, 10, 11, 1949, Appendix pp. 651, 652, 653.
33. John Earl Haynes and Harvey Klehr, *Venona*, note p. 417.
34. Ibid., p. 175.
35. Max Shlafrock, "Deportation Notes," undated, sent to author, October 22, 1991.

A.M. two men stopped me on Fresnos Street and insisted that I go with them to *Gobernación*. . . . They showed me their credentials and referred to me as 'Señor Max.' I begged and pleaded with them to let me stop off and notify Carmen [Otero, my lawyer], to no avail. They assured me that I only had to answer a few routine questions, and then they would release me. When we got [there], I was hustled into a room where I waited until I almost froze. It was so miserably cold."

After being held at *Gobernación* for several hours, he was ushered into an office and, in his faltering Spanish, answered questions concerning his daily routine, his politics and political activities in Mexico. He was also interrogated about his businesses, a chicken farm and a woodworking shop, and asked to identify the stockholders.[36] He was then presented with a typed deposition and instructed to sign it.

"[Following] the questioning and the signing of the statement, I had been moved to a warmer room which faced the courtyard of *Gobernación*. Looking out an open window, I saw [my lawyer] Carmen. I yelled, and she came up, but they wouldn't let her talk to me. Pretty soon, I saw Enos at the other end of the room. About half an hour later, I saw Sam in another corner. We were not permitted to [speak]. . . ."

At some point in the course of the long afternoon, his lawyer returned bearing a sheepskin coat against the cold and a small amount of cash. In the meantime, Enos Wicher had been allowed to leave. (Shlafrock later learned that his business partner's release had been secured by Paul Murray, a close friend of the American Ambassador and the president of Mexico City College where Enos taught engineering.) At about 10:00 P.M. the Mexican authorities informed him that he and Sam were being deported immediately. Each was allowed a phone call. Max's daughter Shelley, fifteen years old at the time, still remembers what happened next: "My dad left the house one morning and . . . I remember he called home, and he said they [had] picked him and Sam Novick up. . . . 'They're deporting us to the border,' he said. [He asked us] to pack some clothes for him, that he'd be at the house in X

36. Max believes the purpose of these questions was to prove that he had acted illegally because he owned bearer stock in two corporations, which was against Mexican law.

amount [of time.] They [Max and the agents from *Gobernación*] came to the house . . . to get his suitcase and everything else. [Meanwhile] my mother [had] called Albert [Maltz,] Charlie [Small] [and] Fred Vanderbilt Field, who lived in our same *barrio* (neighborhood). I can't remember who else was there, but three or four [friends] were and they tried to offer a bribe to [these big guys with guns, who were with him.] . . . [but they] wouldn't take it. [We] did manage to put money in my father's suitcase figuring that if something happened. . . ."[37]

With the three inspectors taking turns at the wheel of Sam's car and driving at break-neck speeds, the five of them pulled into Nuevo Laredo the following afternoon. Their escorts delivered them to the local immigration office that evening, and following a series of phone calls to their superiors in Mexico City, decided that Max, but not Sam, who lacked sufficient identification, would be delivered across the border.

Max remembered that the inspectors asked him if he wanted to walk or take a cab: "I decided to take a cab across the bridge. . . . They got into the cab with me and rode half way across. They got out and waited on the bridge until I arrived on the other side. A customs inspector came up to the cab and asked for my papers. . . . After looking at my meager identification, he told me to pay off the cab driver and come inside. He then proceeded to question me as to where I live, how long have I been in Mexico, and why. He then asked how come I had no draft card, no citizenship papers. 'Oh, now I get it,' he remarked with glee, 'you've been deported from Mexico.'"

Following a thorough body search—"They were looking for drugs," Max believed—the Chief Naturalization Officer, whom Max described as a nice man with a fatherly manner, interrogated him. Max admitted to having been deported from Mexico for violating Mexican immigration laws by investing money illegally. Upon being asked why he had gone to Mexico in the first place he said he had been harassed by witch-hunters for over a year and could take it no longer. After conversing for more than an hour, the Naturalization Officer suggested he return to Mexico.

Max wrote: "Tired and hungry, not having slept in thirty-six hours, I took my suitcase and walked back to the Mexican

37. Shelley Shlafrock, interview with author, January 18, 1993.

side. They would not permit me to enter. Back I went to Mr. Wilkinson [the Naturalization Officer] and he told me that until my citizenship had been confirmed, they couldn't let me in. He told me to go back and tell the Mexican authorities that he couldn't accept me. . . ."

After being batted back and forth across the border several times, Max was eventually driven to a Mexican jail where, in his own words: "I spent the most miserable night of my life. It was a large cellar room full of drunks—no benches, no cots, no nothing except walls, a concrete floor, bars, one toilet that didn't flush, one urinal, and the place smelled awful. . . . I walked back and forth all night watching these poor creatures vomit, fall into it and sleep that way for hours. It was a real nightmare."

He was bailed out the following morning, Friday, December 20, by the Mexico City DFS inspectors, and escorted back across the bridge to Laredo where, once again, he was refused entry until his American citizenship could be confirmed. But, upon returning with his Mexican captors to the Regis Hotel in Nuevo Laredo, he discovered that Sam had disappeared. Upon asking about his friend's whereabouts, he was told Sam had been returned to the United States. Exhausted after his night in jail, Max bathed, slept and, upon reading the local newspaper, "discovered that Sam and I were the most dangerous Communist spies in the world!"

Over the next few days, under headlines like "Expulsion of Two Americans Who Were Financing Communist Agitators," Max learned that he and Sam had flown to Nuevo Laredo on a local airline, were the leaders of a Red espionage network operating throughout the continent, and had violated the General Population Law by owning the companies they claimed to be employed by.[38]

On Saturday, Max was moved from the Hotel Regis to a

38. "Expulsion of two Americans who were financing communist agitators," *Excélsior*, December 21, 1957; Max Shlafrock gave me copies of twenty one articles which appeared in nine different newspapers between December 21, 1957 and January 29, 1958. Additional headlines included: "Mystery surrounds ouster case here— Injunction granted early Sunday," *Laredo Times*, December 23, 1957; Jose Rodriguez Solis, "Red millionaires turn up— They are still here thanks to the law of *amparo* that protects their civil rights;" *El Diario de Nuevo Laredo*, December 27, 1957; "The Secretariat of the Interior carries out another raid— More deportations,"*El Diario de Nuevo Laredo,* January 5, 1958.

shabby, well hidden rooming house on one of Nuevo Laredo's side-streets and, from there, to yet another establishment. Then at 3:00 A.M. on Sunday morning he was awakened, ordered to pack, and ushered into a waiting automobile belonging to a local *Gobernación* employee. One of the original Mexico City DFS agents joined them, and the two other inspectors followed in Sam's car. (Sam may have been with them but Max never saw him.) After driving for approximately four hours they pulled up in front of the Hotel de los Reyes located on the outskirts of Monterrey. They checked into the hotel and went to bed.

That Sunday afternoon, for the first time since Thursday, Max and Sam were reunited but were not allowed to speak. Not until a few days later would Max learn what Sam had known all along: A Federal Judge had granted them temporary injunctions, ie. *amparos*[39] thanks to the intervention of a Mexico City attorney. But when a federal court representative arrived at the Hotel Regis in Nuevo Laredo to deliver the *amparo* he discovered they had vanished. In order to prevent the injunctions from reaching Max and Sam, the *Gobernación* officers, who continued to maintain contact with their superiors in Mexico City, had whisked them off to Monterrey. Speculation in the press heightened: They had left the country, been jailed, made the whole thing up or, perhaps, been kidnapped.

Meanwhile, the small community in exile in Mexico City, alarmed at what they supposed was the instigation of a campaign directed against them, mobilized in screenwriter Albert Maltz's home to decide what steps they should take. After contacting the authorities and discovering that no official deportation orders had been issued through *Gobernación*, they reached the conclusion that the detentions had been instigated by a small group acting on their own or following the instructions of a third party. If these staged deportations were successful, they might set a precedent for subsequent ones.

Fearing the men might be deposited and apprehended on the other side of the border, they identified and contacted two Texas-based lawyers who were willing to defend them in the

39. Habeas corpus does not exist in Mexico. Instead, under certain circumstances, one can obtain a writ from a judge, referred to as an *amparo*, in order to prevent an arrest.

United States.[40] At the same time, they appealed, through intermediaries, to ex-President Lázaro Cárdenas to mediate on their behalf, hired an influential Mexico City attorney to intervene at the highest echelons of government, and initiated the process for obtaining an *amparo*.[41]

I believe, in the end, that the extensive press coverage was partially responsible for successfully preventing Shlafrock's and Novick's deportations; that, and the Laredo authorities' apparent lack of enthusiasm at the prospect of Max's re-entry into the United States. In addition, the pressure exerted by the political expatriate community was also helpful. (Albert Maltz later estimated that they had spent approximately $10,000 to keep the two men in Mexico.)

In any case, their captors decided to leave Monterrey and return the two men to Nuevo Laredo. They checked them into the Hotel Regis on Tuesday afternoon. Shortly after, Raul Ugalde, a young lawyer and recent graduate of the University of Mexico, arrived. Max explains: "He gave Sam a copy of the *amparo*, told us that tomorrow, Christmas day, we would have to appear before the Judge, and that Grace [Sam's companion], was here. We got up, dressed, and accompanied the lawyer to the Reforma Hotel where we met Grace, Dascha [her close friend and Raul Ugalde's wife] and Licenciado de la Garza, [a lawyer]. After hugs and kisses, we went into the hotel restaurant for supper."

They met with the judge the next day.[42] He set bond at Mex$25,000, approximately $2,000 each, and gave instructions to turn them over to the Nuevo Laredo immigration authorities, thus relieving the Mexico City agents of their responsibility. Nuevo Laredo's Chief Immigration Officer, however, was reluctant to recognize the *amparos*. Only after a lengthy dispute, did he relent. But he then insisted they report to him four times a day. (He would later agree, grudgingly, to three daily appearances.)[43]

40. Obtaining legal representation could be difficult because many lawyers, preferring to avoid the controversy and negative publicity involved in politically charged cases, refused to handle them.
41. Joel Gardner, *The Citizen Writer in Retrospect: Oral History of Albert Maltz*, p. 294.
42. "District judge explains Constitutional guarantee for the injunction granted to the millionaires," *El Diario De Nuevo Laredo*, December 29, 1957, p. 1. The Mexico City press accused the Judge of recognizing the *amparos* because he was a Communist and had accepted a bribe.
43. "The Red Millionaires Want to Leave—They may do so, but under the surveillance of *Gobernación* agents," *El Diario De Nuevo Laredo*, January 11, 1958, p. 1.

"This afternoon we went to the movies," Max wrote on Tuesday, December 31, 1957: "We saw three horror pictures. That, I hope, will end the horrors for 1957 and the future. I'm lonely and sad, but still hopeful that 1958 will be a better year, not only for me, but for all mankind; that peace will prevail throughout the world so that little people, like me, can live peacefully."

I wish I could write that Max's New Year's wish came true. On one hand, the judge did grant him and Sam permission to leave Nuevo Laredo on January 11 in the custody of *Gobernación* officials, providing they checked in periodically with immigration authorities in Mexico City. On the other, the second half of 1958 proved to be the most critical year many would face during their time in Mexico.

Max Shlafrock, however, would not be around to find out. He sold what little he possessed, returned to Miami the following April with his wife and daughter, and, despite enormous reversals, was able to eke out a living in the city he had left thirty-nine months earlier.

For those who remained, the New Year ushered in a period of political upheaval and labor unrest, followed by episodes of severe repression. From April through December, teachers, university students and electricians joined by telegraph, oil and railroad workers, protested throughout the country.[44]

Arnoldo Martínez Verdugo, former Secretary General of the Mexican Communist Party from 1963 until 1981, was closely involved in the disturbances, and he remembered them well. When I interviewed him at his offices at the Study Center for Labor and Socialist Movements (CEMOS) he explained: "1958 was an exceptionally important year for the trade union movement—1958 and 1959, actually. There were two huge uprisings during this period which culminated in particularly violent reprisals: the elementary teachers strike and, the more important of the two, the general railroad strike, which paralyzed the entire system."

As a writer, editor, a former political prisoner and, up until

44. Enrique Krauze, *La Presidencia Imperial,* p. 200. Up until recently political unrest during an election year was not uncommon. Once the president in power had designated his successor he became a 'lame duck' creating a power vacuum lasting six months or more. Until the new president assumed office in December, interest groups scrambled to be heard by the new administration.

recently, the opposition government's delegate for Coyoacan, Martínez Verdugo has been an acute observer of the Mexican political scene for over forty years. He is charismatic, direct, and earnest but not without a sense of humor. He looked older than his years—he was in his sixties at the time—until he smiled and removed his glasses to massage the bridge of his nose, a gesture he repeated frequently. He told me that the movement began in 1958: "[But] by March of 1959, it was repressed. So was the Party. Its office was occupied by the police [and all its files confiscated.] On March 28, 1959 more than nine thousand people throughout the country were detained . . . there was no place to put them and then, little by little, they were released until they ended up processing those remaining—more than five hundred—and condemned them to sixteen years, ten years, five years. . . . A great repression. . . . They then expelled a Soviet Embassy group, accusing them of contributing money to the [railroad] syndicate. Totally false. It was a very strong syndicate. Money was no problem."

Referring to the same period, Mexican writer and intellectual Alonso Aguilar, recalled how in the fall of 1958, when the railroad strikes were at their peak, several North American political expatriates were arrested. According to Aguilar: "At least a few were deported. . . . although I understand that they weren't directly accused of having in any way fomented this movement.[45] There was an attempt, probably resulting from pressure by some North American Agency—the FBI or the CIA—to legitimize the actions taken against them by demonstrating that in these and other conflicts shaking Mexico . . . there was Communist infiltration. In this concrete case, the Mexican police collaborated with its neighbor which, without any doubt, was the one which took the initiative and decided to employ a typically McCarthyite measure."[46]

Martínez Verdugo expressed it this way: "I assume that it [the detention of Americans] was a joint venture between the local authorities and the North Americans. The Mexican government wouldn't have dared seize foreigners, particularly North American foreigners, unless they believed a crime had been

45. They were accused of fomenting the movement but since no one was formally charged and tried the government never had to present evidence against them.
46. Alonso Aguilar, interview with author, July 9, 1996.

committed. . . . I think, in these cases, the Embassy suggested [that certain measures be taken.] That's my impression, but it's possible that it's no more than that, a personal impression."[47]

He was not alone. Even the press shared this impression, as was borne out by the following article which appeared below the caption, "Many FBI Agents in Mexico for Special Consultation."

The unidentified journalist speculated on the large number of foreign observers present at police headquarters during a series of detentions conducted in September 1958: "[Many], perhaps, are curious tourists, but we know that many FBI agents have come to observe the communist uprisings. For the United States, in particular, and for that agency, Mexico is regarded as a center of reunion for communist espionage agents."[48]

I have no doubt that it was easier to justify the arrest and deportation of foreigners in an atmosphere fraught with tension. Placing the blame on 'alien elements' provided the government with the opportunity to deflect criticism from local problems. In other words, foreigners made good scapegoats.

On Saturday, September 6, 1958 and for close to a week, scores of 'international agitators,' accused of having financed internal rebellion and intervening, either directly or indirectly on behalf of striking students and teachers and railroad, oil, and telegraph workers were apprehended. Throughout the country, but predominantly in Mexico City, Poles, Yugoslavs, Czechs, Spaniards, South and Central Americans, and U.S. citizens were rounded up by the *Dirección Federal de Seguridad* (DFS), the Secret Service, and the Federal Judicial Police. The operation was reputed to be the largest mass detention and deportation of political dissidents Mexico had ever known.[49]

Sculptor and graphic artist, Elizabeth Catlett, remembers the roundups: "My younger son was sick with a high fever, and we had to go to a wedding celebration up around Insurgentes and Boston [Street] . . . so I decided I couldn't go but Pancho [her husband, artist Francisco Mora], had to because he always

---

47. Arnoldo Martinez Verdugo, interview with the author, August 14, 1992.
48. "Hay 208 detenidos en la jefeatura de policia por los sucesos del sabado," *Excélsior*, September 8, 1958, pp. 1, 8. The thought that "curious tourists" would be hanging around police headquarters borders on the ridiculous.
49. Paul P. Kennedy, "Curb Alien Reds— U.S. Leftists Among Groups Hit in Government Raids to End Series of Riots," *New York Times*, Sept. 11, 1958, p.

played the guitar and sang. I was telling him how to get there, and the two kids were watching TV. [He] left around 10:00 P.M. . . . I had just turned on the news to see what had happened with the [railroad workers]. That very week, I think, they [the government] decided . . . to break the strike . . . they had a big fight. I heated some alcohol [for my son]. I had it in one hand and a wash cloth in the other, when somebody knocked at the door.

"I went to the door and there were three men. I said, 'My husband said not to let anyone in when he's not here so you have to come back another time.' [One guy] said, 'We're from *Gobernación*, and we want to see your papers and. . . .' I went to shut the door. All of a sudden he grabbed me by the arm and twirled me around, his arm up under my chin and, by that time, my little boy, my biggest son, he was about eleven, and the maid who's small, were standing at the door, and my son jumped on him, and he knocked [my child] down, and my feet weren't even on the floor, and I'm heavy. One had me by one arm, one had me under the chin, and the other was behind, and I started yelling, and we got down to the next landing . . . and my son came out, and I said, 'Call.'"

They drove Elizabeth to the detention center for foreigners on Miguel Schultz Street, handed her over to authorities, and checked her name off a list which, in her words, "looked like a list straight from the Embassy of practically everybody Left in Mexico." The names were listed in alphabetical order, and three—Lewis, Blasenheim and Bright—had already been checked off: Alan Lane Lewis, whose name appeared as Lewis Allen (sic.), was a former N.Y. theater director, a scenario director at Fox, and a producer for Paramount.[50] At the time of his arrest, Lewis was sitting out the blacklist in Mexico and running the UNAM's (University of Mexico's) theater department. Bernard Blasenheim was an American construction contractor. Not regarded as political, he was associated with the ACGM through some of his business associates and friends. Blacklisted screenwriter John Bright, was one of the

50. Patrick McGilligan and Paul Buhle, *Encyclopedia of the American Left, IL*, p. 573-575; There was another 'Allen' whose name also appears on ACGM lists. Robert Francis Allen, a journalist, was with the press corps in Spain during the Civil War. It's possible that this too may have been responsible for the confusion.

founders of the Screen Writer's Guild and a member of the Hollywood section of the Communist Party.

Shortly before Elizabeth's name was checked off the list at the detention center, handicraft store owner May Brooks and her husband, Sam, Zeiss's representative in Mexico, were thinking about having a cup of tea before retiring. Just then, the phone rang. "It was Moira Bright," May told me, calling to say her husband had been taken away by armed agents.

"We lived in Polanco then and Schon [our lawyer] lived close by, so Sam said, 'Moira, don't worry about it. I'll tell Schon to get after this, and we'll find out where Johnny is and we'll . . . pay off, and he'll come home. O.K.?' So Sam, very relaxed, goes out and says, 'Listen, get some tea up, and I'll call you when I'm leaving [Schon's].'"

Within minutes after he'd left, three men drove up in a station wagon, rang the bell and asked for Sam. She told them she had no idea where he was. They decided to wait.

"They get back into their car. They're sitting there, and they have a ballad playing [on the car radio]. It happened to be one of those revolutionary ballads about Pancho Villa. . . . And I thought, 'Only in Mexico would you have this kind of irony. Here you have the cops waiting to arrest us, and they're listening to a ballad about Pancho Villa.'"

When Sam called to say he was on his way home, she told him about the agents parked in his driveway and urged him to stay away at all costs. His lawyer agreed. Sam would leave town immediately. May pulled out her telephone directory and proceeded to call anyone she could think of who might be in danger. But for some, Bernard Blasenheim, Alan Lane Lewis, John Bright, and Elizabeth Catlett, the first names on the list, the call would come too late.

Why would they, in particular, have been singled out? The obvious reason was that their names appeared on the ACGM lists. But naturally, there was much speculation about the four who were seized: Elizabeth Catlett told me that during the early days of the railway workers' strike she had introduced a European journalist, interested in covering the event for his paper, to the Union's lawyer, a friend of her husband's. But she could think of nothing else which in any way linked her to the disturbances. Some felt Blasenheim's detention had nothing to do with his politics but, rather, with his having made enemies in high places; others believed a former employee had denounced him out of spite. Alan Lane Lewis's connection with the University of Mexico during a time of student unrest may well have been responsible for his apprehension. (I was told that Lewis's photograph was superimposed onto a group shot of student dissidents and used against him.) Jean Butler told me that Hugo thought Bright was targeted because he was a heavy drinker and tended to show-off and exaggerate his importance. Yet, in the final analysis, no one will ever know for sure.

Within a day or two of their detentions the three men were summarily deported. Their families followed shortly after and would never to return to Mexico. The community was thrown into a panic. Some, along with David Drucker, suspected American secret service agencies of encouraging the anti-subversive campaign in the belief that the ACGM had masterminded the flight of British agents Guy Burgess and Donald Maclean to Moscow via Mexico. But there were no hard answers, only conjecture, along with the belief that everyone 'on the list,' some of whom had been previously identified in the press, would continue to be vulnerable.[51]

Whatever the reasons, the knowledge that the Mexican government's change in policy might eventually affect their ability to remain in the country was cause for concern. While well aware that hostilities had increased following the Stern incident, they were, none-the-less, taken off guard by the intensity and suddenness of the attacks. When John Bright was, in Jean Buler's words, "deported [in his carpet slippers] without enough money in his pocket to make a phone call," every one of the political expatriates knew they could be next.[52]

As it turned out, Elizabeth Catlett had been. She later learned that, following her seizure, her eldest son had located a family friend, artist Pablo O'Higgins: "He . . . told Pablo that some policemen came and took me away and that Pancho was at a party, and he told Pablo, he didn't know the address but [had heard me give his father directions]: '. . . you drive on

51. David Drucker, interview with author, May 20, 1991. In 1951 Russian spies Guy Burgess and Anthony MacLean avoided arrest in the United States by escaping to Moscow. However, it seems unlikely that U.S. agencies would wait seven years to strike back.
52. Jean Butler, interview with author, August 2, 1991.

Insurgentes to Boston, and you take a right and on the left-hand side on a corner building about three blocks down, if you look in the window, you'll see my father playing the guitar on the ground floor.'

"Pablo went, and he found them and broke up the party and took Pancho to look for a lawyer. [Meanwhile our friends] Juan Carrasco [a neurologist] and his wife, [Carmen, Albert Maltz's secretary] came by the lockup and brought me some cigarettes and some money. . . . And I knew Blasenheim was there, and Johnny Bright sent me some food, and Sunday passed. They brought me some sketch pads and stuff, and I was reading *Brave New World*, the only book there in English."

Unlike the others, she was fortunate. "They were threatening me with deportation, me and my children. And I said, 'but my children are Mexican.' I made up my mind . . . to become a [Mexican] citizen." Her husband and their circle of friends appealed to the Mexican authorities, to prominent figures on the left like Vicente Lomabardo Toledano, and finally to the Secretary of Education, who was familiar with Elizabeth's work. He arranged for her release. On Monday night, without prior warning, she was handed over to officials, and along with a Spanish prisoner, transported to *Gobernación* offices and given permission to leave. Newspapers claimed that authorities let her go upon learning she had obtained Mexican citizenship through marriage.[53] But, in fact, she did not apply for citizenship until after the event.

Alphabetically, the next on the deportation list was David Drucker: He told me: "I got a call from Alan Lewis's wife [Brooke] on a Saturday night about eleven o'clock, and she said, 'The immigration authorities are here at the house and they want Alan to go down to the Department of Immigration to verify his papers,' or something like that. 'Can you get me a lawyer?' So, I call Charles Small. We couldn't find anybody, and the next time I spoke to Brooke she said they had taken him to the Department of Naturalization. . . .

"On Sunday morning, at seven o'clock . . . our maid came up to our bedroom and said, 'There are two gentlemen at the door who would like to speak to you.' Now, it was only at that

53. Paul P. Kennedy, "Curb Alien Reds—U.S. Leftists Among Groups Hit in Government Raids to End Series of Riots."

moment that I . . . realized something was up so I—in my pajamas—got into a pair of pants and jacket and went over the back fence, which was next to the San Angel Inn [Restaurant], and, fortunately, the door to the little chapel there, on the left hand side as you come in, was open. I was able to get out, and I circled around and ended up at the house of a Mexican friend and subsequently people began to come in who apparently had also been called on."[54]

Among those who, in Drucker's words, "had been called on," were public health nurse Lini (Fuhr) de Vries, identified by Elizabeth Bentley as the woman who had recruited her into the Party; Hans Hoffman, a psychologist with the *Hospital Infantil*, (Children's Hospital) and, formerly, a close friend of physicist Robert Oppenheimer's brother, Frank;[55] Sam Novick, whose attempted deportation the previous year had failed, and poet-turned-carpenter, George Oppen. Also singled out for deportation were Miami refugee and silver shop owner Charles Small, medical translator Asa Zatz and the Sterns' former employee, Ralph Scott. (Having accompanied them to Mexico in 1953 Scott remained in the country after their departure and ran a dry cleaning business purchased with their assistance.) Although he had departed six months earlier, Max Shlafrock's name was also on the list, and the newspapers assured their readers of his imminent arrest. There were others, as well.

A few—the Halperins and Fred Field, for example—were tipped off by friends; the Hoffmans were vacationing in Valle de Bravo, and screenwriter Albert Maltz was in Los Angeles. When agents knocked on Maltz's door his house-guest, Helen Sobell, in Mexico to raise funds for her husband's defense—he had been incarcerated for conspiracy to commit espionage following the Rosenberg trial—answered. "We don't want you," they told her, having, of course, no idea who she was. "We want Albert Maltz."

For the next few weeks, Americans with a history in left-wing politics made themselves scarce: David Drucker moved

54. David Drucker, interview with author, May 20, 1991.
55. Robert Oppenheimer headed the Manhattan Project, the U.S. program that developed the atomic bomb. He and his brother Frank had been associated with the Party in the past and were under investigation by the FBI. Rumors of their collaboration with the Russians proved false.

into a friend's hacienda near Pachuca. The Halperins were taken to the Cuernavaca home of Domingo Lavin, a leading Mexican industrialist. When someone told May Brooks she too might be in danger she contacted a family friend, composer Conlon Nancarrow, who drove her and her two children to Acapulco. (They figured that, as an American, she would be more likely to go unnoticed in a town packed with tourists.)

Only upon return to Mexico City, would she discover that her husband, Sam, had also been in Acapulco, within walking distance from where she was staying. He and Fred Field were both living in the vacation home of a member of Mexico's Electricity Commission. According to May: "They hated the sun, and they hated the beach, so they were indoors all the time, and Fred played his recorder and . . . there were some books so [Sam read] all day long, and they'd walk out at night, and take walks on the beach and come back together. He said Fred was terrible to live with. All he wanted to eat was spaghetti and there was a lot of spaghetti, and he listened to a lot of recorder music and read what he could, and so they passed the time.[56]

Within days of the hasty arrests and deportations, the local branch of the Communist Party staged a demonstration at the office of Mexico's major newspaper, *Excélsior*. Under the leadership of painter David Alfaro Siqueiros, protesters denounced the FBI presence in the country, a raid on Communist Party offices, and the arbitrary apprehension and expulsion of political exiles and other foreigners residing in Mexico.[57] Nothing came of it, of course, but once strike leaders throughout the country had been arrested and jailed, the strike broken, and one phase of the disturbances curbed, the 'network of foreign agitators' no longer served any purpose. Thus, one by one, the Americans who had disappeared, reemerged, although a few refused to come out of hiding until they had received their lawyers' assurances that they were no longer in danger of deportation.

While most feared being expelled from Mexico, screenwriter Albert Maltz, in Los Angeles during the detentions, worried about getting back in. (The press had learned of Helen

56. May Brooks, interview with author, February 16, 1993.
57. "Protestan los Comunistas por el encarcelamiento de 11 personas," *Excélsior* September 12, 1958, p. 3.

Sobell's presence in his home which, according to Maltz, they were referring to as a "safe-haven for foreign spies.") Newspapers reported that Mexican police had been posted along the border to bar Maltz's reentry. If this was true, they were unsuccessful. He did return, uneventfully.

However, after he arrived in Mexico, he feared deportation, and gave his attorney a letter addressed to the incoming president, Adolfo López Mateos. In it, he summarized his background and expressed his willingness to leave Mexico voluntarily, if he were requested to do so. But he stressed his interest in remaining and explained why he didn't deserve to be expelled. The letter was signed by two prominent film personalities: One had just been elected to congress; the other was López Mateos's cousin.[58]

Of course, each situation differed. Some political expatriates, among them David Drucker, were without documents. (The government had requested and seized his during the round-ups, he told me.)[59] His daughter, Susan, remembered spending long afternoons in lawyer Carmen Otero's office, often in the company of Maurice Halperin's son, David, waiting to receive an 'all-clear' so their parents could come out of hiding and return home.

After three weeks, Susan's parents did, but the Halperins were offered no alternative to deportation. Apparently, not all expulsion orders were reversible. Since Maurice, denounced in the press for having expedited the Stern's departure, was in hiding, David, his twenty-one year old son, was given full responsibility for negotiating a deal. Anxious, perhaps, to avoid the publicity which had accompanied earlier deportations, he arranged for his parents to leave voluntarily. Through a contact with close ties to former President Lázaro Cárdenas, the Halperins were allowed to return to their Mexico City home. In exchange, they agreed to leave the country by November.

But where could they go? Hesitant to return to the United States for fear he might be subpoenaed, Maurice consulted two powerful Mexican acquaintances, Lombardo Toledano, the left-leaning labor leader, and Narcisso Bassols, a former cabinet minister and Mexican Ambassador to the Soviet

58. Joel Gardner, *The Citizen Writer in Retrospect.* p. 907.
59. David Drucker, interview with author, May 20, 1991.

Union. The two were instrumental in Halperin's decision to leave Mexico for the Soviet Union.[60]

At the same time Mexico's stance toward the political expatriates toughened, a major shift was taking place in American policy, one which would offer additional options. After 1947, the State Department had begun withholding passports on the basis of political affiliation. With the 1950 McCarran Act (Internal Security Act), equating Communism with subversion, they established a judicial rationale: To provide anyone who might intend to engage in activities detrimental to the United States with the means of traveling abroad was contrary to the nation's best interests. While attempts were made to limit this edict, it wasn't until the 1958 Supreme Court decision in the case of artist Rockwell Kent that the Passport Office's authority to deny travel documents on political premises was significantly curtailed.[61]

In the summer of 1958, shortly after the precedent-setting Kent decision, the State Department held a five-day briefing with U.S. Embassy and consulate personnel in Mexico and informed them of the changes. In the past, as reported by the *New York Times*: ". . . members of this [the politically dissident] American colony, while free from United States investigative procedures, were nevertheless pinned down so far as Communist activities were concerned. Their travel has been restricted largely to Mexico itself, and they have been under continuing surveillance here by the Mexican Foreign office and secret police."

Now, however, they would be able to obtain travel documents, move freely world-wide, and solicit the protection of the U.S. government. The article predicted that, ". . . one or more North American Communists now residing in Mexico may soon apply. . . ."[62]

In fact, many political expatriates did just that. Maurice Halperin solicited his passport immediately following the

---

60. Don Kirschner, *Cold War Exile: The Unclosed Case of Maurice Halperin*, Missouri: University of Missouri Press, 1995, pp. 178-179.
61. David Caute, *The Great Fear: The Anti-Communist Purge Under Truman and Eisenhower*, pp. 249-250. Decisions in the Walter Briehl and Weldon B. Dayton cases also contributed to this outcome.
62. Paul Kennedy, "Passport Ruling Sifted In Mexico," *The New York Times*, June 29, 1958, p. 26.

Supreme Court decision and was told that, in spite of the ruling, his attempt might still be unsuccessful. He consequently contacted Leonard Boudin, Rockwell Kent's lawyer, who filed a suit on his behalf. His petition came through shortly before he left Mexico.[63]

At about the same time, the Butlers and the Oppens also solicited their passports. Mary Oppen recalls that after their initial request was delayed, they consulted a lawyer who had publicly proclaimed his willingness to undertake any case of this nature. Once he had written a letter on their behalf, they received their passports.[64] Others, Miami dentist David Prensky, for example, waited it out and received his documents without incident during the '60s.

A passport made a major difference. Now, those formerly "pinned down" in Mexico could go almost anywhere and that, of course, was an added incentive to leave: In 1959 the Oppens followed their daughter Linda, who had returned to the United States for college a year earlier; in 1960 the Butlers seized the opportunity to work in Europe and left for Italy; the Maltzes returned to California in the summer of 1962. My parents, on the other hand, were among those who continued to reside in Mexico, but took advantage of their newly acquired freedom and began to travel.

By 1959, while we were no longer as likely to be detained, deported or attacked in the press as frequently as in the past, the American government continued to encourage and, in general, receive Mexico's full cooperation in matters related to the political expatriate community. Although Mexico would assume a more liberal stance internationally, as illustrated by that country's refusal to sever ties with Cuba in 1961, López Mateos continued to resist progressive reforms within the country.[65] Some attribute his conservative stance, in part, to the warm working relationship he sustained with Winston Scott, CIA Chief of Station from 1956 on. (When Scott remarried in 1962 López Mateos was a witness at his wedding.)[66]

---

63. Don Kirschner, *Cold War Exile: The Unclosed Case of Maurice Halperin.*
64. Mary Oppen, *Meaning: A Life,* Oakland, CA: Black Sparrow Press, 1978, p. 202.
65. Barry Carr, Marxism and Communism in Twentieth-Century Mexico, Lincoln & London, University of Nebraska Press, 1992, p. 233.
66. Jefferson Morley, "CIA Son," *Washington Post,* March 17, 1996, p. 1. Following his retirement in 1969, Scott wrote his memoirs, *It Came to Little* but upon his death

Needless to say, we, more than other expatriate communities, were keenly aware that the CIA operated in Latin America. But I doubt if, even in our wildest dreams, we came anywhere close to understanding the extent of their presence in Mexico.

Under Scott's administration the CIA operated LITEMPO, a complex program which provided a series of support systems for Mexico's non-military security forces. It engaged in joint operations and intelligence exchange, was instrumental in improving the country's ability to collect information and maintain public security, and established a secret communications network for Mexico.

In addition to its sophisticated infrastructure, some members of its staff were able to exercise enormous influence over the executive branch of government. Winston Scott, for example, continued on close terms with López Mateos's successor, Diaz Ordáz. However, even Scott was occasionally frustrated: Luis Echeverria, Diaz Ordáz's Secretary of *Gobernación*, disapproved of the CIA role in Mexico and was a reluctant partner. But, when instructed by his president to cooperate, he grudgingly complied. By the time he became President in 1970, Scott had retired.[67]

If Mexico's policies, from the executive on down, faithfully reflected North American interests, it was only logical that the media, both Mexican and foreign, would do the same. ACGM "subversion," for example, was periodically reported in the press, and few political expatriates managed to keep their names out of the papers. (My parents were the exception.)

Fred Field, on the other hand, was mentioned frequently. A March 20, 1961 *Newsweek* article by Harold Lavine identified him as having attended the Communist sponsored Latin American conference in Mexico City. According to Field: "I was living in Mexico as the guest of the government and if I was to stay, I had to conform to its rules. There weren't many: I could not work in a bar, I could not invest in any media enterprise, and I could not own property within a certain number of meters of the coast."

---

two years later, the CIA immediately confiscated all his personal papers as well as the manuscript. His son's attempts to retrieve them have, so far, been unsuccessful.
67. Philip Agee, *Inside the Company: CIA Diary,* Toronto, New York & London: Bantam Books, 1975, pp. 268, 539-540.

He explained that, above all, foreigners had to avoid becoming involved in local politics, and that attending a conference on national sovereignty could be so interpreted.

The September, 1958 roundups were still recent enough to serve as a reminder of the steps the government was willing to take when they believed firm action was warranted. Understandably, Field was outraged and worried about the possibility of official reprisals so he wrote *Newsweek's* editor demanding a retraction. The editor informed him that Lavine stood behind his story. Shortly after, Field learned of a mutual friend who was hosting a party Lavine was expected to attend and arranged to have himself invited. He waited until the journalist, who had a reputation for overindulging, had imbibed heavily and then approached him and asked where he had obtained his information.

Field recalls: "His first answer was that he had seen me there himself. A little more pressing and he admitted that he had not attended but that the information came to him from a completely reliable source. What was that source? He couldn't reveal that to me. We stayed on that plateau for several more bourbons. But very late, the next morning, in fact, Lavine finally told me that his information had come from the FBI."[68]

Maurice Malkin, a disenchanted former Party member, who wrote at length, and often inaccurately about the ACGM, also placed Field at the conference, so if one believes Field, perhaps Lavine was not the only one the FBI gave information to. (Either that or Malkin also read *Newsweek*.)

Malkin reported: "U.S. representatives at that conference included well known American communists Fred V. Fields (sic.), Samuel J. Novick, Albert Maltz and Catherine Cole, a member of the Party in Los Angeles County. Other American traitors hid their identity because they were afraid of being questioned by the authorities upon their return to the United States."[69]

Needless to say, such smears were irritating but dissidents are vulnerable targets. Preferring not to call attention to themselves, they had little legal recourse. Occasionally, however, they did fight back.

68. Fred Vanderbilt Field, *From Right to Left*, p. 292.
69. Maurice Malkin, *Return to My Father's House*, ed. Charles W. Wiley, New Rochelle, New York: Arlington House, 1972, p. 211.

On September 19, 1960 *U.S. News & World Report* published an article under the headline "The Underground Railroad—To Russia." HUAC chairman, Representative Francis F. Walter (Democrat) of Pennsylvania, identified seventeen people as past or present members of the American Communist colony in Mexico.[70] Also identified by name was Spanish Civil War veteran Bart van der Schelling and his wife, Edna Moore, the American School music teacher. She decided to ignore the article. On November 7, 1960 a second article appeared. Although she was not named, the unidentified journalist accused ACGMers of collaborating with the Soviet Embassy by assisting Soviet spies who fled the States via Mexico.[71]

Meanwhile, rumors were circulating throughout the school and the American community that the Board had decided to terminate Edna's contract. In a letter dated November 10, 1960 she appealed to congressman James Roosevelt, who was known for his relentless opposition to the HUAC. After filling him in on the details, she explained her position: "This sudden preposterous attack on me is ridiculous, false and cruel. . . . So despite my exemplary record I am threatened with the loss of my job. As a school teacher of modest means, I have no resources to combat these charges, if indeed there is any way for an individual to fight his or her way out of the strangling circumstances of being publicly smeared by this truly Un-American committee."

Edna was dismissed by the school on November 30. On that same day she approached Rosalind Beimler, a personal friend and her principal, and explained that, fearing the worst, she had contacted Roosevelt.

When I interviewed Rosalind Beimler in her Cuernavaca home over thirty years later she still remembered the incident in some detail. The former American School administrator, who went on to become a highly regarded psychoanalyst, told me: "[After] she came to me and told me what she was being accused of . . . in this newspaper article or magazine, I felt she

70. "The Underground Railroad—To Russia," *U.S. News & World Report*, September 19, 1960. The following individuals were singled out: Frederick Vanderbilt Field, Hugo D. Butler, Joan Abelson, George Pepper, David and Esther Drucker, Albert Maltz, Bart and Edna Van der Shelling, Dr. Jake Levine and, until they fled to the USSR, Martha Dodd Stern and Alfred J. Stern. The Liebers, Steins and Halperins were also mentioned, but the first had left in 1954, the others in 1958.
71. "Underground Railway for Reds Begins at U.S. Border," *U.S. News & World Report*, November 7, 1960, p. 82.

had nothing to do with any of that, and she was a very fine person, and I believed her. Well, first of all, I had heard that he [James Roosevelt] was in town, by chance . . . because I was a friend of the editor of *The News*. I called him immediately and I said, 'Do you know where he [Roosevelt] is?' [He told me he was at a luncheon]. . . . So I said [to Edna], 'Let's just get in the car, and let's catch him there.' And so we did. . .they finally let us in. I think we looked respectable, and we said we'd wait and he said 'No, no, no . . . let's talk about it right now.' He said, 'You know, I'm not particularly *persona grata* with the CIA or the FBI or whatever it was. . . . I don't know whether I can get into her files or not, but if I can I will, and I'll check it out for you and let you know.'"[72]

Roosevelt notified Edna within days that the HUAC files contained no mention of her whatsoever, and suggested she use his letter to clear her name with the Board of Directors.[73] The letter was not sufficient. The damage had already been done. Out of work, black-balled in the community, and living on a pittance—her husband Bart had suffered two major heart attacks and could no longer work on a steady basis—she approached, on the recommendation of friends, the Philadelphia law firm of Dorfman, Pechner, Sacks & Dorfman. They agreed to take her case on a contingency basis, billing Edna solely for expenses.[74]

At the time, the memory of San Miguel Allende's Stirling Dickinson and his 1957 triumph over *Time* magazine loomed large in the collective consciousness of the community in exile. Some of us thought that, perhaps, his case had set a precedent of sorts. But, unlike Dickinson, Edna was not a conservative Republican, born into a prominent family with close ties to one of the country's more prestigious law firms. Nor did she have the means to travel to the United States seeking redress. In addition, the slur against her was a direct quote by a Congressman on the floor of the House of Representatives and, as such, was privileged. In other words, Edna could not sue Representative Francis F. Walter. She could, however, sue *US News and World Report*.[75]

72. Rosalind Beimler, interview with author, September, 1991.
73. James Roosevelt, letter of December 13, 1960 to Edna Moore Van der Schelling. In a February 25, 1961 NBC television appearance Roosevelt referred to Edna, though not by name, as an example of someone wrongly accused by HUAC investigators.
74. Philip Dorfman, letter to Edna Moore Van der Schelling, January 9, 1961.
75. Ibid.

After her lawyers had filed her suit, the magazine responded with a Motion for Summary Judgment on the basis of jurisdiction: Since she was no longer a resident of any particular state, nor a foreigner, she could not bring action in a federal court, which requires diversity of citizenship.[76]

When the decision was handed down by Judge Joseph S. Lord III on Feb. 4, 1963 he upheld *U.S. News & World Report* in the belief that this particular case could not be tried at the federal level. In dismissing Edna's action he also observed that she would be unable to appeal in another jurisdiction because the statute of limitations was about to run out.[77]

Upon hearing the verdict, Edna wrote Harry Lore, attorney for Dorfman, Pechner, Sacks & Dorfman, "We are planning to borrow money [to cover expenses] since we don't have it at the moment. However, it will be forthcoming, and if Mr. Dorfman and you want to keep on being bothered with my case, I definitely would like to appeal this opinion, which I think is unjustified and unfair."[78]

On December 10, 1963 their petition was denied, leaving them with one final option, a Supreme Court appeal. They submitted a Petition for Certiorari to the highest court and requested that the judgment be reviewed. One last time, their appeal was turned down. Adding insult to injury, the successful party, in accordance with the law, submitted a bill for $494.35 to cover their printing expenses and other costs. (Dorfman settled for $250.)

In his final letter, Philip Dorfman wrote Edna: "This unhappy news is as distressing to us as it must be to you. There may, however, be some small consolation in realizing that whatever could have been done, was done in connection with your meritorious claim. But the vagaries of litigation are such that often the just are defeated because of technicalities which apply equally to all claims, regardless of their merit."[79]

In the early '60s, Edna and Bart returned to the United

76. Harry Lore, attorney for Dorfman, Pechner, Sacks & Dorfman, letter to Edna Moore Van der Schelling, September 2, 1962.
77. Joseph E. Lord, III, Opinion in the United States District Court for the Eastern District of Pennsylvania, Edna van der Schelling v. U.S. *News & World Report, Inc.* Civil Action No. 29692, February 4, 1963.
78. Edna Van der Schelling, letter to Harry Lore, February 9, 1963.
79. Philip Dorfman, letter to Edna Van der Schelling, April 21, 1964.

States. Earning a living in Mexico had become more challenging; conditions back home were more favorable to their return than in the past, and Bart's heart condition had worsened. By then, he had established a modest reputation as a Primitive painter. Returning to the United States or going elsewhere was becoming economically and politically more feasible for them and others like them. The ground was shifting.

"We should have known bad times were coming," people joked years after the political repression that characterized the second half of 1957 and most of 1958. "The Gods warned us, but no one was listening." Legend has it that a major calamity in Mexico is invariably preceded by a natural disaster. When Hernán Cortes and his small band of *conquistadores* invaded Mexico, bringing in their wake disease, destruction and political upheaval, no one was particularly surprised. The ancient deities had spewed forth one portent after another: tidal waves, drought, volcanic eruptions, floods and earthquakes.

In July 1957, in anticipation, no doubt, of the political unrest and official repression that followed, an earthquake struck Mexico City. Several buildings collapsed, water mains burst, and power failed city-wide. The Angel, a historic landmark celebrating Mexico's independence from Spain and the triumph of liberty over tyranny, was destroyed when the monument's one hundred and eighteen foot pillar shuddered and cracked sending the gilded angel, wings unfurled, tumbling from her perch. For an instant, those few bystanders in the vicinity caught their breath and crossed their fingers. Maybe the angel would flap her wings and glide to safety. A miracle? Of course. Along with its near-perfect climate, natural beauty and vast variety of resources, Mexico takes great pride in its miracles, and they occur with startling regularity. But not this time. This time the angel lost her balance, plummeted to the ground, and carpeted the Paseo de la Reforma in chunks of bronze. For many, the symbolic toll far exceeded the material damage.

Not surprisingly, the government restored the monument to its rightful place at the top of its towering pillar within a year. But dissidents, expatriates and natives alike, would have to wait somewhat longer for the dust to settle and for some semblance of political normalcy to return.

Chapter Seven

Saying *Adios*: Leaving Mexico

When we arrived in Mexico City in 1950 it was already a mega-lopolis. Balanced on the bones of an ancient civilization, its soil cradles the remains of mighty rulers and confines the uneasy spirits of its deities. As a result, Mexico's past is always obtruding: Ancient temple courtyards buckle under the weight of steel girders and thrust their columns upward, piercing concrete and glass. On our expeditions to the pyramids, my sister and I searched for pottery shards and *cabecitas*, little clay heads. Construction workers sold my father figurines and clay pots, which they dug up in the vacant lot a half a block from his office. Years later, subway builders shifted tons of soil and debris and plunged headlong into major ceremonial centers, uncovered the country's only round pyramid, and salvaged an immense stone disc representing the turquoise-skirted water goddess, *Chalchiuhtilicue*.

In the same way the past obtrudes on the present, Mexico suffuses your spirit, fogs your vision, clings to you like dust. Thus, you may leave Mexico, but Mexico never leaves you. And yet, despite that, the urgency of practical considerations: earning a living, educating one's children, attending to medical problems—was too great for many political expatriates. Not even the pull of ancient deities could restrain them. Acting on the same impulses—political, economic and social—which had led them to choose Mexico in the first place, almost all, including my parents, ended up leaving the country that had provided them refuge, be it for three months or thirty three years.

Ironically, many decided to leave just as the anti-Red furor generated by social unrest in the late '50s was beginning to subside. Once López Mateos's government had successfully consolidated its control over the country by jailing key opposition leaders, discouraging significant internal reforms, and forming new alliances, official interest in the ACGM—though not in the local resistance movements—waned. On the other hand, even if the government had wanted to, it would not have been easy. We may not have recognized it at the time, but we belonged to a vanishing species: The few who might have qualified were either leaving the country or fading away. Newcomers were scarce, and the handful who arrived were as likely to be greeted by those leaving Mexico as by those intending to remain.

For the ones who remained, however, life would continue much as before. They raised their children, worked, took classes, met people outside their immediate circle, and developed new interests. The financially solvent began purchasing homes in Mexico City or acquired a weekend retreat and were more likely to leave Mexico for an occasional trip than in the past. While they maintained contact with old friends, their dependency on each other declined and, throughout the '60s, the community drifted apart as some moved across town, left Mexico City altogether or, as was the case with a few living in the provinces, sought out larger city centers. A number grew old in Mexico and left their bones there; some remain in the country today.

Each case differed, of course. Obviously, those who remained for three or four years—the nomads—were, generally, not as touched by the country nor as committed to it as the old-timers would become. A large proportion of nomads were screen-writers and other Hollywood refugees, most of whom left during the '50s. These included Leonard Bercovici, Bernard Gordon, Ian Hunter, Ring Lardner Jr., Robert Rossen, Dalton Trumbo, John Wexley, Mike Kilian, and film maker Joseph Losey's former wife, Louisa Stuart. Though not part of the Hollywood contingent, journalists Charles Humboldt and A.B. Magil, writer Janos Szekely, a.k.a. John Pen; photographer Elizabeth Timberman, and literary agent Max Lieber also left in the early '50s, either returning to the United States or continuing on to Europe.

While they had many reasons for leaving, most of them left because there was no work, and they couldn't earn a living. (Years earlier five of the Hollywood Ten easily had been unable to pay legal expenses and support their families. So when Dalton Trumbo and Lester Cole received a breach of contract settlement from their studio they shared it with the others.)[1] Some had suffered financial setbacks resulting from devaluations, inflation or poor investments, and a number had little or no savings and were unable to generate steady incomes.

Writer Crawford Kilian wrote that: "Mike, [my father], was working for peanuts at Channel Two, putting the whole station on the air; [my mother] was working at Greengates School for our tuition costs and no salary. (She subsequently switched to the American School Foundation, where she received modest remuneration, and remained there until leaving Mexico in 1954.) We had a maid and a succession of fairly nice houses and apartments, but we were broke and painfully insecure."[2]

The Lardners told me they decided to leave in July, 1952 after only six months in Mexico. Ring's mother had suffered a stroke and could no longer take care of herself or her large Connecticut home. Frances explained: "We really had a lovely time in Mexico. . . . We took Spanish lessons, we had fun with our friends, the kids enjoyed the American School, we had really interesting and funny experiences, but we began to realize it was no place for us. We couldn't make a life there because I couldn't work, he couldn't work . . . and we just knew we'd be better off in a country where our language was the language of the country because that was a serious factor." They also hoped that once back in the States Frances, an actress, might be able to find a job in television or in the theater.[3]

Others managed to stay on for a few more years. The Kahns remained until 1955. According to Gordon's wife, Barbara: "For a time we managed financially. Living was inexpensive, and my husband wrote articles for *Holiday,* but a bad investment wiped out whatever assets we had and brought on my husband's heart attack. Rest and treatment helped but, at that point, we decided to return to the States. The boys were now nine and twelve, and we wanted them to have an American education. They were fluent in Spanish, but still we were *Norte*

1. Lester Cole, *Hollywood Red: The Autobiography of Lester Cole.* Palo Alto, Ramparts Press, 1981, p. 301.
2. Crawford Kilian, memoir, first draft, pp. 6-7.
3. Ring Lardner, Jr. and Frances Chaney, interview with author, May 25, 1991.

Americanos, and home beckoned. In August of '55 we joined my father, a widower. . . ."[4]

Aside from the economic worries besetting many of those who left shortly after arriving, the writers were likely to be affected by a concern unique to their profession. Novelist Howard Fast, who spent the summer of 1954 in Mexico, explained it this way when he pleaded with screenwriter Albert Maltz to return: "Come home with us. . . . You're a writer, You can't remain here and write well. This is an alien place to us, no matter how kind and generous they are. We have no roots here, and we don't have our language. Our lives are our language."[5]

While Fast's argument did not convince Maltz—he remained in Mexico for an additional eight years—he had apparently questioned his decision to leave the States years earlier. In a 1951 letter to his friend Herbert Biberman, Maltz wrote, "I continue to swing like a goddamn pendulum between the urge to return home and join the political fight, and the urge to stay in Mexico and write. Writing, after all, could itself be a weapon that reaches very wide."[6]

For screenwriter Dalton Trumbo, in Mexico just slightly over three years, remaining politically inactive was also a source of conflict. According to Jean Butler, "Dalton missed political activism—living on the edge, the excitement of commitment—whereas others might be warier after past experiences and want to remain uninvolved." However, he too was spending what little remained of his savings and began to worry about the financial consequences of staying on.

When Trumbo moved down to Mexico in 1950, it had taken him and his family, and the Butlers, who had accompanied them, two weeks to arrive: On the eve of their departure, Nicky, the Trumbo's eldest daughter, had come down with fever and a strep throat and they postponed the trip for three days. When they finally set off, their caravan consisted of the Butler's twelve year old Cadillac—every elegant detail intact down to its crystal bud vases—the Trumbo's almost new Packard, followed, in turn, by Dalton driving a jeep hauling a

4. Barbara Kahn, Commencement Address. Barbara Kahn's correspondence with author, July 11, 1991 to 1998.
5. Howard Fast, *Being Red*, p.333.
6. Larry Ceplair and Steven Englund, *Inquisition in Hollywood*, p. 415.

trailer, which contained his books and a motion sickness prone sheep dog. They decided to cover no more than two to three hundred miles a day and make occasional stops at points of interest so as not to tire the seven kids, the eldest of whom was thirteen. What they hadn't bargained for were the three day streptococcal layovers as each child fell ill, extending what is ordinarily a two or three day drive into a two week odyssey.[7]

His return to the United States with his two eldest children was far worse. Upon reaching Matamoros, he discovered that the trailer he had stored there had been broken into. Then, as he was about to cross the border, customs officials on the Mexican side appropriated his pre-Columbian artifacts, (removing antiquities from the country is illegal), provided him with a receipt, and sent him over to the American side where police detained him because he was driving without license plates. As he was about to drive off the battery went dead, the car refused to start, and a wrecking truck hauled them away to a motel in Brownsville. There were no vacancies. After the fourth try—it was 3:00 A.M. by then—he and his children found a place to stay. When he returned to Matamoros the following day, he discovered that lawyers could not help him retrieve his archeological pieces, and he returned to the States, procured a U.S. drive-through permit, drove back to Matamorros, and shipped his pre-Columbian collection back to Mexico City.[8]

His son, Chris, about thirteen at the time, recalled being stuck in a Brownsville motel while his father negotiated with customs: "Nicky and I discovered that the Mexican ten centavo piece worked like a quarter in the coin driven television at the motel. I imagine it worked the same magic in other machines too. As I recall, we were caught in this enterprise and 'real' money had to be put up. I was also glad to be in a country where the chocolate didn't taste of cinnamon. Beyond that, the trip was relatively uneventful; just an unemployed, blacklisted writer with scant prospects, two kids, a cat, and a dog hauling a trailer across the southwest toward an uncertain future."[9]

For the Trumbos and most of the other screenwriters, Mexico had been economically unfeasible. The Butlers were

7. Jean Butler, *Those Happy Few*, p. 28, pp. 20A-20D.
8. Dalton Trumbo, *Additional Dialogue*, pp. 286-90.
9. Chris Trumbo, letter to author, October 14, 1995.

among the few who had managed to eke out a living as writers and among those who remained the longest. Their decision to leave after nine years in the country was triggered by a string of events. When the September 19, 1960 issue of *U.S. News & World Report* was released and they were among the twelve families named in an article purporting to expose an American communist conspiracy in Mexico, their daughter Mary was mercilessly bullied by classmates. The article's appearance revived fears that the arrests and deportations which had occurred in 1958 might be resumed. Shortly after, they were given the opportunity to collaborate on a film script in Italy. For years, their ability to travel had been curtailed, but now they could no longer be denied passports on political grounds, so there was nothing to keep them from accepting the offer and moving on.

By then, many of their friends had left, and Hugo was becoming increasingly discouraged by what he perceived as an anti-foreign bias in both the screen industry and the country itself. There were other concerns, as well: Their eldest daughters had reached adolescence, and the Butlers were increasingly troubled by Mexican *machismo*. In addition, Mexico City, which despite its size, had boasted no more than half a dozen traffic lights during the early '50s and seemed more an extended village than a city, had pretty much disappeared. Aggressive driving, a rising population, an increase in crime, and the rapidly deteriorating environment would make their decision to move to Italy all the easier.[10]

Three years later, they returned to Mexico, briefly, and in 1964, moved to California. By the time they arrived, there was no doubt that, during their absence, changes had been taking place in the United States as well.

Of course, this did not mean that many of those returning would not be harassed or blacklisted,[11] but, it was clear McCarthyism was on its way out. A few writers would now begin to market scripts under their own names, and those exercising

10. Jean Butler, *Those Happy Few*, p. 146.
11. Bernard Weinraub, "Blacklisted Writers Win Credits For Screenplays," *New York Times*, Arts and Leisure, April 3, 1997, p. 1. In April 1997 the Screen Writers Guild announced that twenty-four film credits had been restored to ten blacklisted writers working under cover during the '50s and '60s. In the future, studios, will be asked to give formerly blacklisted writers credit on newly released prints and videos. As many as one hundred films are believed to have been written or co-written by blacklisted writers.

other professions were more likely to procure jobs, start a business, or return to school without fear of being shadowed or subpoenaed. In short, the risks inherent in returning had now lessened.

This had not been true less than ten years earlier. In 1955, when screenwriter Gordon Kahn and his family left Mexico and relocated in Manchester, New Hampshire, they were confronted with one difficulty after another: His wife, Barbara, had taught there previously, but when she applied for a teaching position the superintendent told her she had been instructed, despite her determination to hire her, to refuse her the job.

Within months, in February of 1956, Gordon was subpoenaed to appear at a New Hampshire hearing on communist subversion called by the state attorney general, who was interested in running for a national office. The FBI shadowed them, tapped their phone, and questioned their friends. The hearing was not scheduled until June, but in the meantime, the Supreme Court tried and dismissed a similar case. As a result, the charges against Kahn were dropped.

His son James was not so lucky. Upon his graduation from Harvard Medical School, he was refused a security clearance, which barred him from practicing Public Health, his field of choice. (Today he has a private practice with a specialty in tropical diseases.)[12]

James was not the only medical student to be denied clearance. After the Halperins left Mexico and moved to the Soviet Union in 1958, their son David attended the University of Chicago Medical School. As part of his studies, he arranged to work with a prominent Moscow surgeon for a few months so he could spend some time with his parents. Shortly before leaving, he learned that the FBI had notified the school of his "defection to the Soviet Union." Upon being informed that his return to the university might be compromised should he decide to go, he canceled his plans.

In 1961 he was called before the draft board. As a physician, he would have been inducted as an officer. Instead, he was rejected from the service and assigned the 1-y classification reserved for those judged "morally and mentally unfit." At the

12. Barbara Kahn, Commencement Address. Barbara Kahn's correspondence with author, July 11, 1991 to 1998.

top of his draft card someone had penned in a small "p" for "political."

By 1962, his parents were living in Cuba, and he was completing his residency at the Hines Veterans' Administration Hospital outside Chicago. Then, without warning, he was dismissed from his position. He appealed the dismissal through a lawyer, approached a number of well connected insiders, and was subsequently reinstated. Only years later, based on information in his FBI files and on a conversation with the former chief-of-surgery at Hines, would he learn that he had been fired as a result of FBI pressure aimed, not at him personally, since he was an exemplary student with no political history, but against his father.[13]

Max Shlafrock told me that when he left Mexico in April 1958, following the unsuccessful attempt to deport him, he was stopped upon arrival in New York, transported to a detention center, and held until an informal interrogation before the U.S. Immigration Service could take place. He was subsequently permitted to return home until the formal hearing a month later, at which time his citizenship was established beyond question, and he was released from custody.[14]

Although the small community continued to shrink, some of us chose to remain. Not I. In 1959, in the belief that Mexico had nothing to offer me, I applied to Michigan State University and, to my utter astonishment, was accepted despite substandard grades and mediocre SAT scores. During the summer preceding my enrollment, I harbored illusions of becoming a writer, a journalist or an English teacher, marrying someone my parents disapproved of, and settling down in some small American town. In short, I yearned for a life diametrically opposed to my parents'. By the time my cab pulled up in front of West Mayo Hall, my illusions had evaporated. I discovered that East Lansing, while minutes away from Michigan's capital, was merely an appendix of the University. It was more provincial than anything I had known in Mexico. At its heart was a football stadium. (The year I arrived Bubba Smith was playing for the Spartans, and we had a fine football team.) The College of

13. Don S. Kirschner, *Cold War Exile: The Unclosed Case of Maurice Halperin*, pp. 165-176.
14. Max Shlafrock, letter to author, May 6, 1997.

Agriculture, one of the best in the country, dominated the campus. It ran a model dairy farm—cows grazed in the fields surrounding MSU—and cultivated a vast expanse of farmland. As a result, the quality of dormitory food was exceptional, and I gained twelve pounds during my first year there.

Town consisted of one main street lined by a few stores, the dry cleaners, the Sputnik doughnut shop, a bank and a cafeteria. Most social life radiated around sporting events or was confined to the sorority and fraternity houses. (By then, my parents' politics had marked me: I refused to pledge, on principle.) In any case, there was only one Jewish sorority on campus, and I had been warned away from the others. I was assigned a room with the only other 'foreign student' in the dorm. Dorothy Hata was the daughter of a prosperous Hawaiian grocer, and her life-long dream was to become "the most beautiful woman in the world." We did, in fact, get along fairly well. That was not the problem.

Even if I had been raised in the Bronx I would have felt out of place at Michigan State. Perhaps I would have been better off in a more cosmopolitan setting. But the things I missed I would have missed no matter where I went. Things like salsa and tortillas with every meal, the smell of sun-dried sheets, a view hedged in by mountains, the words which only existed in Spanish, the reassuring whistle of a night watchman making his rounds, even my identity as a *gringa*. I would have missed those regardless of where I attended school. Here, invariably, whenever I mentioned having lived in Mexico, people would ask, "Oh, in Sacramento or Albuquerque?" (That someone they might meet on a daily basis could have lived outside the country was simply inconceivable.) Everything was sterile and predictable. I wrote my parents, "This place is sooooooooo boring. Nothing ever happens." After two and a half years at MSU and six additional months in New York City working as a secretary, I allowed my parents to wheedle me into returning to Mexico.

Despite personal circumstance and changing conditions, which had caused many to leave the country by the mid-'50s, I discovered, when I returned in 1962, that some old-timers still hadn't budged. (I sometimes felt as if I hadn't either: I moved back into my old bedroom in our Pedregal home. My old clothes still hung in the closet; my childhood books were still on the bookshelf and, from the garden, I had an unimpeded view of the mountains.)

Many of those oldtimers never would return to the United States. Over the years producer George Pepper, Zeiss optical representative Samuel Brooks, former CIO leader Charles Small, writer Cedric Belfrage, and more than a half dozen others died in Mexico and were buried there.[15]

Today a handful of political expatriates or their spouses, less than ten, still live in the country: Mary Belfrage, Anita Boyer, May Brooks, and sculptor Elizabeth Catlett are among them. With the exception of Anita, all live in Cuernavaca. Each has resided in the country for more then thirty-five years and will probably never leave.

In the long run, however, the majority did. Those who remained for more than ten years, such as former Amtorg counsel David Drucker, one-time U.S. Embassy employee Marion Davis, former Mexico City College instructor Jeanette Pepper, medical translator Asa Zatz, silver shop proprietor Berthe Small, and one-time Secretary of the Civil Rights Bail Fund, Fred Field, all returned to the United States in the '70s and '80s.

By then, the consequences of urban decay, which had troubled the Butlers, had taken its toll. Fred Field described the conditions which, in the end, played a role in driving him and other old-timers out: "The place . . . virtually ceased to exist as I first knew it. To describe more precisely what happened: smog, garbage, too many people with shattered dispositions, and hundreds of thousands of automobiles, buses and trucks finally took over." In addition, he and his wife, Nieves, worried about providing the best possible medical treatment for their daughter, Xochitl, who has cerebral palsy.[16]

Whether their inability to earn a living, anxiety over their children's prospects or disenchantment with Mexico's political

15. Others who died in Mexico included former labor organizer Gray Denton Bemis; Mildred Price Coy, who had headed the China Aid Council; historian Harold Coy; public health nurse Lini de Vries, businessman Samuel Novick, former Spanish Civil War nurse Frederica Martin, film maker Bill Miller, composer Conlon Nancarrow; Ray Spencer, staff executive of the Motion Picture Artists Committee and founder of the Hollywood Theater Alliance, both cited by the HUAC as Communist fronts, and contemporary dancer and choreographer, Waldeen.
16. Fred Vanderbilt Field, *From Right to Left*, pp. 259-262.

corruption, environmental decay, or deficient medical attention was responsible, they were reacting to an immutable fact of life: They were growing old. They wanted to simplify their lives. Perhaps they had cleaved to Mexico all those years because they felt secure and loved the natural beauty, the people, the climate, and the quality of life. Or maybe the magnetism exerted by the ancient deities had rendered them incapable of tearing themselves away.

Ultimately those who left returned to a country significantly altered from the place they had fled thirty, fifteen, or even ten years earlier. By the late '60s the integration movement was in full-swing; opposition to the Vietnam War was mushrooming; people started to recognize that the words 'feminism' and 'femininity' did not mean the same thing; and challenges to Cold War legislation had increased. In short, some of the very things they had fought for years earlier were becoming fashionable.

Yet despite this, they were in for a certain amount of culture shock. Readapting to the American way of life after a long absence—while far easier than their original adaptation to Mexico—was still a challenge: How does the dishwasher work? Can I make a right turn at a red light? How do I go about getting a credit card, a driver's license, a bank account? And what are TV dinners?

Upon their return, some started small businesses, went back to work, took classes or became involved in a wide variety of causes. They supported legal assistance programs and free choice, lobbied for a moratorium on nuclear testing and worked for the War Resisters' League, the National Emergency Civil Liberties Committee, and the Screenwriter's Guild. They became involved in literacy drives, the feminist movement, and First Amendment issues. With few exceptions, they didn't re-join the Party but, despite years of political inactivity in Mexico, most became involved in local or national issues upon returning to the States. To one degree or another, politics would always dominate their lives.

When they had left the United States originally, they did so out of political conviction or because outside pressures had grown unbearable and were unlikely to improve anytime soon. Politics, of course, played a major role in their decisions to leave. But I don't think their politics changed drastically as a result of having left. Certainly, had they remained in the States, some would have had greater access to the CP press. They may have participated in Party politics to an extent that was impossible in Mexico, and the Party may have played a more prominent role in their lives. However, by the time many political expatriates left home, the U.S. Party had already gone underground, its power had diminished considerably, its membership was shrinking, and what leadership remained, had grown less effective.

Accordingly, political expatriates were more likely to be influenced by international events such as the 1956 revelation during the 20th Congress of Stalin's atrocities, or the Hungarian uprising that same year, than by having absented themselves from the States. In the long-run, virtually all those in Mexico, with few exceptions, ended up leaving the Party. I imagine the majority of them would have reacted much the same had they remained in the States.

Others had never belonged or dropped out years before leaving home. Yet, while many expressed their disillusion with Party politics and were highly critical of Soviet leadership and the outcome of events under Communist rule, they continued to think of themselves as Marxists. I think this was true of my parents. The same ideals that had attracted them to the Party years earlier stayed with them for as long as they lived.

They were not alone. When I asked Fred Field, for example, if he thought Communism was dead he replied: "No. I don't think anything that is leading toward a better world [can die.] Where would I go if I weren't a Party member?" He explained that the word, 'Communism' has been used very loosely: "Even the Party now uses it [but they] don't know what they're talking about. . . . What has happened in the Soviet Union? Why did it happen? Certainly what happened is not what, when we started out, we thought [it]was. That's perfectly clear. And that's very true also of what happened to Mao Zedong's Communism. What do you call a present Chinese government . . . run by a very small group, whose sons go to the best universities, get the best jobs, etcetera, etcetera very much as has happened in the Soviet Union [where] the bureaucracy ran the place, but [which] still isn't capitalism either?"

He was writing a text on the subject, he told me. "But I'm doing this for my own benefit; I want to complete my life feeling that I've understood what I did, if nothing else. But if anybody else is interested, fine."[17]

Max Shlafrock wrote, "I never lost faith in the left movement. Neither did any of the people I was associated with. I am still confident in ultimate victory. . . . Marxism is alive and well. They [have to] discover how best to make it work, and I think they will."[18]

On the opposite side of the spectrum some, like Spanish Civil War veteran Eddy Lending, repudiated Communism even before leaving the United States in 1950. "I was a gadfly in the movement, a Don Quixote tilting at windmills," he told me during an interview. "I became disenchanted while I was in the army of the whole vicious, criminal movement, which [is what] it was."

He tried locating the people he had recruited into the Party in order to explain that he had made a terrible mistake, but his words fell on deaf ears. "They saw me as a traitor and a renegade," he told me, "and it's a tribute to many of those friendships that they survived the political/philosophical schism." (I remember, shortly before his death, that my father learned of Eddy's political change of heart. When he did, he was shocked.)[19]

Although many gave up on the Party, the movement and the Soviet Union, Lending's position was the most extreme. Edna van der Schelling told me, "I really started getting upset with them [the Soviet Union] when Stalin signed the non-Aggression pact with Germany in '39."[20] However, to my knowledge, neither she nor her husband, Bart, nor any of the others ever despaired of their political commitment to the degree that Lending had. Linda Oppen wrote me that her parents, George and Mary, were shocked at the extent of Stalin's atrocities revealed at the Twentieth Congress. "But the earlier Stalin-Hitler pact caused them more shock, though they remained Marxists always. The Party was not ideologically or intellectually important to them afterward."[21]

17. Fred Field, interview with author, August 7, 1992.
18. Max Shlafrock, letter to author, August 8, 1991.
19. Edward Lending, interview with author, August 6, 1991.
20. Edna van der Schelling, interview with author, August 1, 1991.
21. Linda Oppen, letter to author, December 2, 1991.

Jean Butler admitted that, because the Soviet Union had tried to implement socialism, they felt it was fulfilling a significant role in world history. Yet, despite that, they never believed Russian society was perfect and, given its history, knew it would take time to overcome its autocracy and anti-Semitism. But, for the Butlers, the Twentieth Congress revelations were less surprising than for others who had been more committed to the movement.

New Masses and *Mainstream* writer Charles Humboldt, for one, was profoundly affected. Jean Butler remembered: "[He] was dreadfully upset and very turned off at the . . . Twentieth Party Congress. So it caused some terrible heartaches for a lot of people and, after that, their only loyalty was to each other. That's what evolved out of those revelations, and you kept hoping that maybe with a different leader things would be a little different in the Soviet Union, that it wouldn't be a place of tyranny."[22]

In his oral history, Albert Maltz claimed that although he continued to believe in the ideals of a world without exploitation and in a planned economy: "The shock effect of the [Twentieth Congress] report on me, and I know on many others, was absolutely disemboweling. I can indicate one aspect of its effect by saying that for six months I could do no writing . . . I also felt that what had occurred in the Soviet Union was the greatest tragedy of all human history, a much greater tragedy than the murder of people in the Nazi holocaust because the Nazis had made clear that they had certain enemies that they wanted to get rid of, whereas in Soviet society with its magnificently proclaimed ideals there was such gross hypocrisy hidden behind the ideals in what was done by individual to individual."[23]

Historian Eric Bentley took Maltz's premise one step further when he wrote: "The Russian disaster would be many times worse than the German because it is more than a disaster, it is also a tragedy, the greatest historical tragedy of the past hundred years, because, beyond all the physical suffering, it represented the desolating disappointment of the great hope of our era: the hope of Socialist humanism, the hope, to put it modestly, of a

22. Jean Butler, interview with author, August 2, 1991.
23. Joel Gardner, *The Citizen Writer in Retrospect: Oral History of Albert Maltz*, pp. 877, 880.

society which, through Socialism, shall be less oppressed, less insecure, less miserable."[24]

In one of her letters Berthe Small expressed a similar disillusion: "I keep thinking of what [your parents] Mike and Belle would have to say about the present state of affairs in the USSR (to say nothing of Charles) and, smart as they were, I think they would feel the same sense of confusion and a certain loss of the dream we cherished and struggled for. My own bitterness is not directed at the changes themselves, which were necessary, but at the forces of reaction which are also being unloosed, so that the baby is being thrown out with the bath water."[25]

Belle and Mike lived in Mexico for thirty-two years, far longer than most but, like Fred Field and many of the others, were concerned about pollution and health care. Originally, hoping to escape the environmental blight plaguing Mexico City, they moved to Cuernavaca during the '70s but even the provinces were growing increasingly problematic. In addition, they missed the intellectual stimulation provided by a large city and felt increasingly isolated. The turning point, I think, was the night my mother was stung by a small albino scorpion and rushed back to Mexico City for treatment because the local hospital had run out of antivenin. "I can't remember these things happening before. Do you?" my mother asked me.

I think they had already made up their minds to leave the country long before they screwed up their courage to tell me. I was the only one left by then, my sister Judy and brother Paul having moved to the States years earlier.

I often wonder what induced me to remain in Mexico. (So few of us did.) I was attached to the country, of course, and felt less like a foreigner here than I had in the States. In short, Mexico was home to me. There was no going back: I earned a Degree in Education at the University of the Americas, formerly Mexico City College, and upon graduation, I returned to the American High School to teach English literature. After marrying my Mexican husband, Mauricio, in 1965 and giving birth to two children, Ricardo and Laura, any chance that I might

---

24. Eric Bentley, ed., *Thirty Years of Treason*, p. 944.
25. Berthe Small, letter to author, December 15, 1997, in reference to the breakdown of Communism in the Soviet Union.

follow my siblings' footsteps and return to the States was gone.

In the spring of 1982 Mauricio and I were sitting with my parents on the screened-in porch above the swimming pool of their Cuernavaca home. The smell of chlorine and newly mowed grass and fragments of our children's conversation—they were speaking Spanish—reached us sporadically accompanied by the occasional splash of a volleyball hitting water. "Do you think we'll have much trouble selling the house? The market's not all it should be," my father asked Mauricio.

"Well, after a devaluation property values generally decline. You'd do better to wait awhile."

"Hey, what's this about selling this house? Why would you sell the house?" I asked.

Silence. Then both my parents spoke at the same time. "Well, we figure this might be a good time to leave Mexico. You kids have all left home, and we no longer have to worry about running a business, and the house is awfully big. . . ." said my father.

"And Mexico's not what it used to be."

Yes, times had changed but so had my parents. They were no longer the single-minded young adventurers who, with $1,000 in savings, two children, and very little else except equal parts of idealism, optimism, and trepidation about remaining in the United States, had arrived in Mexico in 1950. By 1982, they had managed several successful small businesses, raised three children, and prospered economically. Upon their retirement, they traveled widely throughout Mexico and Latin America, Europe and Asia, and both returned to school. My father graduated *magna cum laude* with a B.A. in art history, and my mother studied literature and anthropology.

Despite the direction their lives had taken, they never lost their idealism, although they became disenchanted with the totalitarian side of Communism, I think. They would have said that what occurred in the Soviet Union and elsewhere was not the Democratic Socialism they envisioned when they committed themselves to working for the Communist Party and a more egalitarian society. Ultimately, this commitment had led to their leaving the United States.

Some thirty two years later, they left Mexico for entirely different reasons. They had aged and, like their contemporaries, they worried about the altitude, health facilities, and medical insurance and knew they would both qualify for Medicare if they returned to the States. Their move to Oakland in 1982 at the height of the Reagan period was, no doubt, a product of the same naiveté that had brought them to Mexico in 1950. This time, while no longer confronted with the language barrier, they probably knew as little about California as they had about Mexico. However, my father was determined to become a Berkeley student. That he never inquired about their admission policies prior to moving didn't faze him. They rented an apartment, shipped their paintings and some furniture up from Mexico, and moved in. My father then informed the university of his intentions. Only after he discovered that Berkeley was not as eager to admit him as he was to attend, did they move to San Francisco and become students at the University of San Francisco's Fromm Institute.

They gravitated toward others like themselves, bridge-playing political progressives with a love of art and music. My mother started to write a bit; my father rented a studio where he could continue to paint and sculpt, hobbies he had taken up in Mexico. They both started wearing berets. My father grew a mustache, allowed his sideburns to grow, and wore sports jackets over blue jeans and khakis. They joined the Gray Panthers, canvassed for local candidates with strong civil rights records, supported environmental programs, attended the opera, and traveled.

Belle and Mike, unlike their ancestors, Jews who changed addresses more often than they changed shoes and who left behind no mark more permanent than a pencil scrawl, died in the same country where they were born, in 1986 and 1989 respectively. According to their instructions, they were cremated. They left no instructions regarding their ashes. I don't imagine they gave it much thought. I certainly hadn't, but after my father's death I seriously considered returning them to Mexico. I would have buried my mother's in the garden of the house my father had built in the Pedregal. I believe it would have pleased her to know she had left something behind, symbolically at least, in a place where she had spent nearly half her life, the better half, I think.

My father's ashes I would have scattered all over downtown

Mexico City from the top of its tallest building, the *Torre Latino Americano*, not as a symbolic gesture, but in the knowledge it would have appealed to his sense of humor. He would have grinned at the knowledge that this way they'd never be rid of him. (Although with all the pollution they probably would never have noticed.)

Of course, I know, as I always have, that my parents and their political friends acted in good faith. Some were truly heroic in stature. I still believe some of their contributions have been long-lasting and significant. They raised national awareness on a wide variety of issues, made great strides in advancing the causes of women, African-Americans and other minorities, and were responsible for upgrading working conditions and fomenting adult education. They have, in fact, paved the way for subsequent social reform.

However, I am appalled by what I have since learned about the authoritarianism, excesses and dogmatism exercised by some American Party leaders and the atrocities and abuses of power committed by totalitarian governments in Communism's name. It has led, not only to our "throwing out the baby with the bath water," but to our throwing our faith away. We no longer believe we can reinvent the universe.

My parents did not live long enough to witness the collapse of Soviet Communism. But I did, and I'm sometimes astonished at the intensity of my own sense of loss and, though I hesitate to use the word, betrayal. When I began this research over nine years ago it was with the mindset of a pilgrim embarking on a sentimental journey: Julius Rosenberg's innocence was without question, all government informants were unreliable, the Soviet archives were closed to scholars, and *Venona* was a misspelling of a city in Italy. I believed my project would deal with two types of protagonists: the pursuers and the pursued. The first would consist of the FBI, the congressional committees and the informers, all of whom were prevaricators acting out of personal interest in order to strengthen the forces of reaction; the second included people like my parents, other political expatriates, and anyone whose association with communism, however slight, had landed them in trouble. I had a lot to learn.

We have lost our innocence. I certainly have, but I am not

alone. In speaking of McCarthyism, Keith, my anonymous intelligence source, wrote the following: "It would seem to me that there are aspects of this period that still rankle both ways. I certainly wouldn't advocate ignoring the injustices that were done to many truly innocent liberals by McCarthy, over-zealous Congressional committees, and other government agencies. I sincerely believe that, over the years, most of the people involved in the enforcement side of this issue regret the injustices. I was practicing law in Chicago during McCarthy's hey-day but later worked very closely with the people who had been deeply involved. They now recognize the mob psychology that influenced them during those days and regret their over-zealousness. I think a lot of their remorse (if that is the right word . . . maybe chagrin is more appropriate) is that they have become more educated about the world and the need for more toleration or appreciation of the views of others."[26]

We may agree that "more toleration or appreciation of the views of others" is desirable but I think, as more information about the American Party's and international communism's abuses becomes known, some are using it to justify the unjustifiable—McCarthyism. The wrongs committed in communism's name are being employed to keep the Cold War on the front burner. McCarthyism's reach was so wide it affected individuals on both sides of the political divide.

In an entirely different way, the influence exerted by Mexico on the political expatriates and, to a much greater extent, on their children, is incalculable. Those youngsters, like myself, who remained for any length of time, left Mexico much changed by their exposure to the people, way of life, language, government and world-view. As a result of their experience, they will never be quite the same.

Johanna Friedman, businessman Samuel Novick's daughter, wrote that she loved the country and people and became: " . . . bicultural and bilingual . . . a totally different person. . . . [There] was hunger and deprivation, [all around me] while we lived in luxury. So much beauty and so much injustice. I now take nothing for granted."[27]

David Drucker's daughter, Susan, wrote of having mixed

26. Keith, letter to author, March 8, 1993.
27. Johanna Friedman De May, letter to author, March 18, 1999.

feelings, about politics, on one hand; about living in Mexico on the other: "The shocking thing to me about my father's stories about Amtorg, the CP and his party card—was precisely that it implied a connection I had always assumed . . . *not* to exist. . . ." Yet she recognized that she was much enriched by the experience: "I only wish it were less schizophrenic, and that I had managed to integrate those years with the rest of my life."[28]

Dr. James Kahn, screenwriter Gordon Kahn's eldest son, was nine years old when he arrived. He remembered an occasion when Jean Butler stopped her car to make way for a long military convoy: "I told her, 'I don't mind waiting because they're Mexican,' and I asked Jean if my feeling that Mexico was a magical place was justified or was it because I was vulnerable? After a thoughtful pause, Jean replied, 'No, it was magical.' I felt Mexico changed my life. It was the biggest character builder, but at the same time, I felt guilty for missing so much of the United States. . . . I was plucked out of the great American vortex of materialism and waste and pop culture. Once that pattern was broken it never returned. . . . Upon returning [to the States] . . . I discovered myself to be five years to the side of what had occurred there—not five years behind. I wouldn't have understood how good Mexico was to us if I hadn't returned [to the States]."[29]

Lynne Kalmar, Kurt Odenheim's daughter, remembered Mexico as a "Wonderful place to be a teenager [in. There was] no peer pressure for drugs, sex, alcohol, etc. [and there were] cheap activities for teenagers, movies, dancing. . . ." Although she felt the adults thought it restrictive and elitist and were troubled by the pollution, she believed it was ". . . more internationalist, more sophisticated in some areas [but] more naive in others. I can live anywhere and will never really belong anywhere, although I can survive in almost any culture and social strata."[30]

They—Johanna, Susan, James, Lynne, and others I am still in touch with, left many years ago. At times I think of myself as the last of the 'Commie Kids' remaining in Mexico, although I know I'm not. I have heard that one of Lini de Vries' daughters

28. Susan Drucker Brown, e-mail to author, January 5, 1998; October 23, 1995.
29. James Kahn, telephone conversation with author, July 24, 1991.
30. Lynne Kalmar, letter to author, June 22, 1992.

and Elizabeth Catlett's, May Brooks's and Martha Dodd Stern's sons live in Mexico City or Cuernavaca; the daughter of a Hollywood couple lives in Tepoztlán, and Maurice Halperin's son, David, practices medicine in Chiapas. But in the final analysis, less than a dozen of us still reside in Mexico.

Occasionally, I wonder why I do. The conditions that drove others out—economic instability, the escalating population, pollution and insecurity—are far worse now than they were in the past. My children left Mexico over fifteen years ago; most of our family members have died or left the country, and my husband sold his business five years back. Practical considerations no longer tie us down.

A few months ago, after endless conversations about the decreasing quality of life, Mauricio and I decided to spend a month in Miami, a prelude to leaving Mexico for good. In the past few years I had often thought of leaving, usually following one unpleasant incident or another: An acquaintance was kidnapped or mugged or—of far less import—friends insisted I was incapable of understanding Mexican politics because I wasn't Mexican or the driver of the car behind me honked his horn, passed me on the right, rolled down the window and shouted *pinche gringa* because I refused to run the red light.

So we rented an apartment in North Miami, where the streets are spotless and traffic comes to a standstill when, for example, a swan and her cygnets wander off a golf course and try to cross the street. The stoplights always work, the super markets provide motorized wheelchairs with shopping baskets for those who need them, and no one drives above the speed limit. Even the fallen leaves are so artistically arranged I could swear they ask for landing clearance before they hit ground. The streets don't smell of sewage or diesel fuel. (Of course, they don't smell like fresh tortillas or roses or mangos either.)

In general, everything lived up to our expectations. I actually began to have expectations—something I'd managed very well without in Mexico—and grew short-tempered on the few occasions when things didn't turn out as I thought they should. I felt completely safe. I even stopped locking the car door and placing my handbag on the floor. I started buckling my seatbelt. Everything was orderly, civilized, clean and tedious. We were never surprised. In Mexico something as commonplace as standing on line at the bank, stepping off the sidewalk or buying a taco can be full of surprises. (Just this morning I read in the paper about a man driving peacefully down the *Periferico* just as someone jumped off a bridge spanning the freeway, crashed though his windshield and died. The driver survived.) True, some surprises are decidedly unpleasant—but others can be instructive, surreal, inspirational or just plain goofy.

I started to think that if we did leave Mexico, it would probably be for the wrong reasons: There's a tendency to abandon one place for another in the belief we will end up, not only in a new location but in a new life, that we will turn into someone else. (I remembered my mother packing her *Settlement Cookbook* and her knitting when she left New York believing, no doubt, that once in Mexico she would master those skills that had eluded her for years.) No matter where we live, each of us inhabits our own little pocket of joy or sorrow. The older you get the truer this is. The young, at least, are more adaptable and likely to grow in unexpected directions.

While all of us who lived in Mexico during the McCarthy years may have retained our individual identities, Mexico left no one untouched. We developed new insights and interests and, as a result, choices. It broadened our outlook and changed our habits: We grew to love highly seasoned food, unrestrained color and bold design and *mariachi* music sung slightly off-key. Today we are less easily embarrassed by overt demonstrations of affection or strong emotion than we once were, and we have lost some of our earnestness and high regard for fastidiousness, punctuality and rational thought. We've learned to take nothing for granted and know, no matter where we live, that what might be considered bizarre or surreal elsewhere is merely routine in Mexico.

For me, Mexico did much more than that. It gave me a story. In part, maybe that's why I've remained there as long as I have. It is where the story is, and as long as I hang around, I can keep an eye on it, piece it together and write it down.

Epilogue

A Personal Note: Why I Wrote This Book

I am still here and so is my story, but the Mexico we knew, the conditions that created us, the things we, and in particular, our parents represented, are rapidly disappearing. Inevitably, our stories will too. They already have. We are a vanishing species.

I would like to believe that by recording these voices I've found a way to hoodwink the Angel of Death. An ancient ritual—the Orthodox Jews, Hmong and others still practice it—is to choose a new name for the dying, in the belief Death will be fooled and the 'death warrant' rendered undeliverable.[1] By writing out these histories and producing a book I am 'renaming' these accounts, changing them into something else, something more likely to evade Death, to escape oblivion. This is true of all creative acts I suppose. Nothing can revive the past, it will never be what it was, but at least it will BE—for a while anyway.

That is what I would like to believe, but I have yet to fully understand, and probably never will, why getting this all down in writing has dominated my life to the extent that it's become an obsession.

I suppose, in part, it stems from the nature of our time in Mexico. History is always elusive, but some histories are more elusive than others. Certainly, this is true of the events recounted here. Since secrecy, inevitably, is an offshoot of exile, there is much we'll never know: Our time in the country, more like a sneeze than pneumonia, has made little difference in the permanent scheme of things. In the end, the country is not

1. In *The Spirit Catches You and You Fall Down: A Hmong Child, her American Doctors and the Collision of Two Cultures*, (New York: Farrar, Strauss & Giroux, 1998), Anne Fadiman writes that the Hmong will change a child's name in order to fool the *dab* that has stolen its soul.

much changed—if at all—for our having lived there. In fact, I originally considered naming this book, *The Invisible Exile*.[2]

Undoubtedly, some political expatriates were more successful at invisibility than others, but even in the case of those who weren't, stories tend to die with their owners, and their owners are dying. I would become even more aware of this in the course of writing this book.

Although I was fortunate to establish contact with John Menz, Bill Miller, Conlon Nancarrow, Waldeen Falkenstein, David Drucker, Fred Field, Maurice Halperin, Ring Lardner Jr., Harry Schaeffer, Edna Moore Van der Schelling, and Stirling Dickinson prior to their deaths, Ray Spencer, Ian Hunter, Martha Dodd Stern and Fredericka Martin eluded me.

So did my parents, and on some level I was angry at them for dying—worse yet, for abandoning me—and, no doubt, for the commission of crimes, some imaginary, some real. The anger, and along with the anger, guilt—for feeling angry I suppose, for not caring enough when they were alive, and for not having made things easier for them when I could have—surfaced following their deaths. I always supposed it originated with our having fled New York in October of 1950.

So that became my point of departure, and I started searching for answers and writing them down in the belief that once I understood what, if anything, they had done and why they had done it, I could forgive. And they would forgive me too, because at some level we 'entertain the vain notion that the dead will listen to us, which is why much of what we write is meant for them.'[3]

If I sometimes felt as if I were writing for the dead, I also knew I was in debt to the living. Every time I approached someone for an interview there was an implicit understanding: If you give me your answers I will write them down. Although I know they probably would have given them to me anyway, I felt an obligation to fulfill my side of the bargain: Some had been my friends for many years; others I'd met in the course of the

---

2 I later changed the title to *Gathering of Fugitives*, a phrase I filched from Bruce Cook, *Dalton Trumbo*, p. 226.
3 Marta Kornbluth, "Los Libros de los Muertos" in *Miriam's Daughters: Jewish Latin American Women Poets*, Santa Fe, New Mexico: Sherman Asher Publishing Company, 2001, p. 134

writing. I'd grown fond of them and didn't want to disappoint them. But there were times when I seriously questioned my own sanity in having embarked on this project and considered dropping it. That's when knowing they were counting on me to finish made me persevere.

I doubt I would have been driven to write this book and to persevere when I was much younger—in my thirties or early forties—because, in effect, the young don't really believe they are going to die. I know I didn't. But my parents died when I was approaching fifty—I'm thankful to them for hanging around as long as they did—because only with age had I developed the obstinacy and hard-headedness required to see this through. By then, I was old enough to recognize that, yes, I was going to die, but I knew I had a fairly good chance of living long enough to finish the research and the writing, no matter how slowly I worked. (Of course, I had no idea I would spend between nine and ten years on this book.)

Thus, after Belle and Mike died, when I became aware of how little I knew, I was haunted by a feeling of loss, not only for my parents, but for their story, and I wandered out in search of it. At least, that's what I tell myself. But sometimes, when I'm feeling even less rational than I usually do, I'll let my imagination squirm loose from its leash. That's when I believe it was the story that came searching for me and took me by the hand like the ghost in the Mexican ballad and legend, *La Llorona*, the weeping woman. She is the eternal wanderer who haunts the life of her lover, shadowing his every move for all eternity.

Maybe now that I have come to terms with my own private *Llorona*, the story of my parents and the other American political expatriates who sought refuge in Mexico during troubled times, she will go away and let me be.

Appendices

Appendix I

Identification of Subjects

A wide variety of personalities played key roles in this story. Listed below, in the order in which they appear in the text, are some of those who participated in the drama of U.S. exile in Mexico. (An italicized description of sources used follows each name. The term 'written documentation' refers to books and books in progress, some written by the subjects themselves, articles in periodicals, etc.)

Prologue: Why We Fled the Bronx

—Meyer (Mike) and Belle Zykofsky are my parents. Few outside their families, a small circle of friends, and the FBI, who investigated them over a period of 18 years in connection with charges of conspiracy and espionage, have ever heard of them. They were born in the United States, children of impoverished East European immigrants and, as adolescents, were attracted by the Communist Party's Popular Front and participated enthusiastically and openly in left-wing politics. My father ran for a New York City Assembly seat for the American Labor Party (ALP), a progressive political pressure group, and was chairman of their Parkchester branch. (For a short time, the ALP exerted considerable influence on New York's local politics.) Then, in the fall of 1950, they fled the Bronx for Mexico not to return to the United States to live, until thirty two years later.
(Interviews with their friends, family and FBI documents.)

Chapter One: The Impulse

—Although avant-garde composer Conlon Nancarrow is celebrated for his contributions to twentieth century music, his political history is less well known. He began his residence in

Mexico in 1940 as a protest against the U.S. Government for refusing to renew his passport. Their reason? He had been a member of the Communist Party and served for two years in the Abraham Lincoln Brigade, the American volunteer corps which supported Spain's popularly elected Government in opposing Franco during that country's Civil War. He died in Mexico City in 1997.
(Interview with Conlon Nancarrow and written documentation.)

—"They called me a premature and exaggerated anti-fascist," Spanish Civil War veteran Wiliam Colfax Miller told me. He arrived in Mexico in 1939 having heard that a man with his military experience could become a general in the Mexican Army. He never became a general, but shortly after his arrival, he met Ramón Mercader, the man who killed Leon Trotsky, and by the time he died in Ajiic, Mexico in 1994, had left his mark on the Mexican film industry. An actor, cameraman, director, and producer, he participated in over 150 films and published the *Mexican Motion Picture Directory* for 25 years.
(Telephone interviews with Bill Miller, personal correspondence and written documentation.)

—While still a student at the University of Texas, economist and academic John "Brick" Menz's political activism attracted the FBI's attention: "My name became a household word on campus. . . . That's when we moved to Mexico to work at Mexico City College." Once there, he continued to fuel the FBI's suspicions. He made front page news when he marched down the Paseo de la Reforma between Diego Rivera and David Alfaro Siqueiros in support of U.S. presidential candidate Henry Wallace.
(Telephone interview with John Menz, personal correspondence and written documentation.)

—Dancer, teacher, choreographer and writer, Waldeen—Falken-stein was her surname but she rarely used it—is credited with introducing contemporary dance to Mexico, staging the earliest 'mass' ballets, and leaving her mark on a series of original and authentically Mexican works. Arriving in Mexico for the first time in 1931, she returned intermittently until settling there in 1948 and was still residing in her adopted country when she died in 1994.
(Interview with Waldeen and written documentation.)

—According to Asa Zatz, a former Yale Drama School student who specialized in theatrical lighting, wrote and directed for film and theater, and eventually became a translator of medical texts, going to Mexico was a result of his wife Waldeen's migration. Following their divorce he stayed on. However, the FBI claimed that during the war he had been employed by the Office of Strategic Services, a precursor of the CIA, and fled to Mexico seeking refuge from Congressional committees and, perhaps, from court action.
(Interview with Asa Zatz, personal correspondence and written documentation.)

—Today a highly regarded sculptor and graphic artist, Elizabeth Catlett originally went to Mexico in the '40s to study at the "Taller de Gráfica Popular," (Workshop of People's Graphic Art). Following the breakup of her marriage to American artist Charles White, she married Mexican painter Francisco Mora and remained in Mexico. But when she returned to the United States in 1947 to give birth to her first child, she found herself under investigation for her support of civil and labor rights and her earlier involvement with the George Washington Carver School, on the Attorney General's list of Red Front organizations. After authorities tried to deport her from Mexico in 1958, she became a Mexican citizen and presently resides in Cuernavaca.
(Interviews with Elizabeth Catlett and written documentation.)

—Philip Stein, a scenic artist for Columbia Pictures, was jailed, fired from his job, and barred from the studios following the United Scenic Artist's strike, one of a series of turbulent confrontations between a progressive union, Conference of Studio Unions, and the studios. He and his wife, Gertrude, a teacher, moved to San Miguel Allende in 1948 where he studied at the Art Institute on the G.I. Bill. They later settled in Mexico City and, for the next decade, Philip worked closely with muralist David Alfaro Siquieros.
(Interview with Philip and Gertrude Stein, personal correspondence and written documentation , FBI documents.)

—Though not a political expatriate himself, Mexican writer, journalist and economist, Alonso Aguilar befriended a number of them. Fired from his post at the National Bank of Foreign Commerce by President Ruiz Cortines, allegedly for his ties to the left, he was an active participant in Mexico's intellectual life during the '50s and '60s: He taught at the University of Mexico, was director of the Center for Mexican Studies (CEM), edited *Indice*, was co-founder of "Editorial Nuestro Tiempo" and director and founder of *Estrategia* magazine. However, it was as General Coordinator of the National Liberation Movement, which encouraged political unity among members of Mexico's fragmented left, that he became *persona non grata* in the United States. *(Interviews with Alonso Aguilar and written documentation.)*

Chapter Two: Perforated Lives

U.S. resident aliens who feared they might be deported:

—Dutch born Bart van der Schelling had been a circus clown, a political visionary, an opera singer, and an officer in the International Brigades during the Spanish Civil War. Fearing deportation from the United States, he arrived in Mexico in 1950 where he tuned pianos for a living until a heart attack forced him to retire. Although more than fifty at the time, he started painting, achieving some recognition as a primitive artist. He and his wife, Edna Moore, returned to the United States in 1962 after she was fired from her job at the American School for political reasons. *(Interview and personal correspondence with his wife, Edna Moore.)*

—Although not a Communist, Canadian Anita Boyer, who regards herself as apolitical, had a penchant for marrying them, and not just any Communist. Both her first and second husbands, Raymond Boyer and Frederick Vanderbilt Field, were millionaires, achieved notoriety for their political radicalism—the first in Canada, the second in the United States—and went to prison. Pressuring Anita with the threat of deportation was a way of striking back at her second husband, heir to $72 million and a member of the Institute of Pacific Relations (IPR) Board. (Field helped establish and finance its magazine, *Amerasia*, and was the Secretary of the Civil Rights Bail Fund.) Although Anita agreed to leave the United States in 1953, the immigration agent who permitted her voluntary departure rather than deportation, which would have barred her re-entry into the United States indefinitely, lost his job. *(Interviews with Anita Boyer; interview, personal correspondence with Fred V. Field and written documentation.)*

—Between 1950 and 1955 British subject, Cedric Belfrage, writer, co-founder and editor of *The National Guardian*, was denounced as a Soviet courier by government witness Elizabeth Bentley, called to testify before both the House and the Senate, and jailed by immigration authorities on two occasions. Deported to England, he traveled extensively, finally settling down in Cuernavaca, Mexico in 1963. Once there, he and his wife, Mary, operated a guest house that became a meeting place for the politically expatriated and their friends.
(Interview with Mary Belfrage and written documentation.)

Party or Party press envoys:

—Charles Humboldt a.k.a. as Clarence Weinstock, was well known in Party circles for his close association with the *New Masses* and *Mainstream* magazines. Originally in Mexico to study mural painting, he lived there between 1952 and 1954 with Elizabeth Timberman, an accomplished photographer. Despite biographers' claims that his stay in Mexico lasted only a few months, residents here dispute that.
(Interviews with friends and written documentation.)

—The *Daily Worker* sent A. B. Magil, his wife and daughter to Mexico in the summer of 1950, but when the newspaper ran out of funds nine months later, the Prague based news agency, Telepress, hired him. However, the Magils left precipitously within the following year upon discovering that plainclothesmen had been interrogating their child about her father's activities. In 1954 Abe returned to cover a Party convention, was abducted by agents, detained for four days, and then deported.
(Interview with Harriet and A.B. Magil , personal correspondence and written documentation.)

—During the second half of 1950, the Communist Party smuggled scholar, writer and journalist, Abraham Chapman, his wife and two daughters out of the United States and into Mexico. Shortly after, the family was sent to an isolated village where they were hidden by a poor Mexican family. Within a few months, Chapman had been spirited out of Mexico, and by the end of 1950 the family was reunited in Czechoslovakia.
(Personal correspondence with his daughter, Anne Kimmage, and written documentation.)

—When the Party warned that they might be singled out for a major investigation, May and Samuel Brooks left New York for Paris, where they remained for a year. Since 1949 May had organized the Party underground for Manhattan. She was particularly vulnerable to attack because her contact, John Lautner, turned government informant. A year later, they left Paris for Mexico. After Sam died in 1962 May remained there.
(Interviews with May Brooks.)

Those accused of conspiracy and espionage:

—Maxim Lieber was a leading literary agent who represented Howard Fast, Albert Maltz and a number of prominent social realists including Erskine Caldwell. Named by Wittaker Chambers, a longtime friend, during the Alger Hiss trial, he refused to cooperate with the FBI, took his family to Mexico and later settled in Poland where he worked in Polish publishing. Disgusted with conditions there, he returned to the United States after seven years.
(Interviews with friends and written documentation.)

—Martha Dodd, writer and daughter of William Dodd, President Roosevelt's Ambassador to Germany prior to WW II, chose Mexico rather than risk the inevitable subpoena. She and her husband, Alfred K. Stern, a Chicago financier, prominent in left-wing activities, had been accused of espionage by informant Boris Moros. Settling in Mexico at the end of 1953, they remained for close to four years until learning that the American government was attempting to secure their deportations from Mexico. They then purchased fraudulent Paraguayan passports and fled to Czechoslovakia never to return to the United States.
(Interviews with friends, written documentation procured through the Library of Congress, and FBI documents.)

—Professor, journalist and writer Maurice Halperin headed the Latin American division of the Office of Strategic Services in 1943, but resigned in 1946 when Elizabeth Bentley brought his name to the attention of the FBI. In 1953, he was called to testify before the Senate Internal Security Committee, accused by informer Nathaniel Weyl of representing the Texas and Oklahoma wings of the CPUSA at Communist meetings in Mexico, and suspended with pay from Boston University pending an

investigation. He opted to move to Mexico before the hearings could be held. During a 1958 clamp-down on political expatriates in Mexico, attempts were made to deport him, and he left Mexico voluntarily for the Soviet Union in 1958. The recently revealed Venona Decrypts, intercepted wartime intelligence cables between the U.S.S.R. and its embassies, indicate that Halperin passed material to the Soviets during WWII.
(Personal correspondence with Maurice Halperin and his biographer, Don Kirschner, and written documentation.)

—As a founding member of the National Lawyers Guild, legal advisor to the Soviet run Amtorg Trading Corporation, and the executive director of the American-Chinese Export Company, David Drucker and his wife, Esther, a folk singer, were bound to be singled out for investigation by the FBI. In 1952, two years after his passport was confiscated, he moved with his family to Mexico City. David was targeted for deportation by Mexican authorities in 1958 but managed to elude arrest. He returned to the United States in 1976.
(Interview, telephone interview and personal correspondence with David Drucker; interview with his daughter, Emmy; personal correspondence with his daughter, Susan; written documentation and FBI documents.)

The blacklisted Hollywood writers and political activists:

—One of the Hollywood Nineteen, Gordon Kahn wrote *Hollywood on Trial*, a journalistic account of the Hollywood Ten hearings, which terminated his own career. *Boy's Town* and *All Quiet on the Western Front* were among his screenplays, and he collaborated with artist Al Hirschfeld on a book about New York speakeasies, *Manhattan Oases*. Under the pseudonym Hugh G. Foster he contributed regularly to *Holiday Magazine* . Following his death, his only novel, *A Long Way from Home*, was published.
(Interview with his son, Tony, personal correspondence with his wife, Barbara, and written documentation.)

—At the time of his indictment as one of the Hollywood Ten, Albert Maltz was well established as a writer: he had published two novels, three plays, and seven screenplays. The author of a collection of short stories, his work had appeared in *The Best Short Stories* in 1936, 1939 and 1941, and he received the 1938

O'Henry Memorial Award for the best American short story. Well known for his outspoken defense of Popular Front causes, Maltz would settle in Mexico for 12 years after being released from prison.
(Interviews with friends and written documentation.)

—George Pepper's highly visible position as executive secretary for the Hollywood Independent Citizens Committee of Arts, Sciences, and Professions, a leading Popular Front alliance of liberals and radicals, placed him in the front lines when attacks against the progressive community intensified. Although he switched careers and turned to movie production, this would not prevent U.S. authorities from removing his passport. He and his wife, Jeanette, an economist and statistician, would leave Hollywood in 1951. Following his death in 1969, Jeanette returned to the States.
(Interviews with Jeanette Pepper, personal correspondence and written documentation.)

After his release from prison, screenwriter Ring Lardner Jr., convicted for contempt of court as one of the Hollywood Ten, and his wife, blacklisted actress Frances Chaney, found in Mexico a haven where they could live cheaply and well. There, surrounded by their closest friends, they picked up the pieces of their shattered lives, but then, after only six months in Mexico, decided to return to the United States.
(Interview with Ring Lardner Jr. and Frances Chaney, personal correspondence and written documentation.)

Those who arrived following hearings into Communist conspiracy in Miami:

—Up until his death, labor leader Charles Smolikoff (Charlie Small) was known for his reckless enthusiasm and untiring support of a multitude of causes. He and his wife, Berthe, a former teacher, also active in union work, had been forced out of the leadership during the Transportation Workers' Union purges in 1948 and were running a small store in Miami Beach. Both were arrested and jailed for contempt during the Miami "Little Smith" trials in 1954. Released before his wife, Charles was instructed by his attorney to leave for Mexico immediately and wait there until she and the children could join him.

(Interviews with Berthe Small, personal correspondence and written documentation.)

—Max Shlafrock was a construction contractor, active in the Jewish community, and the recipient of an official commendation for building excellence from the Miami municipality. He was called to testify on two occasions: in New Orleans before the Eastland Committee and in Miami. During this second hearing, he stood on the Fifth Amendment and was sentenced to a year in prison for contempt, but was released within a few weeks. After fraudulent evidence linking him to the Party was presented in court, he successfully cleared himself of the charges but was, none-the-less, unable to continue working as a Miami contractor. On two occasions, Mexican agents, presumably in the employ of the FBI, attempted, unsuccessfully, to deport him from Mexico. *(Personal correspondence with Max Shlafrock and written documentation.)*

—Dr. David Prensky, a Miami Beach dentist, was identified by government witness Paul Crouch, as a Party member. He had been active in progressive causes including the American Veteran's Committee and Freedom House. Although he believes he could have continued his private practice in Miami, he and his wife decided to try living in Mexico "for a while." They remained for over 28 years. *(Interviews with David Prensky, personal correspondence and written documentation.)*

Chapter Three: Bridging the Cultural Gap

—Though few in the community were aware of his literary reputation and knew him only as a West Coast Party activist, George Oppen went on to win a Pulitzer Prize in poetry. During his stay in Mexico he earned his living as a furniture maker. *(Interview with George Oppen's daughter Linda, personal correspondence and written documentation.)*

—Jean Rouverol and Hugo Butler were known, not only for their screenplays, but for their commitment to the Screenwriters' Guild, resented by Hollywood studios for effectively negotiating higher wages and fairer deals for writers. Upon hearing he was to be subpoenaed, Hugo crossed the border into Ensenada until Jean and their four children could join him.

(Interviews with Jean Rouverol, daughter Mary and son Michael, and personal correspondence with all three, written documentation and FBI documents.)

—At the end of 1951, Dalton Trumbo, one of the Hollywood Ten and probably one of Hollywood's better known screenwriters, was released from prison. Soon after, he and his family joined the Butlers and drove to Mexico City. Unable to earn a living there, the Trumbos returned to the United States after three years. In 1960, Dalton officially broke the blacklist after Otto Preminger openly acknowledged having hired him to script the Academy Award winning film *Exodus.*

(Personal correspondence with Dalton Trumbo's daughter, Nikola, and interview and personal correspondence with his son, Chris, as well as written documentation.)

—When Spanish Civil War nurse Lini Fuhr de Vries, a.k.a. Lini Fuhr, recruited Elizabeth Bentley into the Communist Party in 1935, she had no way of knowing that a decade later Bentley would accuse her of conspiracy. Arriving in Mexico in 1949 with her young daughter and little more than the clothes on her back, de Vries collaborated closely with Mexican government public health officials in Oaxaca, taught anthropology and public health at the University of Veracruz, and became a citizen of Mexico, where she resided until her death in 1982.

(Interviews with friends and written documentation.)

—A Spanish Civil War veteran and old family friend, Edward Lending was disenchanted with Communism by the time he arrived in Mexico in 1950. While stating that his reasons for leaving the States were essentially non-political, he had been identified as a former Party member, and he continued to stay in contact with the expatriate community.

(Interview and personal correspondence with Edward Lending and FBI documents.)

—One would assume that Margaret Larkin would be better known, given her background as a folk singer and preserver of the Ella May Wiggins' Gastonia Songs, her varied publications, including three books, and her union activities. Married to screenwriter Albert Maltz, she accompanied him to Mexico where she wrote *Seven Shares in a Gold Mine.* The book dealt with

an aborted attempt to sabotage the plane in which she and her daughter were traveling to Oaxaca along with a group of workers who had been heavily insured by their employer.
(Interviews with friends and written documentation.)

—A citizen of Mexico, playwright, journalist and professor Carlos Prieto was a close friend to many of the political expatriates and shared some of their political convictions.
(Interviews with Carlos Prieto.)

—Mike Kilian, son of character actor Victor Kilian, was one of the few to arrive in Mexico with employment. But during his absence from the States his father was subpoenaed in his stead, his marriage disintegrated and he lost his job with Mexico's newly inaugurated television industry. Three years later, he returned to California without his family, without a job and with few prospects.
(Interviews with friends, personal correspondence with his son, Crawford, and written documentation.)

—Kurt Odenheim had been a Communist Party organizer in the late '20s and early '30s. Although he left the Party in '37, his former loyalties would mark him. As a resident alien, he feared deportation and, therefore, fled to Mexico in 1954. Once there, he established a company to supply radio and phonograph cabinets to major outlets. He never returned to the United States.
(Interview with his daughter Lynn Kalmar, interviews with friends.)

Chapter Four: Lying Low

—Keith, a pseudonym, is a retired CIA Senior Operations Officer with wide experience in Mexico and Latin America during the '60s. A historian and scholar, he has published several books on espionage.
(Interview with Keith and personal correspondence.)

Former covert operations officer in Mexico, Ecuador, Uruguay and Washington, Philip Agee resigned from the CIA in 1969. He wrote *Inside the Company* and *On the Run*, detailing U.S. intelligence operations.
(Personal correspondence and written documentation.)

—The San Miguel Allende Art Institute was run by Stirling Dickinson, an upstanding member of a prominent Chicago

family. Politically conservative and well regarded by the American Community and local authorities, he was deported from Mexico in 1950 on trumped up charges and, seven years later, viciously attacked by the press and labeled as the man who "keeps open house for Communists and fellow travelers."
(Personal correspondence, written documentation and FBI documents.)

—Morton Sobell's two month stay in Mexico was, perhaps, the briefest exile and, certainly, the most controversial. Two and a half weeks prior to Julius Rosenberg's arrest, Sobell rented an apartment in Mexico City. When he learned of Rosenberg's detention, he tried to find transportation from Mexico to Europe, but was kidnapped by Mexican agents working for the Americans and, along with his family, handed over to American authorities. Sobell achieved notoriety when he was convicted of conspiracy to commit espionage in collaboration with the Rosenbergs and was subsequently imprisoned.
(Personal correspondence and written documentation.)

—One of the twelve top Party leaders indicted in 1948 under the Smith Act, Gus Hall, in a failed attempt to avoid prison and escape behind the Iron Curtain, was apprehended by U.S. agents in Mexico City within 24 hours of having crossed the border. Sentenced to an additional three years in prison for having fled bail, he was not released until 1959. Today, he is the official leader of the Communist Party in the United States.
(Written documentation.)

—As Secretary General of the Mexican Communist Party from 1963 until 1981, writer, editor, and Director of the Study Center for Labor and Socialist Movements (CEMOS), and up until recently, Delegate of Coyoacan for Mexico City's opposition government, Arnaldo Martinez Verdugo has been an acute observer of the Mexican political scene. His understanding of the political scene in Mexico during the past decades provides insight into his government's policy toward Americans in exile.
(Interviews with Arnaldo Martinez Vergugo and written documentation.)

Chapter Five The Temperature Rises

—Writer-historian Ralph Roeder settled in Mexico in 1943 and

received Mexico's Aztec Eagle Award, the most prestigious prize given a foreigner, for his two volume biography on Benito Juarez, but this did not prevent Mexican agents from arresting and detaining him for ten days. He had many friends among the political expatriates and was the brother-in-law of Jacob "Pop" Mindel, who headed the Party's Marxist cadre school and had been imprisoned under the Smith Act.
(Interviews with friends and written documentation.)

—The Soviet Union's Cultural Attaché in Mexico from 1953 to 1957 and a KGB agent until his resignation in 1957, Yuri Paparov has learned to live with controversy. He claims the underground network he established, directed for the most part against the Americans, remained intact and continued to function for many years with good results. As the 1958 election of President Lopez Mateos approached, newspapers linked him with labor and student unrest, and he was accused of associating with Americans living in exile. Presently a journalist and writer residing in Mexico City, he has collaborated closely with the Leon Trotsky Museum, published extensively in the Mexican press, and translated Latin American literature into Russian.
(Interviews with Yuri Paparov and written documentation.)

Chapter Six Surviving the Heat

—Identified as one of those who spied for the Russians during World War II, Enos Regent Wicher worked for the Wave Propagation Group in Columbia University's Division of War Research. After moving to Mexico he taught an engineering course at Mexico City College.
(Interviews with friends and written documentation.)

—In 1949, following a hearing before the HUAC, Samuel Novick settled in Mexico. As the former president and treasurer of the Electronics Corporation of America, reportedly a heavy contributor to Communist organizations, Novick would have been particularly vulnerable to prosecution had he remained in the United States. Attempts to deport him from Mexico in 1958 were unsuccessful.
(Personal correspondence with his step-daughter, Johanna Friedman, interviews with friends and written documentation.)

Appendix II

Bibliography

I: Unpublished Sources

Manuscript Collections

Martha Dodd Stern Correspondence, Library of Congress Archives, Box 7, Folder 7.

Charles Humboldt Papers, Yale University Sterling Memorial Library, Manuscripts and Archives, Manuscript Group #721 with a finding aid by Barbara M. Riley.

Albert Maltz, *The Citizen Writer in Retrospect*. Oral History of Albert Maltz. Compiled by Joel Gardner under auspices of the Oral History Program of U.C.L.A., 1983, Regents of the University of California.

FBI Files:

Hugo Butler Bufile. In possession of Jean Butler Rouverol.

David Drucker Bufile 105-12761-(57). In possession of Drucker family.

Alfred Stern NY 100-57453-906. In possession of author.

Meyer Zykofsky, Bufile 100-411142. In possession of author.

Interviews with the Author:

Alonso Aguilar, July 9, 1991; October 8, 1996.

Guillermo Arriaga, November 8, 1992.

Rosalind Beimler, September 19, 1991.

Mary Belfrage, March 4, 1992.

Anita Boyer, February 2, 1992; February 14, 1992.

May Brooks, February 16, 1993; July 19, 1994.

John Bruton, October 11, 1991.

Mary Butler, July 28, 1991.

Michael Butler, July 27, 1991.

Elizabeth Catlett , January 17, 1991.

Joseph Crown, January 7, 1993.

David Drucker, May 20, 1991.

Emmy Drucker, May 20, 1990.

Frederick Vanderbilt Field, August 7, 1992.

Moe Fishman, January 20, 1993.

Lic. Juan Manuel Gomez Gutierrez, August 25, 1993.

Louisa Hyun Stuart, May 18, 1991.

Margie Jackson, December 20, 1991.

Susana Jones, January 7, 1993.

James Kahn, July 24, 1991 (Telephone).

Tony Kahn, January 21, 1993.

Lynn Kalmar, November 17, 1991; August 22, 1992 (Telephone).

'Keith' [pseud.], November 12, 1993.

Ring Lardner, Jr. and Frances Chaney, May 25, 1991.

Edward Lending, August 6, 1991.

A.B. and Harriet Magil, January 20, 1993.

Arnoldo Martinez Verdugo, August 28, 1991; August 14, 1992.

Marjorie Mattingly Urquidi, January 6, 1993.

Conlon Nancarrow, August 28, 1996.

Victor Navasky, May 15, 1991.

Carmen Otero, November 27, 1992.

John Page, July 20, 1993.

Yuri Paparov, July 8, 1992; December 10, 1993.

Jeanette Pepper, August 2, 1991; August 7, 1992 (Telephone).

David Prensky, May 11, 1993.

Carlos Prieto, September 19, 1991; October 22, 1991.

Jean Butler Rouverol, July 22, 1991; August 2, 1991; January 20, 1992; February, 1994.

Shelley Shlafrock, January 18, 1993.

Berthe Small, January 17, 1993.

Philip and Gertrude Stein, May 15, 1995.

Chris Trumbo, August 1, 1991.

Edna Moore van der Schelling, August 1, 1991.

Waldeen, January 6, 1993.

Ruth Wright, June 29, 199.1

Asa Zatz, May 20, 1991.

(Note: I respected Keith's request to remain anonymous. Several others also asked not to be named, and I chose not to refer to those interviews in the book nor list them here.)

Letters to the Author: (Unless otherwise specified.)

Philip Agee, April 24, 1996

Department of Justice to the Secretary of State. Microfilm DNA RG 59, Box 28160.

Stirling Dickinson, July 23, 1993; August 12, 1993, September 25, 1993; July 30, 1995; October 15, 1996.

Philip Dorfman to Edna van der Schelling, January 9, 1961; April 21, 1964.

David Drucker, May 2, 1993.

Susan Drucker-Brown, January 5, 1998; October 23, 1995.

Johanna Friedman, March 18, 1999.

Lynne Kalmar, June 22, 1992.

Keith, February 11, 1992; March 8, 1993; December 5, 1994; August 9, 1997;

Lillian Kittner, December 7, 1993.

Edward Lending, August 28, 1991; May 19, 1992; August 5, 1993; January 2, 1996.

Edward Lending to Yoko and David Nancarrow· December 30, 1995.

Harry Lore letter to Edna Moore van der Schelling, September 2, 1962.

A. B. Magil, February 3, 1993; May 5, 1994.

John Menz, December 16, 1992; November 11, 1993; November 27, 1993; January 8, 1994; February 11, 1994.

William Colfax Miller, March, 1993; June 30, 1993; November 6, 1993.

Linda Oppen, December 2, 1991.

Marshall Perlin, March 6, 1991.

David Prensky, June 20, 1997.

James Roosevelt to Edna Moore van der Schelling, December 13, 1960.

Bert Quint to Joseph Ravotto, September 18, 1957.

Max Shlafrock, August 8, 1991; May 6, 1997; November 18, 1997; December 20, 1997.

Berthe Small, December 15, 1997.

Philip Stein, January 22, 1995; January 7, 1998.

Chris Trumbo, October 14, 1995.

Edna van der Schelling to Harry Lore, February 9, 1963.

Alan Wald, March 7, 1992.
Asa Zatz, November 20, 1995.

Other Unpublished Documents

Broadwater, Oscar Jeffers. *The Search for Security: Dwight D. Eisenhower and Anti-Communism in America, 1952-1961.* Doctoral Dissertation. Ann Arbor, Michigan: University Microfilms International, 1989.

Carter, Robert Frederick. *Pressure from the Left: The American Labor Party, 1936-1954.* Doctoral Dissertation. Syracuse University, Syracuse, New York: University Microfilms International, 1965.

Department of State to the American Embassy, Mexico, D. F., August 20, 1954, Control Number #A-238.

Foreign Service Despatch from the American Embassy, Mexico, D.F. to Department of State, August 16, 1954, Control Number 284

Foreign Service Despatch from American Embassy, Mexico, D.F. to Department of State December 21, 1954, Control Number 964.

Foreign Service Telegram signed Raymond G. Leddy, September 7, 1957. Control Number 824.

Graff, Matilda (Bobbi). *The Historic Continuity of the Civil Rights Movement.* Unpublished Dissertation. Monteith College, Wayne State University. Detroit, Michigan: 1971.

Kahn, Barbara. Commencement Address for Alvine High School, Manchester, New Hampshire: June, 1972.

Kilian, Crawford. *Growing up Blacklisted.* An unpublished memoir.

Kimmage, Ann. *An Un-American Childhood.* Early version of manuscript.

Mishler, Paul C. *The Littlest Proletariat: American Communists and their Children, 1922-1950.* Doctoral Dissertation. Boston University Graduate School. Boston, Massachusetts: University Microfilms International, 1988.

Rouverol, Jean, *Those Happy Few,* A work in progress.

Ryan, Jeffrey Robert. *The Conspiracy that Never Was: United States Government Surveillance of Eastern European American Leftists, 1942-1959.* Doctoral Dissertation. Boston College, Ann Arbor, Michigan, 1989.

Shlafrock, Max. *Deportation Notes.* n.d. In possession of author.

United States District Court for the Eastern District of Pennsylvania, No. 29692, *Edna van der Schelling v. U.S. News & World Report, Inc.*, Joseph E. Lord, III presiding. (February 4, 1963)

II: Newspapers and Periodicals

The names and dates of issue of newspapers and periodicals consulted are given in the footnotes.

III: Books, Articles and Congressional Publications

Agee, Joel. *Twelve Years: An American Boyhood in East Germany.* New York: Farrar, Straus, Giroux, 1981.

Agee, Philip. *Inside the Company: CIA Diary.* Toronto, New York and London: Bantam Books, 1975; *On the Run.* Secaucus, New Jersey: Lyle Stuart Inc., 1987.

Aguayo, Sergio y John Bailey. "Servicios de inteligencia en México antes de 1985." *Reforma* Enfoque, Enero 26, 1998.

Albright, Joseph and Marcia Kunstel. *Bombshell: The Secret Story of America's Unknown Atomic Spy Conspiracy.* Nebraska: University of Nebraska Press, 1992.

Alexander, Robert J. *Communism in Latin America.* New Brunswick, New Jersey: New Jersey University Press, 1957.

Anderson, Jack and Ronald May. *Mc Carthy: The Man, the Senator, the Ism.* Boston: Beacon Press, 1952.

Bain, Leslie. "Red Hunt in Miami: Who Formed the Posse?" *The Nation,* August 7, 1954: 110-112.

Bayley, Edwin R. *Joe McCarthy and the Press.* Madison: University of Wisconsin Press, 1981.

Belfrage, Cedric. *The American Inquisition, 1945-1960: A Profile of the McCarthy Era.* Indianapolis, New York: Bobbs Merrill, 1973.

Belfrage, Cedric & James Aronson. *Something to Guard: The Stormy Life of the National Guardian 1948-1967.* New York: Columbia University Press, 1978.

Belfrage, Sally. *Un-American Activities: A Memoir of the Fifties.* New York: Harper Collins, 1994.

Bentley, Elizabeth. *Out of Bondage.* New York: Ivy-Ballantine Books, 1988.

Bentley, Eric (edited by). *Thirty Years of Treason: Excerpts from Hearings Before the House Committee on Un-American Activities, 1938-1968*. New York: Viking, 1971.

Bernstein, Carl. *Loyalties, A Son's Memoir*. New York, London, Toronto, Sydney, Tokyo: Simon & Schuster, 1990.

Bessie, Alvah. *Inquisition in Eden*. New York: MacMillan, 1965.

Buckley, William F., Jr. and L.Brent Bozell. *McCarthy and his Enemies: The Record and its Meaning*. Chicago: Henry Regnery, 1954.

Buendia, Manuel. *El CIA en México*. México, D.F.: s.e., s.f.

Buhle, Mari Jo, Paul Buhle, and Dan Georgakas, Eds. *Encyclopedia of the American Left*. Champaign, Illinois: University of Illinois Press, 1992.

Carr, Barry. *Marxism in Twentieth Century Mexio*. Lincoln and London: University of Nebraska Press, 1992.

Carr, Robert K. *The House Committee on Un-American Activities*. Ithaca, New York: Cornell University Press, 1952.

Caute, David. *The Great Fear: The Anti-Communist Purge Under Truman and Eisenhower*. New York: Simon & Schuster, 1978.

Ceplair, Larry and Steven Englund. *Inquisition in Hollywood: Politics in the Film Community, 1930-1960*. Berkley, Los Angeles, London: University of California Press, 1983.

Chambers, Whittaker. *Witness*. New York: Random House, 1952.

Chernin, Kim. *In My Mother's House: A Daughter's Story*. New York: Harper & Row, 1983.

Chevalier, Haakim. *Oppenheimer: The Story of a Friendship*. New York: George Braziller, 1965.

Cochran, Bert. *Labor and Communism: The Conflict that Shaped American Unions*. Princeton, New Jersey: Princeton University Press, 1977.

Cole, Lester. *Hollywood Red: The Autobiography of Lester Cole*. Palo Alto, California: Ramparts Press, 1981.

Comisión Organizadora del Comité de Defensa de Los Derechos Humanos. *En Defensa de la Soberanía de México*. México, D.F.: s.e., s.f.

Comité Mexicano Pro-Morton Sobell. *La soberanía de México y el caso de Morton Sobell*. México, D.F.: s.e., s.f.

Cook, Bruce. *Dalton Trumbo*. New York: Charles Scribner's Sons, 1977.

Cook, Fred. *The Nightmare Decade*. New York: Random House,

1971; *The F.B.I. Nobody Knows.* New York: Pyramid Books, 1964.

Cooke, Alistair. *A Generation on Trial.* New York: Knopf, 1950.

DeVries, Lini M. *Please God, Take Care of the Mule.* Mexico, D.F.: Editorial Minutiae Mexicana, S.A. de C.V., 1969; *Up From the Cellar.* Minneapolis: Vanilla Press, 1979.

Dmytryk, Edward. *It's a Hell of a Life but not a Bad Living.* New York: Times Books, 1978.

Donner, Frank J. *The Un-Americans.* New York: Ballantine Books, 1961; *The Age of Surveillance: The Aims and Methods of America's Political Intelligence System.* New York: Knopf, 1980; "The Smith Act—Baltimore Version." *The Nation,* November 8, 1952: 426-428; "The Miami Formula: Grass-Roots McCarthyism." *The Nation,* January 22, 1955: 65-71.

Dorfman, Ariel. *Heading South, looking North, A Bilingual Journey.* Harmondsworth, Middlesex, England: Penguin Books, 1998.

Draper, Theodore. *The Roots of American Communism.* New York: The Viking Press, 1957; *American Communism & Soviet Russia: The Formative Period.* New York: Viking Press, 1960.

Durr, Virginia Foster. *Outside the Magic Circle.* Tuscaloosa, Alabama: University of Alabama Press, 1985.

Fariello, Griffin. *Red Scare. Memories of the American Inquisition: An Oral History.* New York, London: V.W. Norton, 1995.

Fast, Howard. *Being Red.* New York: A Laurel Trade Paperback, Dell Publishing, 1990.

Fiedler, Leslie. *An End to Innocence.* Boston: Beacon Press, 1955.

Field, Fred Vanderbilt. *From Right to Left: An Autobiography.* Westport, Connecticut: Lawrence Hill, 1983.

Folsom, Franklin. *Days of Anger, Days of Hope: A Memoir of the League of American Writers, 1937-1942.* Niwot, Colorado: University Press of Colorado, 1994.

Fried, Richard. *Men Against McCarthy.* New York: Columbia University Press, 1976; *Nightmare in Red: The McCarthy Era in Perspective.* New York: Oxford University Press, 1990.

Gall, Olivia. *Trotsky en México y la Vida Política en el Periodo de Cárdenas, 1937-1940.* México, D.F.: Ediciones Era, 1991.

Garb, Paula. *They Came to Stay: North Americans in the U.S.S.R.* Moscow: Progress Publishers, 1987.

Goldman, Eric F. *Rendezvous with Destiny.* New York: Knopf,

1952; *The Crucial Decade—And After: America, 1945-1960*. New York: Vintage Books, 1960.

Goodman, Walter. *The Committee*. New York: Farrar Strauss and Giroux, 1968.

Gornick, Vivian. *The Romance of American Communism*. New York: Basic Books, 1977.

Green, Gil. *Cold War Fugitive*. New York: International Publishing, 1984.

Griffith, Robert. *The Politics of Fear: Joseph R. McCarthy and the Senate*. Boston: University of Massachusetts Press, 1987.

Halberstam, David. *The Powers That Be*. New York: Knopf, 1978.

Handlin, Oscar. *The Uprooted: The Epic Story of the Great Migrations that Made the American People*. Boston: Little, Brown, 1952.

Haynes, John Earl. *Communism and Anti-Communism in the United States: An Annotated Guide to Historical Writings*. New York, London: Garland Publishing, 1987.

Healey, Dorothy & Maurice Isserman. *Dorothy Healey Remembers: A Life in the American Communist Party*. New York, Oxford: Oxford University Press, 1990.

Hellman, Lillian. *Scoundrel Time*. Boston, Toronto: Little, Brown & Company, 1976.

Herman, Donald L. *The Comintern in Mexico*. Washington, D.C.: Public Affairs Press, 1974.

Hiss, Alger. *Recollections of a Life*. New York: Seaver Books-Henry Holt, 1988.

Hiss, Tony. *The View from Alger's Window: A Son's Memoir*. New York: Knopf, 1999.

Hofstadter, Richard. *The Paranoid Style of American Politics and other Essays*. London: Jonathan Cape, 1966.

Hooks, Margaret. *Tina Modotti: An Illustrated Life*. London, San Francisco: Pandora-Harper Collins, 1993.

Horowitz, David. *Radical Son: A Generational Odyssey*. New York: The Free Press-Simon & Schuster, 1997.

Howe, Irving and Lewis Coser. *The American Communist Party, A Critical History*. New York: Frederick A. Praeger, 1962.

Isserman, Maurice. *If I Had a Hammer: The Death of the Old Left and the Birth of the New Left*. New York: Basic Books, 1988. *Which Side Were You On? The American Communist Party During the Second World War*. Connecticut: Wesleyan University Press, 1982.

Kahn, E.J., Jr. *The China Hands*. New York: Viking Press, 1972.

Kahn, Gordon. *Hollywood on Trial: The Story of the Ten Who Were Indicted*. New York: Boni and Gaer, 1948; *A Long Way from Home*. Tempe, Arizona: Bilingual Press/Editorial Bilingüe, 1988.

Kanfer, Stefan. *A Journal of the Plague Years*. New York: Atheneum, 1973.

Kempton, Murray. *Part of our Time: Some Ruins and Monuments of the Thirties*. New York: Simon & Schuster, 1955; *America Comes of Middle Age*. Boston: Little, Brown, 1963.

Kimmage, Ann. *An Un-American Childhood*. Athens and London: University of Georgia Press, 1996.

Kirk, Betty. *Covering the Mexican Front*. Norman, Oklahoma: University of Oklahoma Press, 1942.

Kirschner, Don. *Cold War Exile: The Unclosed Case of Maurice Halperin*. Missouri: University of Missouri Press, 1995.

Klehr, Harvey. *Hey-day of American Communism*. New York: Basic Books, Inc., 1984.

Klehr, Harvey and Ronald Radosh. *The Amerasia Spy Case*. Chapel Hill and London: University of North Carolina Press, 1996.

Klehr, Harvey, John Earl Haynes & Fridrikh Igorevich Firsov. *The Secret World of American Communism*. New Haven, London: Yale University Press, 1995.

Klinkowitz, Jerome (edited by). *Diaries of Willard Motley*. Ames, Iowa: Iowa State University Press, 1979.

Krauze, Enrique. *La Presidencia Imperial: Ascenso y Caída del Sistema Político Mexicano 1940-1996*. México D.F.: Tusquets Editores, 1997.

Kutler, Stanley. *The American Inquisition. Justice and Injustice in the Cold War*. New York: Hill and Wang/Farrar Straus & Giroux, 1982.

Landis, Arthur H. *The Abraham Lincoln Brigade*. New York: Citadel Press, 1967.

Lardner Jr., Ring. *My Family Remembered*. New York, Hagerstown, San Francisco, London: Harper & Row, 1976.

Larkin, Margaret. *Seven Shares in a Gold Mine*. New York: Simon & Schuster, 1959.

Latham, Earl. *The Communist Controversy in Washington: From the New Deal to McCarthy*. Cambridge, Massachusetts: Harvard University Press, 1966.

Lattimore, Owen. *Ordeal by Slander*. Boston: Little, Brown and Co., 1950.

Lazitch, Branco. *Biographical Dictionary of the Comintern*. Stanford: The Hoover Institution Press, 1973.

Levenstein, Harvey. *Communism, Anti-Communism and the CIO*. Westport, Connecticut: Greenwood Press, 1981.

Levine, Issac Don. *Mind of an Assassin*. New York: Farrar, Srauss and Cudahy, 1959.

McCaulliffe, Mary. *Crisis on the Left*. Amherst: University of Massachusetts Press, 1978.

McGilligan, Patrick and Paul Buhle. *Tender Comrades: A Backstory of the Hollywood Blacklist*. New York: St Martin's Griffin, 1997.

MacKinnon, Janice R. and Stephen R. MacKinnon. *Agnes Smedley. The Life and Times of an American Radical*. Berkeley, California: University of California Press, 1988.

McWilliams, Carey. *Witch Hunt*. Boston: Little, Brown and Company, 1950.

Mahoney, Harry and Marjorie Locke Mahoney. *Espionage in Mexico*. San Francisco: Austin and Winfield, 1997; *The Saga of Leon Trotsky: His Clandestine Operations and His Assassination*. San Francisco, London, Bethesda: Austin & Winfield, 1998.

Mahoney, M. H. Women in Espionage: A Biographical Dictionary. Santa Barbara, California: ABC-CLIO, 1993.

Malkin, Maurice. *Return to My Father's House*. Edited by Charles W. Wiley. New Rochelle, New York: Arlington House, 1972.

Manchester, William. *The Glory and the Dream*. New York: Little, Brown and Company, 1973.

Marion, George. *The Communist Trial: An American Crossroads*. New York: Fairplay Publishers, 1950.

Martinez Verdugo, Arnoldo(edited by). *Historia del Comunismo en México*. México, Barcelona, Buenos Aires: Colección Enlace Grijalbo, 1985.

Matthews, Jack. "Children of the Blacklist." *Los Angeles Times Magazine*, October 15, 1989: 10-21.

Matusow, Harvey. *False Witness*. New York: Cameron and Kahn, 1955.

May, Gary. *Un-American Activities. The Trials of William Remington*. New York, Oxford: Oxford University Press, 1994.

Meeropol, Robert and Michael Meeropol. *We are Your Sons*. Boston: Houghton Mifflin, 1975.

Mitford, Jessica. *A Fine Old Cause*. New York: Alfred Knopf 1977.

Morros, Boris. As told to Charles Samuels. *My Ten Years as a Counterspy*. New York: Dell Publishing, 1959.

Musacchio, Humberto. *Gran Diccionario Enciclopédico de México Visual*. México, D.F.: Andrés León, 1990.

Navasky, Victor S. *Naming Names*. New York: Viking Press, 1990.

Neuman, Alma. *Always Straight Ahead: A Memoir*. Baton Rouge and London: Louisiana State University Press, 1993.

Norment, Lynn. "Elizabeth Catlett: Dean of Women Artists." *Ebony*. April 4, 1993: 46-50.

Oppen, Mary. *Meaning A Life: An Autobiography*. Santa Rosa, California: Black Sparrow Press, 1990.

Orellana, Margarita de. "El arte de Gabriel Figueroa, palabras sobre imagenes: Una entrevista con Gabriel Figueroa."*Artes de México*, Numero 2, Invierno, 1988.

Oshinsky, David M. *A Conspiracy So Immense: The World of Joe McCarthy*. New York: The Free Press, A Division of MacMillan, Inc. 1983; *Senator Joe McCarthy and the American Labor Movement*. Kansas City: University of Missouri Press, 1975.

Packer, Herbert L. *Ex-Communist Witnesses: Four Studies in Fact Finding*. Palo Alto: Stanford University Press, 1962.

Paparov, Yuri. *Trotsky Sacrificado*. México D. F.: Grupo Editorial Siete, 1992.

Plau de Plessis, Rachel (edited by). *The Selected Letters of George Oppen*. Durnham and London: Duke University Press, 1990.

Quill, Shirley. *Mike Quill Himself*. Greenwich, Connecticut: Devin Adair, 1985.

Rabinowitz, Victor. *Unrepentent Leftist: A Lawyer's Memoir*. Champaign Illinois: University of Illinois Press, 1996.

Radosh, Ronald and Joyce Milton. *The Rosenberg File: A Search for the Truth*. New York: Hold Rinehart & Winston, 1983.

Reeves, Thomas C. *The Life and Times of Joe McCarthy: A Biography*. New York: Stein and Day, 1982.

Robinson, Ionne. *A Wall to Paint On*. New York: E.P. Dutton, 1946.

Root, Jonathan. *The Betrayers, the Rosenberg Case: A Reappraisal of an American Crisis*. New York: Coward-McCann, 1963.

Root, W. Dirk. "U.S. Intelligence Operations and Covert Action in Mexico, 1900-47." *Journal of Contemporary History*. #22 (1987): London, Newbury Park, Beverly Hills and New Delhi: SAGE, 615-638.

Rorty, James and Moshe Decter. *McCarthy and the Communists*. Boston: Beacon Press, 1954.

Rosswurm, Steve (edited by). *The CIO's Left-Led Unions*. New Brunswick, New Jersey: Rutger's University Press, 1992.

Rouverol, Jean. *Refugees from Hollywood: A Journal of the Black-list Years*. Albuquerque: University of New Mexico Press, 2000.

Rovere, Richard H. *Senator Joe McCarthy*. New York, Hagerstown, San Francisco, London: Harper Colophon Books, 1973.

Rowe, Frank. *The Enemy Among Us: A Story of Witch-Hunting in the McCarthy Era*. Sacramento, California: Cougar Books, 1980.

Ruiz, Vicki. *From out of the Shadow: A History of Mexican Women in the United States*. 1900-1995. New York, Oxford: Oxford University Press, 1997.

Salazar, General Leandro A. Sanchez in collaboration with Julian Gorkin. *Murder in Mexico*. London: Secker and Warburg, 1950.

Saposs, David J. *Communism in American Unions*. New York: McGraw Hill, 1959.

Sayre, Nora. *Previous Convictions: A Journey through the Fifties*. New Jersey: Rutgers University Press, 1995.

Schlesinger Jr., Arthur M. *The Crisis of the Old Order*. Boston: Houghton Mifflin, 1957.

Schmitt, Karl M. *Communism in Mexico: A Study in Political Frustration*. Austin: University of Texas Press, 1965.

Schrecker, Ellen. *No Ivory Tower: McCarthyism & the Universities*. New York and Oxford: Oxford University Press, 1988; *Many are the Crimes: McCarthyism in America*. Boston, New York, Toronto and London: Little Brown and Company, 1998.

Schultz, Bud and Ruth Schultz. *It Did Happen Here: Recollections of Political Repression in America*. Berkeley and Los Angeles: University of California Press, 1989.

Schwartz, Stephen. *From East to West: California and the Making of the American Mind*, New York: The Free Press, 1999.

Seidman, Joel (edited by). *Comunism in the United States: A Bibliography*. Ithaca and London: Cornell University Press, 1969.

Shannon, David. *The Decline of American Communism: History of the Communist Party in the United States Since 1945*. New York: Harcourt, Brace & Co., 1971.

Shipman, Charles. *It Had to be Revolution*. Ithaca, N.Y.: Cornell University Press, 1993.

Simon, Kate. *Etchings in an Hour Glass*. New York: Harper & Row, 1990.

Simpson, John (edited by). *The Oxford Book on Exile*. Oxford, New York: University of Oxford Press, 1995.

Siqueiros, David. *Me Llamaban el Coronelazo*. Mexico: Grijalbo, 1977.

Sobell, Morton. *On Doing Time*. New York: Scribner's, 1975; "Sobell on Venona and the Rosenbergs." Internet, H-DIPLO, http://h-net2.msu.edu/~diplo/essays.htm, September 12, 1997.

Starobin, Joseph R. *American Communism in Crisis,1943-1957*. Berkeley, Los Angeles and London: University of California Press, 1975.

Stein, Philip. *Siqueiros: His Life and his Works*. New York: International Publishers, 1994.

Steinberg, Peter. *The Great "Red Menace:" United States Prosecution of American Communists, 1947-1952*. Westport, Connecticut: Greenwood Press, 1984.

Stone, I.F. *The Haunted Fifties, 1953-1963*. Boston: Little, Brown & Co., 1989.

Sudaplatov, Pavel. *Special Tasks: The Memoirs of an Unwanted Witness—A Soviet Spymaster*. Boston, New York, Toronto, London: Little Brown, 1994.

Sulzberger, C.L. *A Long Row of Candles: Memoirs and Diaries, 1934-1954*. New York: Macmillan, 1969.

Swearingen, M. Wesley. *FBI Secrets: An Agent's Exposé*. Boston, Massachusetts: South End Press, 1995.

Taibo, Pablo Ignacio. *Los Bolshevikis: Historia narrativa de los origenes del comunismo en Mexico*. Mexico, D.F.: Joaquin Mortis 1986.

Tanenhaus, Sam. *Wittaker Chambers:A Biography*. New York: Random House, 1997.

Taylor, Telford. *Grand Inquest: The Story of Congressional Investigation*. New York: Simon & Schuster, 1955.

Theoharis, Athan. *Seeds of Repression*. Chicago: Quadrangle, 1971; *Spying on Americans*. Philadelphia: Temple University Press, 1981.

Thomas, Hugh. *The Spanish Civil War*. New York: Harper and Brothers, 1961.

Trumbo, Dalton. *Additional Dialogue: Letters of Dalton Trumbo, 1942-1962*. Edited by Helen Manfull. New York, Philadelphia: Evans, 1970.

United States Congress, House of Representatives. Congressional Record, "Committee on Un-American Activities Hearings." August 9-11, 1949.

United States Congress. House of Representatives, 87th Congress, Second Session, Committee on Un-American Activities, *Guide to Subversive Organizations and Publications*, December 1, 1961.

Vanden Heuvel, Katrina. "Grand Illusions." *Vanity Fair*, Vol. 54, (September 1991).

Wechsler, James A. *The Age of Suspicion*. New York: Random House, 1953.

Weinstein, Allen. *Perjury: The Hiss-Chambers Case*. New York: Knopf, 1978.

Weinstein, Allen and Alexander Vassiliev. *The Haunted Wood: Soviet Espionage in America. The Stalin Era*. New York: Random House, 1999.

Weisbord, Merrily. *The Strangest Dream*. Toronto, Ontario: Lester and Orpen Dennys, 1983.

White, Anthony. *Siqueiros*. Encino: Floricanto Press, 1984.

Wolfe, Bertram D. *A Life in Two Centuries: An Autobiography*. New York: Stein and Day, 1981.

About the Author

Diana Anhalt comes from a long line of wanderers which helps explain why practically everything she has published in Mexico and the United States deals with exile, expatriation and identity. A former teacher, newsletter writer and editor, her work has appeared or is forthcoming in, among others, *El Nacional*, *The Mexico City Times*, *Grand Tour*, *The Texas Observer*, *Atención*, *Voices of Mexico*, *Jewish Currents*, *Midstream*, *Under the Sun*, *Passager* and *Southwest Review*. She currently resides in Mexico City, Mexico.